Holiday Season Cookbook

WITH MENUS

From Thanksgiving through New Year's
Favorite Recipes© of Home Economics Teachers

© Favorite Recipes Press/Nashville EMS MCMLXXXI
Post Office Box 77, Nashville, Tennessee 37202

Library of Congress Cataloging in Publication Data
Main entry under title:
Holiday season cookbook with menus.
  Includes index.
  1. Cookery. 2. Holidays.
TX739.H66   641.5'68   81-9707
ISBN 0-87197-138-0   AACR2

Dear Homemaker!

At last! A cookbook designed exclusively for the time of the year that you entertain the most — the Holiday Season. From those crisp, cool Fall days when you plan Thanksgiving gatherings through the joyous Christmas season all the way to confetti-tossing, horn-blowing New Year's galas.

You'll find it all in this unique cookbook. Plus! Fabulous menus already planned out for you. Entertaining was never so easy! (Especially with holiday hints and tips you'll find with every set of menus.)

Or, if you like creating your own menus, mix and match with the hundreds of recipes that follow. Festive appetizers . . . super salads . . . tantalizing main dishes . . . an original variety of vegetables and side dishes . . . mouth-watering breads . . . and, of course, dozens of holiday desserts. Every recipe was submitted from Home Economics teachers — all across the country — so you know they're perfect.

The *Home Economics Teachers' Holiday Season Cookbook* is sure to make your holidays easier, merrier . . . and more organized than ever before!

Mary Jane Blount

FAVORITE RECIPES PRESS

Board of Advisors

Favorite Recipes Press wants to recognize the following who graciously serve on our Home Economics Teachers' Advisory Board:

Frances Rudd
Supervisor, Home Economics
  Education
Arkansas Department of Education

C. Janet Latham
Supervisor, Home Economics
  Education
Idaho State Board of Vocational
  Education

Catherine A. Carter
Head Consultant, Consumer
  Homemaking Education
Illinois Division of Vocational
  and Technical Education

Barbara Gaylor
Supervisor, Home Economics
  Education Unit
Michigan Department of Education

Louann Heinrichs
Home Economics Teacher
Greenville High School
Greenville, Ohio

Roberta Looper
1982 President, National
  Association of Vocational
  Home Economics Teachers
Livingston, Tennessee

Phyllis L. Barton
Past President, National Association of
Vocational Home Economics Teachers
Alexandria, Virginia

Contents

Holiday Season Menus 8

Festive Appetizers and Beverages 21

Sparkling Salads 47

Party-Time Main Dishes 63

Harvest-Time Vegetables 83

Treasured Holiday Breads 95

Traditional Holiday Desserts 111

Homemade Holiday Gifts 143

Color Photograph Recipes 155

Index 163

Thanksgiving Menus

How many things we have to be thankful for! And how nice it is to have a holiday to remind us. Thanksgiving is the beginning of the holiday season, but Christmas and New Year's gatherings aren't far behind! So, as you cook and bake for Thanksgiving, plan ahead. Double recipes and freeze leftovers so you'll be prepared for holiday guests who drop in unexpectedly throughout the season.

And remember — use leftovers creatively. If you know your family tires of turkey sandwiches, fix turkey crepes, salads, or even a turkey pie, instead. We bet they won't even know they're eating leftovers!

Maybe this is the year you'd rather have Thanksgiving dinner without a turkey. If so, the *Traditional Dinner Menus* offer variety that your family will surely enjoy. Or, if you're cooking for a crowd, why not have a buffet? Your table will look lovely laden with the Thanksgiving delights found in the *Buffet Menus*. Buffets also allow youngsters to sit with "grown-ups", while family and friends mingle comfortably. If you have a buffet, however, use as many T.V. trays as possible to make eating even easier.

With food costs increasing, covered dish dinners are more popular today than ever. Why not have one for Thanksgiving too? That way, everyone gets the joy of providing for the bountiful feast, and there's much less burden on the hostess. And what fun it is to try everyone's favorite dish! It can be potluck, but the menus suggested here for *Family Covered Dish Dinners* will make sure your dinner is organized and well balanced.

Who says you can't be creative and traditional at the same time? These menus make sure that you will!

THANKSGIVING TIPS

- Best turkey buy is 16-24 pounds. It yields more meat per pound and is moist and tender. Look for one with short legs, plump body and un-bruised skin.

- Never stuff a turkey before freezing. When stuffing, pack it lightly.

- Light your Thanksgiving fire safely by using a drinking straw as a taper.

- Share your Thanksgiving happiness by inviting a forgotten senior citizen, perhaps a neighbor, to share Thanksgiving dinner.

- Cream, to top your pumpkin pie, may be whipped well ahead of serving time if corn syrup is used as a sweetener instead of sugar.

- Use pinking shears dipped in flour to cut festive strips for lattice-topped pies.

- Before starting dinner, ask everyone to share one thing they are most thankful for this year.

- Soak pine cones in a solution of 1 cup baking soda to 1 quart water. Dry for a few days and throw on the fire for a warm, golden glow.

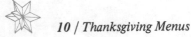

TRADITIONAL
THANKSGIVING DINNERS

Roast Turkey
Cheesy Italian Green Beans, page 84
Apple and Sweet Potato Casserole, page 91
Italian Dressing, page 92
Cherry Surprise, page 128
Pumpkin Custard Pie, page 140

Onion-Orange Salad, page 60
Holiday Ham, page 73
Helen's Sweet Potato Casserole, page 90
Anise Bread, page 105
Curried Fruit, page 116
Rum Balls, page 151

Cranberry Waldorf Salad, page 52
Braised Pheasant, page 78
Perky Potato Salad Mold, page 86
Zucchini Bread, page 107
Ice Cream Pie, page 138

Chocolate Fondue, page 26
Cranberry-Relish Mold, page 38
Gingered Duckling with Orange Rice, page 78
Broccoli Special, page 85
Creamy Scalloped Potatoes, page 87
Delicious Monkey Bread, page 105

Spiced Cranberry-Orange Relish, page 38
Sherry and Spice Game Hens, page 78
Fried Sauerkraut Balls, page 88
Potato Dressing, page 93
Anna's Yeast Rolls, page 100
Christmas Apple Pudding, page 112

THANKSGIVING COVERED
DISH DINNERS

Dill Dip, page 23
Cheese and Olive Filling for Rolls, page 31
Strawberry-Cream Cheese Salad, page 56
Spinach Salad, page 61
Holiday Shrimp and Rice Casserole, page 75
Cherry-Nut Bread, page 105
Cranberry Cake with Butter Sauce, page 124

Tomato and Green Onion Dip, page 24
Yummy Pistachio Salad, page 56
Shrimp Scampi, page 75
Glorified Squash, page 88
Sour Cream Coconut Cake, page 122
Cranberry Bread, page 195

Cranberry-Orange Salad, page 52
Rolled Chicken Breast, page 70
Sweet Potato Pudding, page 90
Bishop Bread, page 102
Fruit Cake Muffins, page 144

Chili con Queso with Tortilla Chips, page 30
Cranberry Conserve, page 38
Turkey Roll, page 78
Thanksgiving Yams with Topping, page 89
Yummy Peanut Butter Pie, page 140
Norwegian Carrot Bread, page 145

Crab Dip, page 23
Cranberry-Pecan Salad, page 52
Turkey and Dressing Casserole, page 76
Sweet Potato Balls, page 90
Fudge Sundae Pie, page 140
Apricot Fold Overs, page 152

THANKSGIVING BUFFETS

Crab Dip for Vegetables, page 23
Party Bacon Sandwiches, page 27
Cheese Loaf, page 28
Pistachio-Coconut Surprise, page 56
Turkey Pie, page 77
Scalloped Asparagus, page 84
Danish Puff, page 102
Unusual Brownies, page 131

Artichoke Dip, page 22
Party Pizzas, page 28
Stuffed Mushrooms, page 37
Snowflake Salad, page 56
Best Ever Brisket, page 64
Gumdrop Bread, page 106
Chocolate Mint Pie, page 137

Green Pepper Jelly, page 22
Oyster Dip, page 24
Sausage Pinwheel, page 33
Diane's Fruit Salad, page 48
Party-Time Chicken, page 66
Greek Holiday Bread, page 106
Spicy Pumpkin Pie, page 141

Diana's Spinach Dip, page 24
Cheddar Cheese Spread, page 31
Crab Pizza Snacks, page 33
Pink Salad, page 49
Perfect Filet, page 64
Pam's Sweet Potato Casserole, page 91
Strawberry Bread, page 107
Peach Cream Freeze, page 118
Cream Cheese Brownies, page 130

Curry Dip, page 23
Party Cheese Ball, page 29
Cheese Quiche Tarts, page 30
Strawberry Nut Salad, page 57
Stuffed Pork Tenderloin, page 74
Sweet Potato Souffle, page 90
Pumpkin Bread, page 107
Holiday Mint Bars, page 131

Christmas Menus

Christmas . . . there's no other holiday like it. There's an excitement in the air that envelopes us — from home to work, throughout the department stores, wherever we go. It's a feeling so unique, it can only be called the "Christmas spirit." A time when families gather . . . friends exchange annual letters . . . secrets are mischievously made . . . and presents lovingly wrapped. Somehow, for each of us, that spirit rekindles every year — when we truly think of others and very little of ourselves.

That's why planning Christmas time is so important — everything must go just right! Here are menus for your most special family get-togethers — *Christmas Eve, Christmas Morning, Present-Opening Parties, Christmas Dinners and Christmas Buffets.* Also be sure to read the following unique holiday tips — they'll save you lots of time during this busy holiday season — just when you need it the most!

A. HOLIDAY SPIRIT

- Divide the weeks left into number of people on gift list. The result is the number of gifts you must buy each week in the remaining time before Christmas.

- Small ornaments with names lettered in gold or silver nail polish make fabulous holiday favors or take-home place cards.

- A centerpiece the entire family can help make is a miniature yule log. In a 15-inch cut of birch, drill two holes big enough for candles of your choice. Let children add their own decorations to the log — small holiday ornaments, pieces of pine, holly or mistletoe gathered on a family outing. Add two small pieces of wood to the bottom for legs and you've got a beautiful centerpiece — even more beautiful because it's one your family made!

B. DECORATING TIPS

- Chill candles for 12 hours before use. This ensures even burning and less drip.

- Line walkway or drive with "luminaries" to light a friendly welcome for evening guests. Fill a small paper sack with 4 inches of sand; place a votive candle in center of sand. It will glow for hours.

- Display Christmas cards by forming a Christmas tree or other decorative patterns by taping cards on a door or wall as they're received.

C. CLEANING TIPS

- Remove Christmas tree resin from hands by dampening and rubbing with baking soda, then rinse well.

- Pouring a strong solution of salt and hot water down the sink will help eliminate odors and remove grease from drains.

- When food spills in the oven, sprinkle the burned surface with a small amount of salt. This will stop smoke and odor from forming and make the spot easier to clean. Also, rubbing damp salt on dishes in which food has been baked will remove brown spots.

- Keep your holiday kitchen fresh smelling by rubbing cutting board with a lime to remove onion and garlic odors and boiling a few cloves or stick cinnamon in small saucepan.

D. BAKING AND COOKING TIPS

- Whip equal portions of Crisco, Crisco Oil and flour together. Store in refrigerator for quick and easy preparation of holiday cake pans.

- Use confectioners' sugar in place of flour when rolling out holiday cookies for crispier, sweeter treats.

- Bread, made with fruit and nuts, should be tested with a straw in the center. Tester should come out perfectly clean when bread is done.

- To keep raisins, currants and other dried fruits from falling to bottom of cake, use small amount of the measured flour to coat before adding to batter.

- Add raw cucumber and carrot strips, green beans and cauliflower to liquid left in pickle jar. Refrigerate for several days for cocktail snacks.

- Milk cartons make splendid freezing containers for stocks, soups, etc. They also serve well for freezing fish, shrimp, or any foods that should be frozen in water.

CHRISTMAS EVE BUFFETS

Chicken Fingers, page 32
Sue's Holiday Punch, page 42
Frozen Christmas Salad, page 54
Ham and Potato Casserole, page 73
Broccoli Puff, page 84
White Christmas Pie, page 141
Banana Nut Loaf, page 144

Party Beef Balls, page 28
Pomander Punch, page 44
Noel Salad Loaf, page 54
Turkey Lasagne, page 76
Copper Carrots, page 85
Christmas Cookies, page 132
Holiday Wreaths, page 134
Christmas Carrot Loaf, page 145

Four-Cheese Ball, page 29
Christmas Pineapple Punch, page 43
Christmas Salad, page 56
Chicken Supreme, page 65
Cranberry Sweet Potato Bake, page 90
German Christmas Stollen, page 98
Frozen Pumpkin Pie, page 140

Milinda's Spinach Dip, page 24
Too Good Eggnog, page 40
Hot Asparagus Canapes, page 34
Stuffed Broiled Mushrooms, page 34
Holiday Swiss Steak, page 64
Peanut Sticks, page 136
Norwegian Christmas Bread, page 146
Almond Stars, page 152

Holiday Vegetable Dip, page 25
Sparkling Christmas Punch, page 43
Christmas Cranberry Salad, page 51
Chicken-Sausage Casserole, page 69
Sour Cream Coffee Cake, page 98
Health Balls, page 133
Christmas Spice Cookies, page 152
Linda's Green Pepper Jelly, page 153

CHRISTMAS MORNING BREAKFASTS

Chocolate Eggnog, page 41
Holiday Eggs Mornay, page 80
Orange Streusel Muffins, page 99

Spiced Tea, page 44
Christmas Morning Eggs, page 80
Holiday Fruit Bread, page 106

Mulled Christmas Cider, page 44
Sausage Crepes, page 73
Pull-Apart Breakfast Rolls, page 101

Connie's Christmas Punch, page 41
Hashed Brown Omelet, page 80
Cottage Cheese Rolls, page 100

Microwave Stuffed Mushrooms, page 37
Golden Party Punch, page 43
Quiche Lorraine, page 81
Bran Brown Bread, page 102

CHRISTMAS PRESENT-OPENING GATHERINGS

Party-Time Sandwiches, page 37
Diana's Fruit Punch, page 41
Chicken Salad, page 58
New York Polish Cheese Coffee Cake, page 97
Three-Generation Christmas Jewels, page 153

Crab Cheese Triangles, page 33
Christmas Pineapple Punch, page 43
Chicken and Almond Casserole, page 66
Cranberry-Orange Bread, page 105
Caramel-Coated Yule Logs, page 126

Rolled Cheese Sandwiches, page 31
Wassail Tea, page 45
Stuffed Bread, page 71
Cherry Coffee Cake, page 97
Peppermint Fudge Pie, page 138

Holiday Egg Rolls, page 22
Wassail, page 45
Christmas Salad, page 50
Homemade Pizza, page 79
Mary's Candy Cane Coffee Cake, page 96
Pecan Sassies, page 141

CHRISTMAS DINNERS

Roast Turkey
Shrimp Dip, page 24
Cheese and Vegetable Chowder, page 38
Tri-Level Christmas Jell-O, page 57
Sausage-Mushroom Stuffing, page 92
Christmas Cookies, page 132
Almond Christmas Cut-Ups, page 152

Holiday Dip, page 24
Crab Bisque, page 38
Merry Christmas Salad, page 55
Tiered Party Salad Mold, page 59
Broken Glass Cake, page 112
Cranberry Casserole, page 115

Creamy Parmesan Fondue, page 26
Fruit Soup, page 39
Yum-Yum Salad, page 57
Thousand-Dollar Chicken, page 70
Old-Fashioned Sweet Potato Pudding, page 90
Christmas Peppermint Dessert, page 115

Crispy Cashew Dip, page 23
Stuffed Mushrooms, page 37
French Onion Soup, page 40
Christmas Garland Jelly, page 50
Ham and Cheese Casserole, page 72
Ambrosia Sweet Potatoes, page 89
Chocolate No-Bake Cookies, page 130

Christmas Dip, page 22
Seafood St. Jacque, page 33
Cranberry Relish, page 38
Christmas Ambrosia, page 112
Meat Roll for Fifty, page 71
Potato Kugel, page 87
Yule Log Cake, page 125

CHRISTMAS BUFFETS

Blue Cheese Ball, page 28
Mini-Quiche, page 31
Evergreen Punch, page 42
Strawberry Salad, page 56
Turkey Stroganoff Sandwich, page 78
Christmas Holly Cookies, page 151

Cheese-Pecan Ball, page 29
Cocktail Ham Balls, page 32
Hot Cider Wassail, page 44
Cranberry-Gelatin Salad, page 51
Chicken Tetrazzini, page 69
Christmas Lane Cake, page 146

Holiday Cheese Ball, page 29
Party Chicken Appetizer, page 32
Cranberry Wassail, page 44
Sour Cream-Fruit Salad, page 49
Ham-Stuffed Manicotti, page 73
Grasshopper Dessert, page 116

Jane's Christmas Punch, page 41
Sweet-Sour Fondue, page 27
Hot Pepper Cheese Ball, page 29
Holiday Gelatin Salad, page 54
Seafood Quiche, page 75
Festive Curried Turkey, page 76
Green Velvet Cake, page 124

Dried Beef Dip, page 23
Cheese and Olive Ball, page 28
Festive Grapefruit Salad, page 54
Sweet and Sour Meatballs, page 71
Cranberry Bavarian Pie, page 137

New Year's Menus

Out with the Old! In with the new! It's time to make (and remake) all those resolutions you *know* you're going to keep this year. Start out by trying brand new serving ideas, menus and recipes found throughout the *Holiday Season Cookbook.*

Begin your New Year's evening early with a delicious *New Year's Eve Buffet* for your close friends. These menus suggest great do-ahead dishes that work well for a formal party or casual gathering.

Or, if you're traditionally a party-goer, suggest this year that your friends end their merry-making at your home for a *Midnight Supper.* How pleased they'll be to wind up their festivities that way! Especially when they see the delicious array of foods you've selected from these menus.

When the guests arrive, ask each one to write down their resolution on a piece of paper. Mix them up and redistribute later so everyone can read a resolution aloud. What fun it'll be to guess whose resolution it is. Have two daring friends? Dress them up as Father Time and Baby New Year's to enter as the clock strikes midnight. It will surely be a party to remember all year.

New Year's day is a grand time to entertain as well. When party hats are put away and serious football fans gather to watch TV bowl games, plan a *New Year's Football Brunch.* Make it a casual affair in the den, basement or wherever your guests can eat and watch television comfortably. It will surely be a welcome afternoon after New Year's Eve festivities. And with a menu suggested here, you'll be cheered as much as the teams!

NEW YEAR'S TIPS

- For colorful ice in New Year's punch bowls, fill balloons with colored water and freeze. Peel off the balloon, and it's ready to use. Use leftover balloons to decorate.

- If you plan New Year's Eve parties and New Year's day gatherings, you get double value from sparkling silver and fresh flowers. A repeated menu makes expense in cooking easier to handle.

- Keep party rooms smelling wonderful by dabbing perfume on light bulbs. When lighted, the warm bulb spreads fragrance throughout the room.

- If, by New Year's you're tired of the Christmas cookies that you've baked, exchange with friends and neighbors. You will all enjoy a brand new assortment!

- Eat by candlelight if your housekeeping chores have been slighted by holiday activities.

- A real football surrounded by fresh flowers makes a creative football party decoration.

- If cigarette smoke makes rooms smell stale, place dishes of vinegar in inconspicious places.

- After New Year's Eve parties, carpet stains may be removed by blotting, not rubbing. Put a little seltzer on the spot and soak a while. Then blot with clean, absorbent material, beginning at the outer edge and working towards center.

- A little white blackboard chalk gently rubbed over spots on white table-cloths provide a quick coverup.

NEW YEAR'S EVE BUFFETS

Chili Relleno Appetizers, page 22
Hot Spicy Cider, page 44
Pecan Salad, page 55
Leftover Turkey Pastry, page 76
Coffee Can Cheese Bread, page 96
Grasshopper Cheesecake, page 114
Lemon Bars, page 134

Pizza Appetizers, page 28
Mulled Christmas Cheer, page 44
Strawberry Jell-O Salad, page 57
Oriental Turkey, page 76
Cherry Torte, page 113
Dilly Bread, page 145

Herb Cheese, page 30
Nonalcoholic Mint Julep, page 42
Elegant Blueberry Party Salad, page 49
Chicken and Dressing Casserole, page 66
Butter Rolls, page 100
Sour Cream-Raisin Tarts, page 119

Cheese Roll, page 28
Holiday Cheer, page 42
Molded Cranberry Salad, page 52
Chicken Casserole, page 66
Never-Fail Biscuits, page 96
Caramel Pie, page 137

Shrimp Dip, page 22
Sangria Punch, page 43
Mandarin Orange Mold, page 55
Easy Ham and Cheese Souffle, page 72
Pumpkin Bread, page 107
Mother's Pecan Pie, page 139

NEW YEAR'S MIDNIGHT SUPPERS

Fondue Italiano, page 27
Spiced Tea and Cider Drink, page 44
Blueberry Salad, page 50
Barbecued Brisket of Beef, page 64
Grits Casserole, page 93
Freezer Kolaches, page 102
Cranberry-Ice Cream Pie, page 138

Fresh Holiday Eggnog, page 41
Pink Delight Salad, page 55
Barbecued Meatballs, page 70
Ham Pockets, page 72
Refrigerator Muffins, page 99
Special Occasion Baked Alaska, page 112

Holiday Cottage Cheese, page 57
Hamburger Quiche, page 71
Wyoming Strawhats, page 72
Angel Biscuits, page 96
Cherries in the Snow, page 114

Cranberry-Lemon Salad, page 52
Cannelloni, page 70
Shrimp Quiche, page 75
Arniece's Nut Loaf, page 106
Pecan Pie Bar, page 135

Cranberry Mold, page 51
Turkey Enchiladas, page 77
Spinach-Mushroom Quiche, page 81
Easy Holiday Punch, page 92
Dinner Cheese Biscuits, page 96
Toffee Bars, page 132

NEW YEAR'S DAY FOOTBALL BRUNCHES

Banana Crush, page 41
Cranberry-Pineapple Salad, page 52
Supreme Chicken Casserole, page 69
Uh-Oh muffins, page 100
Cherry Bars, page 128
Swedish Nuts, page 154

Pineapple Punch, page 43
Cranberry-Apple Salad, page 51
Apricot Chicken, page 66
Bran Muffins, page 99
Theola's Old-Fashioned Fruitcake, page 122
Krazy Korn, page 154

Holiday Cranberry Punch, page 42
New Year's Ham Salad, page 58
Shish Kabobs, page 64
Scalloped Corn, page 85
Holiday Dessert Pudding, page 117
Susan's Cheese Cupcakes, page 126
Hot Buttered Nuts, page 154

Strawberry Fruit Punch, page 43
Mexicali Chili, page 64
Cranberry-Orange-Nut Bread, page 105
Molasses Wheat Germ Candy, page 128
Famous Brownie Pie, page 138

Chili Con Queso Dip, page 22
Sweetheart Punch, page 43
Red-White-Blue Salad, page 49
Meatball Casserole, page 72
Flavorful Tomato Bread, page 101
Dream Cookies, page 133
Sugar-Coated Peanuts, page 154

Football Parties

As the busy holiday season draws to a close, we're filled with all the warm memories of visiting relatives, entertaining friends, and sharing the holidays with our family.

Cold January days make a crackling fire and quiet gatherings with friends more appealing than ever. The breath-taking excitement of football games provide inexpensive entertainment, while the menus for *Football Game Parties*, *Football Game Buffets* and *Tailgate Picnics* suggest simple fare that's easy to prepare and not too heavy.

For a change, why not use tabletop appliances? Guests will enjoy the chance to participate in the meal, and it saves you time in the kitchen.

And don't be afraid to experiment with different dishes. Casual parties like these are an ideal time to be a little daring, and as fun for you as your guests. Start with these menus and watch their smiles of delight!

TIPS

- Cheese makes a great TV snack. Afterwards, to prevent cut cheese from drying, dip the surface in paraffin, wrap in foil, and store in refrigerator.

- Not all guests are expected. Keep an emergency shelf in your cupboard and/or freezer with party crackers, ingredients for fix-it-fast foods or ready-made items. It's also wise to have a few cookies frozen to unwrap and serve for friends who stop by for a short visit. Keep these items hidden or "forbidden" from hungry families.

• Use coffee cups as gelatin molds if your supply runs out before the guest list does.

FOOTBALL BRUNCHES

Doris' Stuffed Mushrooms, page 37
Old-Fashioned Fruit Salad, page 48
Egg Strata, page 80
Italian Cream Cake, page 123

Linda's Apple Salad, page 48
Baked Eggs and Sausage, page 79
Squash Fritters, page 89
Super Cheesecake, page 113

Katie's Spinach Salad, page 61
Zesty Sausage Squares, page 74
French-Fried Sweet Potatoes, page 89
German Apple Cake, page 120

Lime Congealed Salad, page 54
Baked Pancakes with Sausage, page 81
Far-East Celery, page 85
Laura's Gingerbread, page 124

TV TRAY MEALS

Cheery Cherry Salad, page 50
Sesame Seed Chicken, page 69
Spinach Balls, page 87
Jean's Pumpkin Bread, page 107
No-Bake Cocoa Bourbon Balls, page 148
Spiced Pecans, page 154

Sweet-Sour Smokeys, page 33
Pear-Pecan Salad, page 55
Simple Simon Cheese Pie, page 81
Squash Dressing, page 93
Rainbow Cake, page 119

Bacon Roll-Ups, page 27
Christmas Lime Salad, page 50
Holiday Shrimp and Rice Casserole, page 74
Mary Jo's Sweet Potato Casserole, page 91
Amaretto Raisin Bundt Cake, page 122

Fondue Italiano, page 27
Cobb Salad, page 61
Touchdown Curry, page 65
Granny's Sour Cream Pound Cake, page 123

TAILGATE PICNICS

Cheese Crisps, page 30
Pineapple-Cheese Ball, page 30
Frosted Ham Ball, page 32
Norwegian Flatbrod, page 100
Chocolate Macaroons, page 129

Vegetable Dip, page 25
Pasta Salad, page 57
Chicken-Fruit Salad, page 58
Spinach Salad, page 61
Moist Oatmeal Cookies, page 134

Chili-Cheese Roll, page 29
Guacamole Salad, page 48
Taco Salad, page 60
Stir and Drop Sugar Cookies, page 135

Sauerkraut Ball, page 34
Pickled Eggs, page 37
Fruit Medley Elegante, page 48
Party Chicken, page 70
Rich Peanut Butter Cookies, page 135

FOOTBALL BUFFETS

Eggnog Wassail Bowl, page 45
Hot Chicken Salad Ring, page 58
Super Bowl Salad, page 61
Rice-Mushroom Casserole, page 93
Poppy Seed Cake, page 124

Fondue Cheese Puffs, page 26
Shrimp Mold, page 59
Celery en Casserole, page 86
Bread Sticks, page 96
Prune Cake, page 124

Chicken Snacks, page 32
Cinnamon-Applesauce Swirl Salad, page 51
Broccoli Special, page 85
Wild Rice Casserole, page 93
Holiday Ring Cake, page 147

Hot Diggity, page 33
Avocado Salad, page 48
Spinach Torta, page 88
Sour Cream-Noodle Bake, page 91
Easy Holiday Trifle, page 117

Festive Appetizers and Beverages

It wouldn't be a holiday party without lots of tempting appetizers. But, remember, those little delicacies can be dangerous! Serve your guests too many, and the delicious dinner you've planned may go untouched. Rather, keep in mind, finger foods should whet the appetite, not satisfy it.

The sky's the limit when choosing what kinds of cheese, fruits, vegetables and meats to use in appetizers. Just remember never use a food as an appetizer that will be repeated in your main meal.

When planning appetizers for any holiday occasion, choose flavors that contrast in texture and taste as well as are colorful to the eye. This chapter is brimming with delightful dips for your favorite chips . . . fun fondues . . . cheese balls to keep the good times rolling . . . tempting tarts . . . and all sorts of stuffed, spiced and pickled nibbles.

Offer your guests a choice of these party punches as they relax and enjoy their appetizers. Garnish drinks lavishly with fruit kabobs, bright red straw-berries, cherries or any colorful fresh fruit. Use your imagination! Frosty beverages served in cham-pagne glasses always lend a party touch. Cinnamon sticks as stirrers for hot beverages add a perky note.

With appetizers and beverages such as these, your guests will eagerly look forward to enjoying another invitation to your home.

CHILES RELLENOS APPETIZERS

2 cans whole green chilies
1 lb. Monterey Jack cheese, shredded
6 eggs
Salt and pepper to taste
Picante sauce

Slice peppers lengthwise. Spread over bottom of buttered 9 x 13-inch baking dish. Cover with cheese. Combine eggs, salt and pepper in bowl; beat well. Spread over cheese. Bake at 350 degrees until knife inserted in center comes out clean. Cool. Cut into small squares. Serve with Picante sauce.

Beverly Owens, Van Buren Jr. H.S.
Van Buren, Arkansas

GREEN PEPPER JELLY

3 lg. green peppers
6 c. sugar
1 1/2 c. cider vinegar
1 bottle of Certo
1 tsp. cayenne pepper (opt.)
Green food coloring

Remove seeds from peppers; place in blender container. Process in blender until pureed. Combine pepper puree, sugar and vinegar in large saucepan. Bring mixture to rolling boil; boil for 10 minutes. Cool mixture for 5 to 10 minutes. Add Certo, cayenne pepper and a few drops of food coloring; stir well. Cool. Pour into hot sterilized jars. Seal. Excellent garnish on cream cheese. Serve with crackers. Yield: 3-4 pints.

Elizabeth W. Benish, Barrington H.S.
Barrington, Illinois

HOLIDAY EGG ROLLS

1/4 c. vegetable oil
1 lb. lean pork, cubed
1/2 lb. frozen raw shrimp, shelled,
    deveined, chopped
4 c. bean sprouts
2 c. chopped celery
8 green onions, chopped
1 tsp. salt
1 tbsp. cornstarch
2 tbsp. soy sauce
1 pkg. egg roll skins
1 egg, beaten
Oil for frying

Heat vegetable oil in wok or skillet. Add pork. Cook until pork loses color. Add shrimp. Cook for 1 minute. Add vegetables and salt. Cook for 2 minutes, stirring often. Sprinkle with cornstarch; mix well. Stir in soy sauce. Cook for 1 minute. Turn into colander; cool completely. Remove skin from egg roll. Place 2 to 3 tablespoons cooled filling on dough slightly below center. Brush dough edges with egg. Fold 1 corner over filling. Fold 2 opposite corners toward center. Roll toward remaining corner to form cylinder. Fry in deep fat at 375 degrees until golden brown. Drain. Serve with duck or mustard sauce. May cut skins to make small rolls.

Karen Anding Crook, Schaumburg H.S.
Schaumburg, Illinois

ARTICHOKE DIP

2 cans artichokes, chopped
1 c. olive oil
1 c. Italian bread crumbs
1 1/2 tbsp. lemon juice
1/2 c. grated Romano cheese
Salt, pepper and garlic powder to taste
Melba toast rounds

Combine first 5 ingredients in skillet. Season; mix well. Heat until cheese melts. Serve warm with toast rounds.

Susan P. Brewer, Broadmoor Sr. H.S.
Baton Rouge, Louisiana

CHILI CON QUESO DIP

3 tbsp. finely minced onion
Butter
3 oz. chopped green chilies
1 clove of garlic, chopped fine
1/2 lb. Velveeta cheese
1/4 lb. Cheddar cheese
6 tbsp. evaporated milk

Saute onion in small amount of butter in skillet until transparent. Add chilies, garlic and cheeses. Heat over low heat until cheese melts. Blend in evaporated milk. Serve with corn chips.

Dorothy S. Weirick, Cottonwood H.S.
Salt Lake City, Utah

CHRISTMAS DIP

4 oz. blue cheese, softened
1 8-oz. package cream cheese, softened
1/3 c. chopped green pepper
3 tbsp. chopped pimento
1/4 tsp. garlic salt
1/4 c. evaporated milk

Combine all ingredients in bowl; mix well. Chill for 1 hour. Serve with fresh vegetables. Yield: 2 cups.

Judy Fine, Science Hill H.S.
Johnson City, Tennessee

CRAB DIP FOR VEGETABLES

    1 8-oz. package cream cheese, softened
    Thousand Island dressing
    1 6-oz. can crab meat, drained
    Broccoli flowerets, cauliflowerets,
      carrot sticks, green pepper sticks,
      celery sticks

Place cream cheese in bowl; beat until smooth. Add enough Thousand Island dressing to make dip consistency. Cut crab meat into small pieces. Add to cheese mixture; mix well. Place in dip bowl. Surround with assortment of fresh vegetables and crackers. May substitute shrimp for crab.

Betsy-Anne Sheffield, Bloomfield Jr. H.S.
Halifax, Nova Scotia, Canada

CRAB DIP

    1 6 1/2-oz. can crab meat
    1/4 c. lemon juice
    2 3-oz. packages cream cheese, softened
    1/4 c. cream
    1/4 c. mayonnaise
    1/2 clove of garlic, crushed
    1 tsp. minced onions
    1/2 tsp. chives
    Salt to taste
    1/8 tsp. Worcestershire sauce
    2 drops of Tabasco sauce

Marinate crab meat in lemon juice for 1 hour; drain. Combine cream cheese and cream in mixer bowl; mix until smooth. Beat in mayonnaise. Add garlic, onions, chives and salt; blend well. Fold crab into sauce. Add Worcestershire sauce and Tabasco. Serve hot in chafing dish. May also be served cold. Yield: 20 servings.

Betty Carol Stevenson, Liberty Jr. H.S.
Ashland, Virginia

CRISPY CASHEW DIP

    2 8-oz. packages cream cheese, softened
    5 tbsp. finely chopped green onions
    1 c. ground ham
    1/2 c. chopped cashews
    1/2 c. Blue Nun white wine
    1/2 tsp. white pepper

    1/2 c. chopped water chestnuts
    Whole cashews

Combine all ingredients except whole cashews in bowl; mix well. Refrigerate until serving time. Decorate with whole cashews. Serve with crackers or vegetables.

Vicki R. Olson, Stillwater Sr. H.S.
Stillwater, Minnesota

CURRY DIP

    1 c. Hellmann's mayonnaise
    1 tsp. tarragon vinegar
    1/2 tsp. each curry powder, garlic salt,
      onion powder and seasoned salt
    Assorted fresh vegetables

Combine mayonnaise, vinegar and seasonings in bowl; mix well. Refrigerate for 4 to 5 hours until flavors blend. Serve with fresh vegetables: broccoli flowerets and cauliflowerets, carrot, celery and green pepper sticks and radishes.

Sara H. Cavanaugh, Wetumpka H.S.
Wetumpka, Alabama

DILL DIP

    1 pt. Dukes mayonnaise
    1 pt. sour cream
    1 tbsp. dried parsley
    3 tbsp. each grated onion, dillweed
    1 1/2 tbsp. seasoned salt
    Fresh vegetables

Combine all ingredients except fresh vegetables in bowl; blend well. Chill. Serve with fresh vegetables. Will keep 1 month or more in refrigerator. Yield: 4 cups.

April Wilkerson, Southwestern Randolph H.S.
Asheboro, North Carolina

DRIED BEEF DIP

    1 8-oz. package cream cheese, softened
    2 tbsp. milk
    1 sm. onion, chopped
    1/2 tsp. garlic powder
    2 1/2 oz. dried beef, chopped
    1 carton sour cream
    1 c. chopped pecans
    1 box Trisket crackers

Combine first 6 ingredients in bowl; mix well. Place in ovenproof serving bowl. Sprinkle with pecans. Bake at 325 degrees until hot. Serve immediately with Trisket crackers.

Catherine E. Reed, Arab H.S.
Arab, Alabama

HOLIDAY DIP

1 lg. carton cottage cheese
1 8-oz. package cream cheese, softened
1 sm. jar jalapeno cheese spread
1 sm. package ranch-style dressing mix

Place all ingredients in blender container. Blend at high speed until creamy. Serve with chips, crackers and fresh vegetables.

Mary Lou Young, Greenwood H.S.
Greenwood, Arkansas

OYSTER DIP

1 8-oz. package cream cheese, softened
Dash of Tabasco sauce
1 can smoked oysters
1 carton bacon and horseradish dip

Combine all ingredients in bowl; mix well. Refrigerate until chilled. Serve with chips or crackers.

Sandra Tanner, Troy H.S.
Troy, Texas

SHRIMP DIP

2 8-oz. packages cream cheese, softened
1 med. onion, chopped
1 tsp. Worcestershire sauce
1 tsp. seasoned salt
1 bottle of cocktail sauce
1 tbsp. horseradish
1 c. cooked, cleaned shrimp

Mix cream cheese, onion, Worcestershire sauce and seasoned salt. Spread in bottom of casserole. Mix cocktail sauce and horseradish together. Spread over cream cheese layer. Arrange shrimp on top. Chill until firm. Serve with crackers. May substitute 1 cup crab meat for shrimp.

Ann Schroeder, Texas City H.S.
Texas City, Texas

SHRIMP DIP

1 4 1/2-oz. can shrimp, drained,
*   chopped*
1 hard-boiled egg, chopped
1 c. sour cream
1/4 c. mayonnaise
3 tbsp. green onions, thinly sliced
1 tbsp. lemon juice
1 tsp. horseradish
1 tsp. Worcestershire sauce
1/2 tsp. dried dillweed

Combine all ingredients in small bowl; mix well. Cover tightly. Chill thoroughly. Serve with fresh, crisp vegetables. Yield: 2 cups.

Mrs. Carolyn Robertson, Linton-Stockton H.S.
Linton, Indiana

DIANA'S SPINACH DIP

1 pkg. frozen chopped spinach
1 c. sour cream
1 c. mayonnaise
1/2 tsp. dillweed
1 tsp. salad supreme
1 tbsp. dried parsley flakes
1 1/2 tbsp. chopped onions
Lemon juice to taste
Fresh vegetables

Cook spinach using package directions. Drain; squeeze out excess moisture. Combine with remaining ingredients except fresh vegetables; mix well. Refrigerate until chilled. Serve as dip surrounded by fresh vegetables.

Diana K. Dukes, Marion H.S.
Marion, Texas

MILINDA'S SPINACH DIP

2 jars strained baby-food spinach
1 pt. mayonnaise
1/4 to 1/3 c. minced onion flakes
1/4 to 1/3 c. minced parsley
1 tsp. each salt, pepper
Juice from 1/2 lemon

Combine all ingredients in bowl; mix well. Refrigerate overnight. Serve as dip with fresh vegetables or crackers. Will keep for 2 weeks refrigerated.

Milinda Carnahan, Sioux County H.S.
Harrison, Nebraska

TOMATO AND GREEN ONION DIP

1 med. tomato, chopped
1/2 c. lemon juice
1/2 tsp. each salt, pepper
1/4 c. chopped green onions
2 c. sour cream
1/4 tsp. Worcestershire sauce
1/2 tsp. sugar
Fresh vegetables

Marinate tomato in lemon juice, salt and pepper for 1 hour. Squeeze out liquid. Add remaining ingredients except fresh vegetables; mix well.

Serve as a dip surrounded by fresh vegetables.
Yield: 3 cups.

Pat Leeser, Montgomery Co. R-II H.S.
Montgomery City, Missouri

HOLIDAY VEGETABLE DIP

1 c. Kraft Real Mayonnaise
1/2 c. sour cream
1/3 c. finely chopped green peppers
1/3 c. finely chopped radishes
1/4 tsp. onion salt
Assorted fresh vegetables

Combine first 5 ingredients; mix well. Chill.
Serve with carrot sticks, cherry tomatoes, broccoli, cauliflower, green pepper strips, cucum-
bers, radishes, celery sticks, mushrooms and
zucchini strips.

Carolyne E. Ray, West Jr. H.S.
Kansas City, Kansas

VEGETABLE DIP

1 carrot, cut in pieces
1 onion, quartered
1 stalk celery, cut in pieces
1 clove of garlic
1 tsp. salt
1/4 tsp. pepper
2 tbsp. vinegar
1 egg
1 c. oil

Place all ingredients except oil in blender container. Turn on and off rapidly until vegetables
are pureed. Turn blender speed to high. Add oil
gradually in a thin stream, pausing occasionally
to allow mixture to thicken. Place in covered
container. Refrigerate overnight to allow flavors
to blend. Serve with fresh vegetables prepared
for dipping. May also be used as salad dressing.
Yield: 2 cups.

Jane J. McFerrin, Shamrock H.S.
Decatur, Georgia

PARTY CHEESE DIP

1/4 to 1/2 tsp. Tabasco sauce
1 3-oz. package cream cheese, softened
1 pt. sour cream
1 env. dry onion soup mix
1 2 1/4-oz. can deviled ham

Mix Tabasco with cream cheese in bowl; blend
in sour cream gradually. Add onion soup mix
and deviled ham; mix well. Spoon into serving
dish. Serve with halved artichoke hearts, mush-

room halves, cauliflowerets, scallions and
cherry tomatoes. Yield: 2 2/3 cups.

Photograph for this recipe above.

WHITE SPICE DIP

1 c. sour cream
1 tbsp. horseradish
1 tsp. lemon juice
2 drops of Worcestershire sauce
1 tsp. salt
1 tsp. pepper

Combine all ingredients in bowl; mix well.
Serve with apple slices. Excellent for low-
calorie dip.

Photograph for this recipe on page 20.

THREE-CHEESE DUNK

1 c. cottage cheese, well drained
1 c. grated Cheddar cheese
2 oz. bleu cheese, mashed
2 tbsp. mayonnaise
1 tbsp. horseradish
1 tsp. prepared mustard
1/2 tsp. Worcestershire sauce
3 green onions, finely chopped
1/2 tsp. each salt, celery salt
Pepper to taste

Blend cheeses together in bowl. Add remaining
ingredients, mixing well. Pile in serving bowl.
Serve with fruit slices.

Photograph for this recipe on page 20.

CREAMY PARMESAN FONDUE

2 8-oz. packages cream cheese, softened
1 1/2 c. milk
1/2 tsp. each garlic salt, salt
3/4 c. Parmesan cheese

Combine cream cheese and milk in saucepan; blend well. Warm over low heat. Add seasonings; mix well. Add Parmesan cheese slowly, stirring until smooth. Pour into fondue pot over burner. Serve with apple, carrot and French bread cubes for dipping on fondue forks. Yield: 8-10 servings.

Mrs. Joy L. Manson, Miami H.S.
Miami, Arizona

FONDUE CHEESE PUFFS

1 lb. Cheddar cheese, cubed
1 lb. Monterey Jack cheese, cubed
2 eggs, beaten
Bread crumbs
Oil for frying

Dip cheese cubes into beaten eggs. Roll in bread crumbs immediately. Place on tray; refrigerate until serving time. Fill fondue pot 3/4 full with oil; heat oil. Place cheese cubes on fondue fork. Fondue cheese cubes individually for 1 minute.

Myrna Orr, McFadden Jr. H.S.
Santa Ana, California

CHEDDARY APPLE FONDUE

1 lb. Cheddar cheese, shredded
1/3 c. flour
1/8 tsp. each nutmeg, mace, cinnamon
*   and salt*
2 c. apple juice

Toss Cheddar cheese and flour together in large bowl. Mix seasonings together; set aside. Heat apple juice in 2-quart saucepan until bubbly. Reduce heat to low. Add cheese mixture, 1/2 cup at a time, stirring after each addition until cheese is melted. Add seasonings. Cook until thickened, stirring constantly. Pour into fondue pot. Serve with apple slices, zucchini slices, mushrooms, cocktail sausages or French bread cubes. Yield: 2 1/4 cups.

Photograph for this recipe on page 6.

CHOCOLATE FONDUE

2 6-oz. packages semisweet chocolate
*   morsels*

1/2 c. sugar
1 tsp. vanilla extract
1/2 c. light cream
Fruit in bite-size pieces (banana,
*   apple, orange, seedless grapes,*
*   cherries, strawberries, etc.)*

Place all ingredients except fruit in fondue saucepan. Place over direct flame. Stir until chocolate is melted and mixture is smooth. Cover flame partially so that mixture is just kept warm. Spear pieces of fruit with fondue forks or long picks; dip into melted chocolate. Swirl to remove excess chocolate. Yield: 2 cups.

Photograph for this recipe above.

CHOCOLATE FONDUE

24 oz. milk chocolate chips
1/3 c. Creme de Cacao
1/2 to 1 c. cream

Melt chocolate chips in fondue pot on low setting. Add Creme de Cacao, blending well. Add enough cream to make of dip consistency. Keep warm. Arrange assorted dip foods on plate: Bite-sized angel food cake pieces, whole strawberries, whole maraschino cherries, marshmallows, apple slices, banana slices or pear slices.

Linda Tole, R.L. Turner H.S.
Carrollton, Texas

SWEET-SOUR FONDUE

1 lb. bulk pork sausage
2 5-oz. packages party-sized smoked
*   sausage links*
1 20-oz. can pineapple chunks
1 jar maraschino cherries, drained
3 tbsp. each honey, vinegar
1 tbsp. soy sauce
2 tbsp. cornstarch

Shape bulk sausage into 1-inch balls. Brown sausage balls and sausage links in skillet together. Remove sausage from skillet; drain. Reserve 2 tablespoons pan drippings. Drain pineapple, reserving juice. Place reserved juice in fondue pot. May add small amount of cherry juice. Add honey, vinegar, soy sauce and cornstarch to pineapple juice; blend until smooth. Add reserved pan drippings. Bring to a boil, stirring constantly. Add sausage, pineapple and cherries; mix well. Simmer for 15 minutes. Serve warm.

Syd Burnett, Flour Bluff H.S.
Corpus Christi, Texas

FONDUE ITALIANO

1/2 lb. ground beef
1/2 env. spaghetti sauce mix
1 15-oz. can tomato sauce
12 oz. Cheddar cheese, shredded
4 oz. mozzarella cheese, shredded
1 tbsp. cornstarch
1/2 c. Chianti
Italian bread cubes

Brown ground beef in saucepan. Drain. Combine beef with spaghetti sauce mix and tomato sauce in fondue pot. Add cheeses gradually, stirring over low heat until cheese is melted. Blend cornstarch and Chianti together; add to cheese mixture. Cook, stirring constantly until thickened and bubbly. Serve as dip with Italian bread cubes.

Susan Spencer, George Whittell H.S.
Zephry Cove, Nevada
Cathryn E. Springer, Northwest H.S.
Canal Fulton, Ohio

BACON ROLL-UPS

1/4 c. margarine
1 1/2 c. herb-seasoned stuffing mix
1 egg, slightly beaten
1/4 lb. mild pork sausage
1/2 to 2/3-lb. sliced bacon

Melt margarine in saucepan. Remove from heat; stir in 1/2 cup water and stuffing mix. Add egg and sausage; blend thoroughly. Chill for 1 hour for easier handling. Shape into small pecan-shaped balls. Cut bacon into thirds, crosswise. Wrap one piece around each ball. Fasten with wooden pick. Place on rack in shallow pan. Bake at 375 degrees for 35 minutes or until crisp and brown. Drain on paper towels. Serve hot. May be made the day before and refrigerated. Freezes well. Yield: 36 appetizers.

Debra A. H. Bean, Rule H.S.
Knoxville, Tennessee

PARTY BACON SANDWICHES

1 loaf sandwich bread
1 10 1/2-oz. can condensed cream of
*   mushroom soup*
Cheddar or American cheese, cut into
*   1/2-in. cubes*
1 lb. sliced bacon

Remove crusts from bread. Spread each slice with undiluted soup. Place cheese cube in center of bread. Roll up, diagonally. Wrap with 1 slice bacon; secure with wooden picks. Place sandwiches on baking sheet. Bake at 225 degrees for 1 hour and 45 minutes to 2 hours or until golden brown. Serve hot. Yield: 25 servings.

Judy Touby, Scottsdale H.S.
Scottsdale, Arizona

CHAFING DISH MEATBALLS

1 lb. ground beef
1/2 c. dry bread crumbs
1/3 c. minced onion
1/4 c. milk
1 egg
1 tbsp. snipped parsley
1 tsp. salt
1/8 tsp. pepper
1/2 tsp. Worcestershire sauce
1/2 c. shortening
1 12-oz. bottle of chili sauce
1 10-oz. jar grape jelly

Mix ground beef, crumbs, onion, milk, egg and seasonings. Shape into small balls. Melt shortening in skillet. Brown meatballs. Heat chili sauce and jelly in chafing dish until melted. Add meatballs. Simmer for 30 minutes.

Janet Wommack, Hood Jr. H.S.
Odessa, Texas

PARTY PIZZAS

1 can chopped black olives
1 can bacon bits
1 c. grated Cheddar cheese
1 c. mayonnaise
Party rye bread

Combine first 4 ingredients in bowl; mix well. Spread on party rye bread. Bake at 350 degrees for 10 minutes.

Mary Dickey Gill, West Lincoln H.S.
Brookhaven, Mississippi

PARTY BEEF BALLS

1/4 lb. Roquefort cheese
1/4 c. mayonnaise
2 tbsp. Worcestershire sauce
1 tsp. prepared mustard
2 c. crushed corn flakes
1/2 c. milk
1 egg, slightly beaten
1 lb. ground beef
1 1/2 tsp. salt
1/8 tsp. pepper
1/8 tsp. red pepper
Barbecue sauce

Crumble cheese into bowl. Blend in mayonnaise, Worcestershire sauce and mustard. Add remaining ingredients except barbecue sauce to Roquefort mixture; mix well. Shape into 1-inch balls. Broil or panfry until browned. Serve hot on toothpicks with heated barbecue sauce in a dip bowl. Yield: 3 1/2 dozen.

Hassie Hunter Rodgers, Goshen H.S.
Goshen, Alabama

PIZZA APPETIZERS

1 lb. Velveeta cheese
1 lb. Cheddar cheese
1 lb. bulk sausage
1 lb. hamburger
Oregano, garlic salt to taste
Party rye bread

Melt cheeses together in double boiler. Saute sausage and hamburger in skillet until brown and crumbly; drain well. Combine meat and cheese; blend well. Season to taste. Spread on rye bread. Bake at 400 degrees for 10 minutes. May be frozen. Yield: 125 pieces.

Bonnie Schneider, Holgate Jr. H.S.
Aberdeen, South Dakota

BLUE CHEESE BALL

2 oz. blue cheese
1 8-oz. package cream cheese, softened
1 sm. can crushed pineapple, drained
1/2 c. crushed pecans

Combine blue cheese, cream cheese and pineapple in bowl; mix well. Form into ball. Roll cheese ball in crushed pecans. Chill until serving time.

Ruth Cross, Sullivan Central H.S.
Blountsville, Tennessee

CHEESE ROLL

8 oz. Cheddar cheese, grated
1 3-oz. package cream cheese, softened
1/2 tsp. garlic salt
1/2 c. finely chopped nuts
1 tsp. paprika
1/2 tsp. chili powder
Dash of cayenne pepper

Blend cheeses together in bowl. Add garlic salt and chopped nuts. Form into 2 rolls. Mix paprika, chili powder and cayenne pepper together on foil. Roll cheese rolls in paprika mixture until covered. Wrap in foil. Chill until firm. Slice into thin slices. Serve with crackers.

Mrs. Doris S. Johnson, Atlanta H.S.
Atlanta, Texas

CHEESE LOAF

1 lb. sausage
2 lb. Velveeta cheese
1 lb. mild Cheddar cheese
1 sm. jar chopped pimentos
4 jalapeno peppers, chopped

Saute sausage in skillet; drain. Melt Velveeta cheese and Cheddar cheese in double boiler over hot water. Add sausage, pimentos and peppers to cheese mixture; mix well. Pour into 9 x 13-inch baking dish. Chill until set. Slice; serve on crackers.

Brenda Simmons, Dayton H.S.
Dayton, Texas

CHEESE AND OLIVE BALLS

12 oz. sharp cheese, grated
1/2 c. margarine, softened
1 1/2 c. flour
1/4 tsp. paprika
1/4 tsp. cayenne pepper
Olives

Combine cheese and margarine in bowl. Add flour, paprika and cayenne pepper; mix well. Shape small amount of mixture around 1 olive; form into ball. Chill overnight. Bake at 450 degrees for 12 to 15 minutes.

Myrtle Chapman, El Reno H.S.
El Reno, Oklahoma

CHEESE-PECAN BALL

    4 8-oz. packages cream cheese, softened
    1 to 2 tbsp. steak sauce
    1 c. finely chopped pecans
    1 clove of garlic, minced
    Few drops of hot pepper sauce
    Chopped parsley
    Paprika

Combine first 5 ingredients in bowl; blend thoroughly. Form into ball; wrap in waxed paper. Chill until firm. Place on serving dish. Sprinkle parsley in 1-inch strip down center of ball. Sprinkle both sides with paprika. Chill. Let stand at room temperature for 15 minutes before serving. Serve as spread with assorted crackers. Yield: 1 1/2 cups.

Madonna Meeker, Ridgedale H.S.
Morral, Ohio

CHILI CHEESE ROLL

    8 oz. Velveeta cheese, softened
    1 8-oz. package cream cheese, softened
    4 oz. diced green chiles, drained

Roll Velveeta cheese between 2 sheets waxed paper to 1/8 to 1/4-inch thick rectangle. Repeat process with cream cheese. Place cream cheese on top of Velveeta cheese. Spread chiles over surface. Use waxed paper to help roll jelly roll fashion. Cover with waxed paper. Chill. Slice; serve with crackers or tortilla chips.

Marilyn J. Rogers, Roosevelt Jr. H.S.
San Diego, California

FOUR-CHEESE BALL

    1/2 lb. Swiss cheese, shredded
    1/4 lb. Cheddar cheese, shredded
    1/2 lb. cream cheese, softened
    2 oz. blue cheese, crumbled fine
    2 tsp. Worcestershire sauce
    1 sm. onion, grated
    1/2 tsp. salt
    1 tbsp. prepared mustard
    1 tsp. prepared horseradish
    2 tbsp. drained pickle relish

    1/2 c. ground pecans (opt.)
    1/2 c. finely chopped parsley (opt.)

Combine all ingredients except pecans and parsley in large bowl; mix well. Chill. Shape into 1 large or 2 small balls. Roll in pecans or parsley. Serve at room temperature with crackers.

Susanne LeFeber, Lebanon H.S.
Lebanon, Ohio

HOLIDAY CHEESE BALL

    2 lg. packages cream cheese, softened
    1/3 c. chopped onion
    1/4 c. finely chopped green pepper
    1 8-oz. can crushed pineapple
    2 tbsp. seasoned salt
    1 c. chopped nuts
    1 c. finely chopped nuts

Combine first 6 ingredients in bowl; blend thoroughly. Form into ball. Roll in finely chopped nuts. Serve with crackers.

Karen Robinson, Alta H.S.
Sandy, Utah

HOT PEPPER CHEESE BALL

    1 8-oz. package cream cheese, softened
    1/4 lb. Cheddar cheese, grated
    1/4 lb. extra sharp cheese, grated
    1/4 lb. hot pepper cheese, grated
    1/4 tsp. onion salt
    1/4 tsp. garlic salt
    2 tbsp. salad dressing
    1 tbsp. Worcestershire sauce
    Chopped nuts

Combine all ingredients except nuts in bowl; blend thoroughly. Form into ball. Refrigerate overnight. Roll in nuts. Serve with crackers.

Delinda McCormick, Caldwell County H.S.
Princeton, Kentucky

PARTY CHEESE DIP

    1 10-oz. package sharp Cheddar cheese
    1/2 c. sour cream
    1 tbsp. Sherry

Combine all ingredients in large bowl. Mix until smooth. Allow to stand for 1 hour. Serve with assorted crackers and fresh vegetables. Yield: 1 1/2 cups.

Paula R. Brown, Anna H.S.
Anna, Texas

CHILE CON QUESO WITH TORTILLA CHIPS

2 tbsp. butter
2 tbsp. flour
1 c. light cream
1 c. chopped drained canned tomatoes
1/2 tsp. finely chopped garlic
1/2 tsp. salt
1 4-oz. can chopped green chiles
1/2 lb. grated Monterey Jack cheese
1 lg. bag tortilla chips

Melt butter in saucepan. Blend in flour. Stir in cream slowly. Bring to a boil over high heat. Cook for 3 minutes over low heat, stirring constantly. Remove from heat. Combine tomatoes, garlic and salt in chafing dish; heat. Stir in cream sauce gradually. Add chiles. Stir in cheese, a small amount at a time until melted. Serve with tortilla chips.

> *Karen J. Barker, Monterey H.S.*
> *Monterey, California*

HERB CHEESE

1 1/2 lb. sharp Cheddar cheese, shredded
2 tbsp. each minced parsley, chives,
*   thyme, sage and savory*
1/2 c. whipping cream
2/3 c. Sherry

Combine all ingredients in bowl; mix well. Refrigerate overnight. Force through strainer. Yield: 4 cups.

> *Photograph for this recipe on page 20.*

CARAWAY-CURRY SPREAD

2 3-oz. packages cream cheese, softened
1 tbsp. evaporated milk
1 tbsp. caraway seed
1/2 tsp. curry powder
Pinch of salt
Dash of hot pepper sauce

Combine all ingredients in small bowl; mix well. Chill to blend flavors. Serve with apple fingers. Yield: 1 cup.

> *Photograph for this recipe on page 20.*

PINEAPPLE-CHEESE BALL

2 8-oz. packages cream cheese, softened
1 8 1/2-oz. can crushed pineapple,
*   drained*
1 to 2 c. chopped pecans or macadamia
*   nuts*

1/4 c. chopped green pepper
2 tbsp. chopped onion
1 tbsp. seasoned salt

Mix together cream cheese and pineapple. Blend in half the nuts and remaining ingredients. Shape mixture into ball using waxed paper. Roll in remaining nuts to coat outside. Refrigerate for flavors to blend.

> *Nicolette Gabrysiak, Warren Township H.S.*
> *Garnee, Illinois*
> *Nancy A. Manon, Salisbury H.S.*
> *Salisbury, North Carolina*

CHEESE QUICHE TARTS

1 8-oz. package cream cheese, softened
1/3 lb. margarine
2 c. flour
1/2 c. milk
1/2 c. mayonnaise
2 eggs, slightly beaten
1 tbsp. cornstarch
1 c. grated Cheddar cheese
1/3 c. chopped green pepper
1/3 c. sliced green onions

Combine cream cheese and margarine in bowl; blend well. Add flour; mix well. Chill. Line small muffin pans with small amount of mixture. Bake at 400 degrees for 10 minutes. Combine milk, mayonnaise, eggs and cornstarch in bowl. Mix until smooth. Stir in cheese, green pepper and onions. Spoon into pastry shells. Bake at 350 degrees for 20 to 30 minutes. Yield: 48 servings.

> *Dorothy A. Larson, Harrison H.S.*
> *Harrison, Arkansas*

CHEESE CRISPS

8-oz. sharp Cheddar cheese, grated
1 3/4 sticks margarine, softened
2 c. flour
1/4 tsp. each salt, red pepper and
*   paprika*
1 c. Rice Krispies, crushed

Mix cheese with margarine. Sift together flour, salt, red pepper and paprika. Add to cheese mixture; blend well. Add Rice Krispies; mix well. Shape into 1-inch balls. Place on ungreased cookie sheet. Flatten with bottom of glass. Bake at 400 degrees for 10 minutes. Cool on rack.

> *Marvis T. Hinson, R.W. Groves H.S.*
> *Savannah, Georgia*

MINI QUICHES

24 6-inch crepes
1 8-oz. package cream cheese, softened
4 eggs, beaten
1 c. finely chopped spinach
1 c. shredded Swiss cheese
2 green onions, finely chopped
1/4 c. half and half
5 slices crisp-cooked bacon, crumbled

Grease 24 muffin cups. Place crepes carefully in muffin cups. Combine remaining ingredients except bacon; mix well. Spoon 2 to 3 table-spoons into each muffin cup. Bake at 375 degrees for 15 minutes or until set. Garnish with bacon.

M. Van Dan, Alden-Hebron H.S.
Hebron, Illinois

CHEESE-OLIVE FILLING FOR ROLLS

1 lb. cheese, grated
2 sm. cans chopped olives
3 hard-boiled eggs, chopped
2 tbsp. green chili peppers
1/2 c. salad oil
1 sm. can tomato sauce
Baked rolls

Combine first 6 ingredients; mix well. Fill baked rolls. Line pan with foil. Place cheese filled rolls on foil; bring foil over to cover rolls. Bake at 350 degrees for 30 minutes. Serve piping hot. May be made day before; refrigerate or freeze.

Elizabeth Baker, Payson Jr. H.S.
Payson, Utah

MOLDED CHEESE AND LIVER PATE

2 env. unflavored gelatin
4 chicken bouillon cubes
1/4 c. cocktail vegetable juice
1 c. shredded brick cheese
1 tbsp. crumbled blue cheese
1/4 c. sour cream
2 tbsp. chopped celery
1 tbsp. chopped green pepper
1/2 c. chopped mushrooms
2 tbsp. butter, melted
1/4 lb. liver sausage
2 tsp. lemon juice
4 tsp. brandy
1/3 c. chopped pecans

Soften gelatin in 1/2 cup cold water. Heat with 1 cup water in 1-quart saucepan, stirring until dissolved. Add bouillon cubes, stirring until dissolved. Combine 1/4 cup gelatin mixture with vegetable juice; mix well. Pour into oiled 4 1/2-cup mold. Chill until set. Beat cheeses with sour cream in bowl. Add 1/2 cup gelatin mixture, celery and green pepper; mix well. Spoon over congealed layer. Chill until set. Cook mushrooms in butter in skillet until tender. Combine sausage and lemon juice in bowl; mix well. Add mushrooms, remaining gelatin mixture and brandy; mix well. Fold in nuts; spoon over cheese layer. Chill until firm. Unmold to serve. Yield: 20-25 servings.

Photograph for this recipe on page 6.

ROLLED CHEESE SANDWICHES

1 8-oz. package cream cheese, softened
Milk
1 tsp. each garlic powder, onion powder
1 loaf of sliced bread, frozen
2 c. chopped nuts

Place cream cheese in bowl. Add enough milk for thin consistency. Stir in garlic powder and onion powder. Trim crusts from frozen bread. Cut bread into 1 1/2 to 2-inch strips. Roll in cream cheese mixture; roll in chopped nuts. Freeze until serving time.

Janice Dennard, Beckville H.S.
Beckville, Texas

CHEDDAR CHEESE SPREAD

1 3-oz. package cream cheese, softened
8 oz. sharp Cheddar cheese, shredded
1/3 c. milk
1/4 c. margarine, softened
1 tsp. Worcestershire sauce
1 tsp. dried chives
1/2 tsp. dry mustard
1/4 tsp. celery seed
1/4 tsp. salt
1/2 tsp. dillweed or 1/4 tsp. dillseed

Combine all ingredients in large bowl. Beat until creamy. Refrigerate for at least 24 hours. Let stand at room temperature for 1 hour before serving. Good with cocktail rye bread. Will keep refrigerated for 2 weeks.

Diane M. Hanson, Fairfield H.S.
Fairfield, Iowa

CHICKEN FINGERS

2 c. finely chopped boned chicken
1 egg
1/2 c. bread crumbs
1/4 tsp. each garlic powder, salt and
  pepper
1/4 c. tomato paste

Combine chicken, egg, bread crumbs, garlic powder, salt and pepper in bowl; mix well. Shape mixture into finger-sized rolls. Place on lightly oiled baking pan. Bake at 350 degrees for 15 minutes. Mix tomato paste with 1/2 cup water. Pour tomato paste mixture over chicken rolls. Bake for 25 minutes longer or until liquid has evaporated. Yield: 8 servings.

Eileen Beauregard, Sequoyah H.S.
Doraville, Georgia

CHICKEN SNACKS

1/2 c. Italian-seasoned bread crumbs
1/2 c. Parmesan cheese
2 tsp. seasoned salt
1 tsp. each sweet basil, salt and paprika
1/4 tsp. thyme
1/2 c. butter, melted
1 egg
2 lg. chicken breasts, cubed

Combine bread crumbs, Parmesan cheese and seasonings in small bowl. Add butter; mix well. Beat egg with 1 tablespoon water in separate bowl. Dip chicken pieces in egg mixture, then into crumb mixture. Place in baking dish. Bake in 400-degree oven for 18 minutes, turning once after 9 minutes. Yield: 3 dozen appetizers.

Sharon Dietrich, Elmhurst H.S.
Ft. Wayne, Indiana

PARTY CHICKEN APPETIZER

1 1/2 c. mayonnaise
1 tsp. dry mustard
1 tsp. instant minced onion
1/2 c. fine dry bread crumbs
1/4 c. sesame seed
2 c. cubed cooked chicken
2 tbsp. honey

Mix 1/2 cup mayonnaise, mustard and onion together in small bowl. Set aside. Mix bread crumbs and sesame seed. Coat chicken with ᵃyonnaise mixture; roll each cube in bread ᵐb mixture. Place on baking sheet. Bake at ˟ degrees for 12 minutes. Combine 1 cup ᵧonnaise with honey. Place dip in small bowl

surrounded by chicken pieces. Yield: 6-8 servings.

Gerald A. Hils, Keene H.S.
Keene, New Hampshire

COCKTAIL HAM ROLLS

1 lb. lean pork, ground
1 lb. ham, ground
1 c. milk
1 c. bread crumbs
1/2 c. vinegar
1 c. (firmly packed) brown sugar
1 tbsp. mustard

Combine first 4 ingredients in bowl; blend thoroughly. Shape into small meatballs. Place in baking dish. Combine remaining ingredients. Pour over meatballs. Bake at 350 degrees for 25 to 35 minutes or until brown.

Beverly Owens, Van Buren Jr. H.S.
Van Buren, Arkansas

FROSTED HAM BALL

1/2 lb. cooked ham, ground
1/3 c. raisins
1 tbsp. grated onion
1/4 tsp. curry powder
1/4 c. mayonnaise
1 3-oz. package cream cheese, softened
1 tbsp. milk
Chopped parsley

Combine ham, raisins, onion, curry powder and mayonnaise; mix well. Shape into ball; place on serving plate. Chill. Mix cream cheese and milk together until smooth. Spread over chilled ham ball. Sprinkle with parsley. Chill until serving time.

Linda Foley Blake, J.L. Williams Jr. H.S.
Copperas Cove, Texas

PARTY HAM BISCUITS

2 tbsp. mustard
2 sticks margarine, melted
3 tbsp. poppy seed
1 onion, grated
1 tbsp. Worcestershire sauce
3 pkg. small dinner rolls
3 oz. boiled ham, diced
3 oz. Swiss cheese, grated

Combine first 5 ingredients in bowl; mix well. Cut rolls in half. Spread sauce over bottom half of roll. Sprinkle with ham and cheese. Cover with top half roll. Bake at 350 degrees for 10 to 12 minutes. May be frozen and reheated.

Deborah E. Foust, Southeast H.S.
Greensboro, North Carolina

HOT DIGGITY

1 carton sour cream
1 8-oz. package cream cheese, softened
1 tsp. minced onion
1 tsp. chopped green pepper
1 jar dried beef, finely chopped

Blend sour cream and cream cheese in small casserole. Add remaining ingredients; mix well. Place in 200-degree oven until completely heated. Serve as dip with crisp potato chips. May add a small amount of milk if necessary to make of dip consistency.

Mrs. Evelyn Piper, Devils Lake Central School
Devils Lake, North Dakota

SAUSAGE PINWHEELS

2 c. Bisquick
1 lb. sausage

Mix 1/2 cup water with Bisquick to form dough. Divide dough in half; place each half between sheets of waxed paper. Flatten dough with hands to form rectangles. Spread half the sausage over each rectangle. Roll as for jelly roll. Refrigerate until chilled. Slice into 1/4-inch thick pinwheels. Place on ungreased cookie sheet. Bake at 425 degrees for 15 to 20 minutes.

Mary Ann McGovern, Truman H.S.
Independence, Missouri

CRAB-CHEESE TRIANGLES

6 tbsp. butter, softened
1 jar Kraft Oil English cheese
2 tbsp. mayonnaise
1/2 tsp. garlic salt
Dash of Tabasco sauce
1 pkg. frozen crab meat
5 English muffins, split

Combine butter, cheese, mayonnaise, garlic salt and Tabasco in large bowl; mix well. Stir in crab meat. Spread on English muffin halves. Place in freezer for 10 to 15 minutes. Cut into 6 wedges. Return to freezer until serving time. Broil for 5 minutes or until bubbly. Yield: 60 servings.

Margaret Polkabla, Memorial H.S.
Campbell, Ohio

SWEET-SOUR SMOKEYS

1 c. (firmly packed) brown sugar
3 tbsp. flour
1 c. pineapple juice
1/2 c. cider vinegar
2 tsp. dry mustard
1 1/2 tsp. soy sauce
2 lb. miniature hot dogs or smokey links

Combine all ingredients except hot dogs in fondue pot; mix well. Bring to a boil. Add hot dogs; reduce temperature. Serve with toothpicks.

Kathy Porep, Harvard H.S.
Harvard, Illinois

CRAB PIZZA SNACKS

1 stick butter, softened
1 4-oz. jar Old English cheese
1 1/2 tsp. mayonnaise
1/2 tsp. garlic salt
1/2 tsp. seasoned salt
1 6-oz. can crab meat
6 English muffins, split

Combine first 6 ingredients; mix well. Spread mixture on each muffin half. Place in freezer for at least 10 minutes. Broil for about 5 minutes or until mixture starts to bubble. Cut each half into eights. Serve hot. Yield: 96 servings.

Karen A. Ogg, Keene H.S.
Keene, New Hampshire

SEAFOOD ST. JACQUES

2 slices bread, cubed
1/4 c. butter
4 tbsp. flour
3/4 tsp. salt
2 c. milk
Shrimp, scallops, lobster, crab meat,
    cooked
1 c. Cheddar cheese, grated

Place bread cubes in large shells or custard cups. Melt butter in saucepan; blend in flour and salt. Add milk slowly, blending well. Cook, stirring constantly until thickened. Arrange seafood over bread cubes. Cover with sauce. Top with grated cheese. Bake at 350 degrees until sauce is bubbly and cheese is melted. May prepare ahead and refrigerate before baking.

Elsie Fahlg.
John Taylor Collegiate Sch
Winnipeg, Manitoba, Can

HOT ASPARAGUS CANAPES

20 thin slices white bread
3 oz. blue cheese
1 8-oz. package cream cheese, softened
1 egg
20 spears canned asparagus
1/2 lb. melted butter

Trim crusts from bread; flatten with rolling pin. Blend cheeses and egg in small bowl. Spread evenly on each bread slice. Roll 1 spear asparagus in each slice. Fasten with toothpick. Dip in melted butter to coat thoroughly. Place rolls on cookie sheet. Freeze. Slice frozen rolls into 3 equal parts. Place on cookie sheet. Return to freezer. Bake at 400 degrees for 15 to 20 minutes or until lightly browned. Serve hot. Yield: 60 canapes.

Mary Mast, Hibriten H.S.
Lenoir, North Carolina

SCANDINAVIAN CANAPE SQUARES

1 8-oz. package refrigerator crescent
*   dinner rolls*
2 c. shredded Cheddar cheese
1/2 c. each cottage cheese, sour cream
1 tbsp. finely chopped onion
1 c. drained chopped pickled beets
1 4 1/2-oz. can deviled ham
5 hard-boiled eggs
2 tbsp. chopped pimento
1 tbsp. chopped capers
1/2 tsp. each dry mustard, celery salt
Chopped parsley
24 rolled anchovies
24 sm. whole cooked shrimp

Unroll dough onto buttered cookie sheet. Seal perforations to form 13 x 9-inch rectangle. Bake at 375 degrees for 10 minutes or until lightly browned. Cool on wire rack. Beat together Cheddar cheese, cottage cheese, sour cream and onion in small mixing bowl. Place crust on serving tray. Spread cheese mixture over crust. Cover half the cheese layer with pickled beets. Cover remaining half with deviled ham. Chop 3 eggs finely. Combine with pimento, capers, mustard and celery salt in bowl. Spread over ham; sprinkle with parsley. Cut each half into 24 squares. Slice each remaining egg into 3 slices; cut each slice into quarters. Place 1 egg quarter in center of each beet square. Top with rolled anchovies. Place 1 shrimp in center of each egg and parsley square. Arrange on serving tray in alternate patterns. Yield: 48 servings.

Photograph for this recipe on page 6.

SAUERKRAUT BALL

1 lg. can sauerkraut, drained
1 hard-boiled egg, chopped finely
1 c. shredded Cheddar cheese
2 tbsp. mayonnaise
Garlic salt
1 tsp. celery seed
1 8-oz. package cream cheese, softened
Milk
1/4 tsp. Worcestershire sauce

Combine sauerkraut, egg, Cheddar cheese, mayonnaise, 2 teaspoons garlic salt and celery seed. Shape into ball; refrigerate. Mix cream cheese with a small amount milk. Add 1/8 teaspoon garlic salt and Worcestershire sauce. Frost Sauerkraut Ball with cream cheese mixture. Serve with crackers.

Marge Keep, Lincoln East H.S.
Lincoln, Nebraska

STUFFED BROILED MUSHROOMS

24 med. mushrooms
1 sm. onion, chopped
1/4 lb. sharp Cheddar cheese, grated
1 1/2 tsp. Worcestershire sauce
Hot pepper sauce
Pinch of Italian herbs
1/2 tsp. each salt, pepper
1/4 tsp. garlic salt
3 tbsp. dry bread crumbs
1/4 c. margarine
Paprika

Clean mushrooms. Remove stems; set caps aside. Chop stems very fine. Mix with onion and cheese. Add 1 teaspoon Worcestershire sauce, dash of hot pepper sauce, Italian herbs, seasonings and bread crumbs. Melt margarine; add dash of hot pepper sauce and 1/2 teaspoon Worcestershire sauce. Place 1/2 teaspoon seasoned margarine into each mushroom cap. Add remaining margarine to cheese mixture; mix well. Stuff caps with mixture; sprinkle with paprika. Place on broiler pan. Broil until cheese melts. Serve hot.

Nancy Finck, Brattleboro Union H.S.
Brattleboro, Vermont

MICROWAVE STUFFED MUSHROOMS

8 oz. fresh mushrooms
2 tbsp. butter
1/4 c. chopped celery
1/4 c. chopped onion
1/4 c. dry bread crumbs
1 tsp. Worcestershire sauce
1 tsp. parsley flakes
1/4 tsp. salt
1/8 tsp. oregano

Wash mushrooms. Remove and chop stems. Combine stems, butter and vegetables in bowl. Microwave on High for 1 1/2 to 2 1/2 minutes or until vegetables are tender-crisp, stirring once. Stir in remaining ingredients. Mound into mushroom caps. Arrange caps on paper towel-lined plate, placing larger caps toward outer edge of plate. Microwave 1 1/2 to 3 minutes or until thoroughly heated, rotating plate once or twice. Yield: 6-8 servings.

Johnnie T. Broome, Blackshear H.S.
Blackshear, Georgia

STUFFED MUSHROOMS

6 to 8 lg. mushrooms
1/2 c. finely chopped onions
1/4 c. finely chopped red or green pepper
1/4 c. butter
2 slices soft bread, diced
1/8 tsp. each salt, ground turmeric and
* white pepper*
1/4 tsp. ground thyme
6 tsp. grated Parmesan cheese

Remove stems from mushrooms; gently hollow out mushroom caps with spoon. Chop stems. Saute mushroom stems, onions and pepper in butter in skillet. Add diced bread and seasonings; stir well. Stuff mushroom caps with bread mixture. Sprinkle 1 teaspoon Parmesan cheese on each stuffed mushroom. Place on buttered pan. Bake at 350 degrees for 15 to 20 minutes. Serve hot. Yield: 2-4 servings.

Von Esther Squires, Fort Morgan H.S.
Fort Morgan, Colorado

DORIS' STUFFED MUSHROOMS

1 lb. medium mushrooms
1 sm. onion, chopped
1/4 c. chopped green pepper
4 tbsp. margarine
1 1/2 c. soft bread crumbs
1/2 tsp. salt

1/2 tsp. thyme
1/4 tsp. each turmeric, pepper

Cut stems from mushrooms. Finely chop enough stems to measure 1/3 cup. Saute mushroom stems, onion and green pepper in skillet with 3 tablespoons margarine until tender, about 5 minutes. Remove from heat. Stir in bread crumbs, salt, thyme, turmeric and pepper. Melt 1 tablespoon margarine in shallow baking dish. Fill mushroom caps with stuffing mixture. Place mushrooms, filled-side up, in baking dish. Bake at 350 degrees for 15 minutes. Change oven control to Broil. Broil mushrooms 3 to 4 inches from source of heat for 2 minutes. Serve hot. Yield: 3 dozen.

Doris Stiles, Doss H.S.
Louisville, Kentucky

PARTY-TIME SANDWICHES

1 3-oz. package cream cheese, softened
1 can cream of mushroom soup
1 4-oz. can chopped almonds
1/8 tsp. garlic powder
1/2 tbsp. Worcestershire sauce
1 3-oz. can mushrooms, drained, chopped
30 slices sandwich bread, crusts removed
Butter, melted

Blend all ingredients except bread and butter in bowl. Spread 1 tablespoon mixture on each bread slice. Roll as for jelly roll. Secure with 3 toothpicks. Cut into thirds. Chill overnight. Brush sandwiches with butter. Toast in 450-degree oven for 10 to 12 minutes or until golden brown. May be frozen before toasting.

Rebecca Barnes, Owasso Jr. H.S.
Owasso, Oklahoma

PICKLED EGGS

12 hard-boiled eggs
2 c. cooked beets with liquid
1/2 c. vinegar
2 tbsp. sugar
1 tsp. salt
3 whole peppercorns
1/4 bay leaf

Peel eggs. Place in large bowl. Combine remaining ingredients in saucepan. Heat until sugar dissolves. Pour over eggs. Refrigerate. Let stand for 2 days.

Pat Nowaskey, Woodstock Community H.S.
Woodstock, Illinois

CRANBERRY CONSERVE

1 qt. cranberries
1/2 lb. white raisins
2 oranges, quartered
1 c. chopped English walnuts
1/2 can crushed pineapple
1 1/2 lb. sugar

Wash cranberries and raisins; drain thoroughly. Grind oranges in food grinder. Place all ingredients in large saucepan. Boil, stirring constantly, for 8 minutes. Spoon into hot sterilized jars, leaving 1/2-inch head space. Seal with paraffin. May be served hot or cold.

Cora Anne Ferrara, Smithsburg H.S.
Smithsburg, Maryland

CRANBERRY RELISH

20 oz. crushed pineapple
6 oz. frozen orange juice, thawed
1 c. white raisins
1 1/2 c. sugar
2 sticks cinnamon
1/4 tsp. cloves
1 lb. fresh cranberries
1 c. broken walnuts

Drain pineapple, reserving juice. Combine orange juice and pineapple juice. Add enough water to measure 2 cups. Combine juice with all ingredients except pineapple and walnuts in saucepan. Cook over low heat until cranberries pop. Stir in pineapple and nuts. Cool. Store in refrigerator.

Jean Turk, Wheaton North H.S.
Wheaton, Illinois

CRANBERRY RELISH MOLD

1 No. 2 can crushed pineapple
2 pkg. cherry gelatin
3/4 c. sugar
1 to 2 tbsp. lemon juice
1 lb. cranberries, ground
1 sm. orange, ground
1 c. finely chopped celery
1/2 c. chopped English walnuts

Drain pineapple, reserving juice. Combine gelatin and sugar in bowl; dissolve in 2 cups boiling water. Add 1/2 cup cold water, lemon juice and reserved pineapple juice. Chill until partially set. Add pineapple and remaining ingredients. Turn into 2-quart mold. Chill until firm. Unmold. Yield: 12 servings.

Sarah Caudill, Montgomery County H.S.
Ramer, Alabama

SPICED CRANBERRY-ORANGE RELISH

1 1-lb. package fresh cranberries
1 3/4 c. sugar
1/2 c. orange juice
1 tsp. grated orange rind
1/2 tsp. ground ginger
1/4 tsp. ground nutmeg
1/4 tsp. ground cloves or cinnamon
1/2 c. chopped nuts (opt.)

Combine cranberries, sugar and orange juice in saucepan. Bring to a boil. Reduce temperature to simmer; cover. Cook until cranberries burst, 8 to 10 minutes. Remove from heat; stir in remaining ingredients. Refrigerate covered. Serve with meats and poultry. Stores well in refrigerator for several weeks. Yield: 3 1/2 cups.

Becky Burns Drone, Page H.S.
Franklin, Tennessee

CONFETTI SOUP

2 cans Campbell's cream of chicken soup
1 tbsp. chopped pimento
1 tbsp. chopped parsley
1 tbsp. shredded carrot

Blend soup and 2 soup cans water in saucepan; heat, stirring occasionally. Garnish with chopped pimento, parsley and carrot. Yield: 4-6 servings.

Photograph for this recipe on page 39.

CRAB BISQUE

1 can cream of mushroom soup
1 can asparagus soup
1 1/2 soup cans milk
1 c. light cream
1 6 1/2-oz. can flaked crab meat
1/4 c. Sherry
Butter

Combine soups in saucepan. Add milk and cream; blend well. Bring to boiling point over medium heat. Add crab meat; heat thoroughly. Add Sherry and pat of butter just before serving.

Mrs. Dorothy M. Ham, Brantley County H.S.
Nahunta, Georgia

VEGETABLE-CHEESE CHOWDER

12 chicken bouillon cubes
1 lg. onion, chopped
2 c. finely chopped celery

2 c. finely chopped carrots
3/4 lb. butter
1 1/2 c. flour
1 lg. jar Cheez Whiz
2 c. cooked, diced chicken
1/2 pkg. frozen peas (opt.)

Dissolve bouillon cubes in 3 quarts water in large saucepan. Bring to a boil. Add onion, celery and carrots. Cook until tender. Melt butter; add flour, blending to a smooth paste. Add to vegetables in bouillon; blend thoroughly. Add Cheez Whiz; mix well. Cook over medium heat, stirring constantly, until thickened. Add chicken and peas; blend well. Freezes well if peas are added just before serving.

Carol Winter, Millcreek Jr. H.S.
Bountiful, Utah

FRUIT SOUP

1 c. dried prunes
1 c. dried apricots
1 c. raisins
2 apples
1/4 lemon, thinly sliced
1/4 orange, thinly sliced
1 stick cinnamon
1/2 c. sugar
1/4 c. tapioca
1   10-oz. package frozen raspberries, thawed

Place dried fruits in saucepan with water to cover. Bring to a boil. Reduce temperature; cover. Simmer gently for 30 minutes. Add next 6 ingredients. Drain raspberries, reserving 1 cup juice. Add reserved raspberry juice. Stir gently. Simmer, uncovered over low heat, until tapioca is cooked. Add raspberries. Bring just to a boil. Do not stir to avoid breaking fruit. Serve warm or cold with whipped cream.

Annette Cook, Somerset H.S.
Somerset, Wisconsin

FRENCH ONION SOUP

5 c. sliced onions
4 tbsp. margarine
6 bouillon cubes
1 tsp. salt
1/4 tsp. pepper
1/2 tsp. Worcestershire sauce
1 tsp. Kitchen Bouquet
6 slices French bread
1/2 c. shredded sharp cheese

Saute onions with margarine in heavy skillet until lightly browned. Add next 5 ingredients; blend well. Simmer for 30 minutes. Place 1 slice French bread in each bowl; add soup. Sprinkle with cheese. Serve piping hot. Yield: 6 servings.

Diane L. Stelten-Dane, Blair Public Schools
Blair, Wisconsin

TOO GOOD EGGNOG

8 eggs, separated
1/2 c. sugar
6 c. milk
2 c. heavy cream
5 tsp. vanilla extract
2 tsp. rum flavoring
1/2 tsp. ground nutmeg
Pinch of salt

Beat egg yolks in mixing bowl until thick. Beat in sugar gradually. Stir in milk, heavy cream, vanilla, rum and nutmeg; mix well. Beat egg whites with salt on high speed of electric mixer until soft peaks form. Fold into milk mixture. Garnish with nutmeg. Yield: 20 servings.

Photograph for this recipe below.

CHOCOLATE EGGNOG

1/2 sq. Hershey's baking chocolate
2 tbsp. sugar
1 tbsp. malted milk powder
1 egg
Milk
Mint extract (opt.)

Combine chocolate, sugar and 2 tablespoons water in top of double boiler. Cook over simmering water until chocolate melts. Add malted milk powder and egg. Beat until light and frothy. Pour over crushed ice in glass; fill with milk. Add drop of mint extract. Stir briskly before serving. Yield: One 8-ounce serving.

Jane Peters, Sevier County H.S.
Sevierville, Tennessee

FRESH HOLIDAY EGGNOG

1 doz. eggs, separated
1 1/2 c. sugar
4 c. milk
1 c. whipping cream, whipped
1/4 c. Brandy
1/4 c. light rum
1/2 tsp. vanilla extract
1/2 tsp. ground nutmeg

Beat egg yolks in bowl until smooth. Combine egg yolks and sugar in top of double boiler over hot water. Stir in milk gradually. Cook, stirring constantly, until mixture coats spoon. Remove from heat. Refrigerate until chilled. Beat egg whites until stiff peaks form. Fold egg whites and whipped cream into chilled egg yolk mixture. Stir in the Brandy and rum. Chill for several hours to blend flavors. Stir in vanilla just before serving; sprinkle with nutmeg. Yield: Twenty-four 1/2-cup servings.

Von Esther Squires, Fort Morgan H.S.
Fort Morgan, Colorado

BANANA CRUSH

4 c. sugar
1 46-oz. can pineapple juice
Juice of 2 lemons
2 c. orange juice
5 bananas, mashed
4 to 6 32-oz. bottles of 7-Up
1 pkg. frozen raspberries (opt.)
Red food coloring (opt.)

Combine sugar and 6 cups water in large saucepan. Bring to a boil. Cool. Add fruit juices and bananas; mix well. Freeze. Place fruit mixture in punch bowl. Allow to soften slightly; break into slush. Add 7-Up. Add raspberries and enough food coloring to tint as desired. Yield: 25-30 servings.

Patricia Knaus, Skyline H.S.
Salt Lake City, Utah

CONNIE'S CHRISTMAS PUNCH

2 pkg. lime or strawberry Jell-O
6 c. sugar
2 lg. cans pineapple juice
2 16-oz. bottles of lemon juice

Dissolve Jell-O in 4 cups boiling water in large container. Add sugar. Stir until sugar dissolves. Add remaining ingredients and 8 quarts water; mix well. Pour into serving bowl. May be frozen. Yield: 3 1/2 to 4 gallons.

Connie M. Sullivan, Seymour H.S.
Seymour, Tennessee

JANE'S CHRISTMAS PUNCH

5 orange and spice-flavored tea bags
1 6-oz. can frozen concentrated grape juice, thawed
3/4 c. lemon juice
2 c. orange juice
1/2 c. plus 2 tbsp. sugar
1 32-oz. bottle of ginger ale, chilled
2 to 2 1/2 c. vodka (opt.)

Pour 3 cups boiling water over tea bags; cover. Steep for 5 minutes. Discard tea bags; cool tea. Combine tea with next 4 ingredients in large container. Stir until sugar dissolves. Refrigerate until chilled. Combine with remaining ingredients just before serving in large punch bowl with lemon slices.

Jane A. Solinsky, James B. Conant H.S.
Hoffman Estates, Illinois

DIANA'S FRUIT PUNCH

1 qt. pineapple juice
1 qt. apple juice
1 lg. bottle of ginger ale
1 sm. can frozen lemonade
3 bananas, mashed
1/2 gal. orange sherbet

Mix first 5 ingredients in large container. Cover; refrigerate until serving time. Spoon sherbet into punch bowl. Add fruit juice mixture. Yield: 30 servings.

Diana Watson, Paoli H.S.
Paoli, Oklahoma

12/11/89

EVERGREEN PUNCH

1 3-oz. package lime gelatin
2 c. sugar
1 qt. apple cider
2 c. lemon juice
1 1/2 qt. orange juice
1/2 c. lime juice
1 lg. bottle ginger ale, chilled

Dissolve gelatin in 2 cups boiling water in large container. Cool. Add remaining ingredients except ginger ale; mix well. Add ginger ale just before serving. Yield: 5 quarts.

Mrs. Evon F. McLendon
Montgomery County School
Mt. Vernon, Georgia

EASY HOLIDAY PUNCH

1 8-oz. package red fruit-flavored
gelatin
1 16-oz. can frozen lemonade, thawed
1 6-oz. can frozen orange juice,
thawed
1 46-oz. can pineapple juice, chilled
1 qt. ginger ale

Add gelatin to 2 cups boiling water in large bowl. Stir until dissolved. Add frozen juices; stir until well blended. Add 6 cups cold water and pineapple juice; mix well. Pour over ice in punch bowl. Add ginger ale just before serving. Yield: 50 servings.

Mariann Bielke, Marion H.S.
Marion, Texas

HOLIDAY CHEER

1 qt. orange juice, chilled
1 bottle of lemon juice, chilled
1/2 gal. vanilla ice cream
1 liter ginger ale
Mint leaves

Mix fruit juices. Place ice cream in punch bowl. Add juices. Pour ginger ale into bowl just before serving. Garnish with mint leaves.

Gloria E. Moon, Upson H.S.
Thomaston, Georgia

HOLIDAY CRANBERRY PUNCH

1/2 c. lemon juice
2 c. orange juice
3/4 c. sugar
1 1/2 qt. cranberry juice cocktail
2 28-oz. bottles of ginger ale, chilled
2 pt. raspberry sherbet

Combine lemon juice, orange juice and sugar in large container. Stir to dissolve sugar. Add cranberry juice. Refrigerate until cold. Pour into punch bowl. Add ginger ale; blend well. Float sherbet balls on top of punch. Yield: Thirty 4-ounce servings.

Carolyne E. Ray, West Jr. H.S.
Kansas City, Kansas

SUE'S HOLIDAY PUNCH

4 c. sugar
4 6-oz. cans frozen orange juice
1 46-oz. can pineapple juice
Juice of 2 lemons
5 to 6 bananas, mashed
1 c. rum
4 16-oz. cans 7-Up

Mix 6 quarts water and sugar in large saucepan. Bring to a boil. Boil about 3 minutes until thickened. Add orange juice, pineapple juice, lemon juice, bananas and rum. Pour into large container; cover. Freeze. Remove from freezer about 2 hours before serving. Break up mixture into slush in punch bowl just before serving. Add 7-Up. Yield: 5 quarts.

Sue Penney, Manor H.S.
Portsmouth, Virginia

LIME PUNCH

2 pkg. lime Kool-Aid
2 c. sugar
1 46-oz. can pineapple juice
1 can frozen lemon juice
1 qt. ginger ale, chilled
1 qt. vanilla ice cream

Mix Kool-Aid, sugar and 2 quarts water in large container. Add pineapple juice and lemon juice; chill. Add ginger ale just before serving. Place ice cream in punch bowl. Pour juice mixture over ice cream. Yield: 50 servings.

Sammie Lee Pounds, New Site H.S.
New Site, Mississippi

NONALCOHOLIC MINT JULEP

1 1/2 c. sugar
Mint leaves to taste
Juice of 4 lemons
Juice of 6 oranges
7-Up

Combine sugar and mint leaves with 1/2 cup water in saucepan. Boil until slightly thickened. Strain; cool. Add fruit juices. Refrigerate until serving time. Place crushed ice in tall glass. Add 1/4 cup syrup mixture. Fill glass with 7-Up; stir until mixed. Serve immediately.

Patricia A. Parker, Cabool H.S.
Cabool, Missouri

GOLDEN PARTY PUNCH

1 46-oz. can pineapple juice
1 6-oz. can frozen lemonade
1 6-oz. can frozen orange juice
1 to 2 qt. ginger ale

Combine juices in serving bowl. Add four 6-ounce juice cans water; mix well. Add ginger ale just before serving.

Betty Lou Stomm, DeKalb H.S.
Waterloo, Indiana

PINEAPPLE PUNCH

1 48-oz. can unsweetened pineapple
*   juice*
1 lg. can frozen orange juice
1 lg. can frozen lemonade
Orange and lemon slices
3 bottles of ginger ale
1/2 pkg. frozen whole unsweetened
*   strawberries*

Mix fruit juices in punch bowl. Add fruit slices. Add ginger ale just before serving. Add frozen strawberries in place of ice. Yield: 20 servings.

Molly Hillcoat, Stewart Avenue School
Cambridge, Ontario, Canada

CHRISTMAS PINEAPPLE PUNCH

2 c. sugar
2 sm. packages Kool-Aid
1 46-oz. can pineapple juice
2 qt. ginger ale

Combine sugar and 2 quarts water in large saucepan. Heat until sugar dissolves. Cool. Add Kool-Aid and pineapple juice; mix well. Add ginger ale just before serving. Pour over ice ring in punch bowl. Yield: 75 servings.

Pat Duncan, Haltom Jr. H.S.
Fort Worth, Texas

SANGERIA PUNCH

40 oz. cranberry juice
40 oz. grape juice
2 oranges, sliced
1 lemon, sliced
1 jar maraschino cherries

Combine all ingredients in large container; cover. Refrigerate for at least 12 hours.

Cloyann Fent, Perry H.S.
Perry, Oklahoma

SPARKLING CHRISTMAS PUNCH

4 c. sugar
2 pkg. strawberry Kool-Aid
2 pkg. cherry Kool-Aid
1 46-oz. can unsweetened pineapple
*   juice*
1 46-oz. can unsweetened orange juice
2 (or more) bottles of ginger ale

Combine first 5 ingredients in large container. Mix well until sugar and Kool-Aid dissolve completely. Add 2 bottles of ginger ale for each 4 cups concentrate in punch bowl. Decorate punch with ice ring. May freeze concentrate.

Deborah Casados, Mexia H.S.
Mexia, Texas

STRAWBERRY FRUIT PUNCH

3 pkg. strawberry Kool-Aid
1 pkg. raspberry Kool-Aid
4 c. sugar
1 lg. can pineapple juice
1 12-oz. can frozen lemonade
1 12-oz. can frozen orange juice
2 qt. ginger ale
Red food coloring

Dissolve Kool-Aid and sugar in 4 quarts water in large container. Add fruit juices; mix well. Add four 12-ounce juice cans water. Stir in ginger ale. Add enough food coloring to tint as desired. Yield: 2 1/2 gallons.

Delores Hays, Hamilton H.S.
Hamilton, Missouri

SWEETHEART PUNCH

1 3-oz. package strawberry gelatin
1 pkg. strawberry powdered drink mix
2 1/2 c. sugar
1 46-oz. can pineapple juice
1 10-oz. bottle of ginger ale
2 pt. pineapple sherbet

Dissolve gelatin in 1 cup boiling water. Dissolve drink mix and sugar in 2 quarts cold water; stir well. Add pineapple juice to gelatin mixture; mix well. Refrigerate until serving time. Add ginger ale and sherbet just before serving. Yield: 35 servings.

Nora Sweat, West Hardin H.S.
Stephensburg, Kentucky

SPICED TEA

2 cinnamon sticks
1 1/2 c. sugar
15 whole cloves
1 sm. package cherry Jell-O
48 oz. pineapple juice
1 qt. sweetened tea
1 lg. can frozen orange juice
1 lemon, sliced

Combine 1 quart water, cinnamon, sugar and cloves in large saucepan. Simmer for about 15 minutes. Add Jell-O; stir to dissolve. Add pineapple juice and tea. Dilute orange juice using package directions. Add to mixture. Add lemon slices. Simmer until very hot. Strain. Refrigerate until cold.

Patsy S. Coble, Arab H.S.
Arab, Alabama

HOT CIDER WASSAIL

Juice and rind of 3 oranges and lemons
1 oz. cinnamon sticks
1 tbsp. allspice
1 1/2 c. sugar
1 gal. sweet cider

Squeeze juice from oranges and lemons. Place rinds and spices in saucepan. Add 1 1/2 quarts water; cover. Simmer for 2 hours and 30 minutes. Strain liquid over sugar. Add fruit juices and cider. Heat almost to boiling point. Serve very hot.

Frances Morton, Tallulah H.S.
Tallulah, Louisiana

CRANBERRY WASSAIL

2 c. apple juice
1 c. cranberry juice
1 c. rum (opt.)
1 orange studded with cloves
2 cinnamon sticks
1 tsp. whole allspice

Combine all ingredients in large Crock·Pot. Cook on High for 1 hour. Reduce temperature setting to Low; cook for 3 hours or longer. Serve warm.

Helen Struthers, Liberty Jr. H.S.
Ashland, Virginia

MULLED CHRISTMAS CIDER

2 qt. apple cider
1 1/2 qt. cranberry juice

1/2 c. (firmly packed) light brown sugar
8 to 10 3-in. cinnamon sticks
10 to 15 whole allspice
20 to 25 whole cloves

Combine all ingredients in 6-quart kettle. Bring to a boil. Simmer, uncovered, for 30 minutes. Strain; discard spices. Refrigerate cider until needed. Reheat for serving. Serve warm or well chilled. Additional cinnamon sticks may be used as stirrer in each mug. Yield: 12 cups.

Jo Ann Glass, Meade County Middle School
Brandenburg, Kentucky

SPICED TEA AND CIDER DRINK

3 Constant Comment tea bags
1/4 c. sugar
2 c. cider
Cinnamon sticks

Pour 1 quart water into medium saucepan. Bring to a boil. Add tea bags; cover. Steep for 5 minutes. Remove tea bags. Add sugar; stir until dissolved. Add cider. Reheat. Pour into mugs. Add cinnamon sticks for stirrers. Yield: 1 1/2 quarts.

Photograph for this recipe on page 45.

HOT SPICY CIDER

3 c. apple cider
3 tbsp. brown sugar
1/8 tsp. nutmeg
1/4 tsp. whole allspice
1/2 tsp. whole cloves
1 stick cinnamon
2 thin orange slices, cut in half

Combine cider, brown sugar and spices in saucepan. Simmer for 15 to 20 minutes. Strain; pour into serving mugs. Garnish with orange slices. Yield: 4 servings.

Rebecca S. Hughes, J.C. Booth Jr. H.S.
Peachtree City, Georgia

POMANDER PUNCH

2 pkg. orange drink mix
1 c. sugar
6 whole cloves
1 cinnamon stick

Pour 6 cups water into percolator. Place drink mix, sugar and spices in basket. Perk through one cycle. Yield: 1 1/2 quarts.

D'Nelle Phillips, Texas H.S.
Texarkana, Texas

WASSAIL

> 2 qt. apple cider
> 2 c. orange juice
> 1 c. lemon juice
> 5 c. pineapple juice
> 1 stick cinnamon
> 1 tsp. whole cloves
> Sugar or honey to taste
> Orange slices

Combine all ingredients except orange slices in large saucepan. Simmer slowly for 1 hour or longer. Do not boil. Strain before serving. Garnish with orange slices.

> *Mary W. Dick, John Rolfe Middle School*
> *Richmond, Virginia*

WASSAIL TEA

> 3/4 c. lemon juice
> 1 1/2 c. orange juice
> 1 1/2 c. apple cider
> 1 1/2 c. sugar
> 7 whole cloves
> 2 cinnamon sticks
> 1 1/2 tsp. tea

Combine juices and cider in large kettle. Set aside. Combine 1/2 cup sugar, whole cloves and cinnamon sticks in 2 cups water. Bring to a boil. Remove spices. Add spiced water mixture to juices. Add 1 1/2 cups boiling water to tea. Steep for 5 minutes. Strain. Add tea to juices with remaining 1 cup sugar. Add 5 cups boiling water before serving. Heat until piping hot. Do not boil. Serve in mugs.

> *Sandy Nelson, Cavalier H.S.*
> *Cavalier, North Dakota*

EGGNOG WASSAIL BOWL

> 3 qt. commercial eggnog
> 1 1/2 qt. cider
> 1/2 tsp. each nutmeg, cinnamon
> 4 whole cloves
> 1 tsp. grated lemon peel

Combine all ingredients in heavy saucepan. Cook over low heat until heated, stirring occasionally. Serve hot or cold. Yield: 4 1/2 quarts.

> *Photograph for this recipe on page 4.*

Sparkling Salads

Toss it . . . chop it . . . mix it . . . chill it. There's not a more appetizing way to begin a meal than with a sparkling salad. And you won't find a better collection anywhere than in this chapter.

If you enjoy placing a colorful gelatin mold on your holiday table, you'll be pleased to see the fresh variety recipes here. Elegant blueberry, Christmas lime, cheery cherry, Christmas cranberry . . . what cheerful colors! And wait until you taste the hearty meat salads too. Many new ways to dress up chicken, ham, turkey and shrimp that you never thought of before. And, of course, vegetable salads — light, nutritious and easy to fix. Bear in mind, as you plan your menu, the salad "fixin's" most economical during the holiday months.

A tip to remember — as soon as you bring home vegetables, wash them quickly in cold water using a brush if necessary; whirl or towel dry. Place in plastic bag and chill thoroughly — ready at a mement's notice for a fresh colorful addition to your salad bowl.

AVOCADO SALAD

1 avocado, peeled
1 tbsp. olive oil
2 tsp. malt vinegar
1/2 tsp. garlic powder

Slice avocado into bite-sized pieces. Place in small bowl. Add oil, vinegar and garlic powder; mix well. Serve immediately on crisp lettuce.

Jean DeWitt, Eldora-New Providence H.S.
Eldora, Louisiana

GUACAMOLE SALAD

2 avocados, peeled, mashed
1/3 c. chopped onion
1/3 c. Old El Paso chopped green chilies
2/3 c. chopped tomato
2 tbsp. taco sauce
1 tbsp. lemon or lime juice
1 1/4 tsp. sugar
1/2 tsp. garlic powder

Combine all ingredients in medium bowl; mix well. Serve with tortilla chips on crisp shredded lettuce. To keep dip from turning brown bury 1 avocado pit in middle of dip. Yield: 2 2/3 cups.

Paula Neth, St. Teresa's Academy
Kansas City, Missouri

LINDA'S APPLE SALAD

1 No. 2 can pineapple chunks
1/2 c. sugar
2 tbsp. flour
1 egg, beaten
4 slices American cheese
3 or 4 lg. red apples, chopped
1 c. pecans

Drain pineapple; reserve juice. Combine juice, sugar, flour and egg in saucepan; blend well. Cook over low heat, stirring constantly, until thickened. Remove from heat. Add cheese; stir until melted. Combine apples, pineapple and pecans in large bowl. Pour sauce over fruit; mix well. Refrigerate overnight.

Cleo Surles, Columbia H.S.
Decatur, Georgia

FRUIT MEDLEY ELEGANTE

1/3 c. port wine or red cooking wine
1/4 c. orange juice
1 tbsp. lemon juice
1/4 c. sugar
1 c. sliced fresh strawberries
1 c. sliced fresh or canned peaches

6 pear halves, sliced
2 bananas, sliced
4 apples, sliced
1 bunch green grapes, halved

Combine wine, fruit juices and sugar. Stir until sugar dissolves. Combine fruits in serving bowl. Pour wine mixture over fruit; mix well. Chill well before serving.

Debbie C. Mobley, Montgomery Central H.S.
Cunningham, Tennessee

GINGER-FRUIT SALAD

1 pkg. lemon gelatin
1 c. ginger ale
1 3-oz. package cream cheese, softened
1/2 tsp. ground ginger
1/2 c. evaporated milk
1 1/2 c. mixed fruit, diced
1/2 c. nuts (opt.)

Dissolve gelatin in 1 cup boiling water. Stir in ginger ale. Combine cream cheese, ginger and milk; blend well. Add to gelatin mixture; mix well. Chill until partially set. Beat chilled mixture with egg beater for 1 minute or until fluffy. Fold in fruit and nuts. Pour into oiled mold. Chill until firm.

Mrs. Rosemary Harwood, North Stanly H.S.
New London, North Carolina

DIANE'S FRUIT SALAD

1 lg. can peaches
1 pkg. vanilla instant pudding mix
1 can pineapple chunks
3 bananas, sliced
1 can mandarin oranges, drained
1 sm. jar cherries, drained

Drain peaches, reserving juice. Mix reserved peach juice with pudding mix in bowl until well blended. Set aside. Drain pineapple chunks, reserving juice. Pour reserved pineapple juice over sliced bananas; stir to coat. Add fruits to pudding mixture; mix well. Refrigerate until thoroughly chilled. Yield: 8 servings.

Diane Sutton, Amity H.S.
Amity, Arkansas

OLD-FASHIONED FRUIT SALAD

Grated rind and juice of 1 lemon, 1 lime
*   and 1 orange*
1 egg
1 c. sugar

1 c. whipping cream, whipped
1 lg. orange, sectioned
1 lg. banana, sliced
1 lg. apple, diced
1 c. chunk pineapple
1 c. green grapes
1 c. marshmallows

Combine rinds, juices, egg and sugar in double boiler. Cook, stirring constantly, until thickened. Chill. Fold in whipped cream. Combine prepared fruit and marshmallows in large bowl. Add chilled salad dressing to taste; mix well. Chill. Store remaining salad dressing tightly covered in refrigerator.

Anne P. Barrett, Dixon Jr. H.S.
Provo, Utah

PINK SALAD

1 can sweetened condensed milk
1/3 c. lemon juice
1 8-oz. can crushed pineapple, drained
1 11-oz. can mandarin oranges, drained
1 can cherry pie filling
1 9-oz. carton Cool Whip
2 c. miniature marshmallows
1/2 to 1 c. chopped pecans

Beat condensed milk with lemon juice in bowl until thick. Add remaining ingredients; mix well. Chill before serving.

Betty Ambrose, Robert E. Lee H.S.
Midland, Texas

RED-WHITE-BLUE SALAD

1 3-oz. package red raspberry Jell-O
2 env. unflavored gelatin
1 c. sugar
1 c. half and half
1 8-oz. package cream cheese, softened
1 tsp. vanilla extract
1/2 c. chopped nuts
1 3-oz. package black raspberry Jell-O
1 15-oz. can blueberries

Dissolve red raspberry Jell-O in 2 cups boiling water. Pour into 9 x 13-inch baking dish. Chill until set. Soften unflavored gelatin in 1/2 cup cold water. Combine sugar and half and half in saucepan. Heat but do not boil. Add unflavored gelatin, stirring to dissolve. Add cream cheese and vanilla; beat until smooth. Stir in nuts. Spread over congealed layer. Chill until firm. Dissolve black raspberry Jell-O in 1 cup boiling

water. Add blueberries. Pour over cream cheese mixture. Chill until firm. Yield: 12-14 servings.

Julie E. Browning, Mabank H.S.
Mabank, Texas

SOUR CREAM FRUIT SALAD

1 med. jar maraschino cherries
1 sm. jar green decorative cherries, drained
1 sm. can Angel Flake coconut
2 sm. cartons sour cream
3 tbsp. red cherry juice
2 16-oz. cans fruit cocktail, drained
1 8-oz. can crushed pineapple, drained
1 sm. package miniature colored marshmallows

Cut red and green cherries in half. Reserve portion of cherries and coconut for garnish. Place sour cream in large mixing bowl. Add cherry juice; blend well. Add fruit cocktail, pineapple and red cherries; mix well. Stir in marshmallows and coconut. Garnish with reserved coconut, red and green cherries. May be refrigerated, covered, overnight.

Janet Kay Francis, Savoy H.S.
Savoy, Texas

ELEGANT BLUEBERRY PARTY SALAD

2 sm. packages raspberry gelatin
1/4 tsp. raspberry flavoring
1 env. unflavored gelatin
1 c. coffee cream
1 c. sugar
1 tsp. vanilla extract
1 8-oz. package cream cheese, softened
1/2 c. chopped nuts
1 No. 303 can blueberries
1/4 tsp. blueberry flavoring

Dissolve 1 package raspberry gelatin in 2 cups boiling water. Add raspberry flavoring. Pour into 9 x 13-inch pan. Chill until firm. Soften unflavored gelatin in 1/2 cup cold water. Heat cream and sugar in saucepan until hot but not boiling. Remove from heat. Add vanilla and cream cheese; blend until smooth. Stir in nuts. Cool. Pour over first layer. Chill until firm. Dissolve remaining package gelatin in 1 cup boiling water. Stir in blueberries and flavoring. Cool. Pour over cheese layer. Chill until firm.

Diane Gibbs, New Bloomfield R-III School
New Bloomfield, Missouri

BLUEBERRY SALAD

1 15-oz. can blueberries
1 8-oz. can crushed pineapple
2 3-oz. packages black raspberry
    gelatin
1 8-oz. carton sour cream
1 8-oz. package cream cheese, softened
1/2 c. sugar
1 tsp. vanilla extract
1 c. pecans

Drain fruit, reserving juices. Dissolve gelatin in 1 cup boiling water. Add reserved juices with enough water to measure 1 3/4 cups; mix well. Add blueberries and pineapple; mix well. Pour into 9 x 13-inch dish. Refrigerate until firm. Combine remaining ingredients in bowl; blend until smooth. Spread over gelatin. Refrigerate until well chilled.

Lee Anne Moore, Jo Byrns School
Cedar Hill, Tennessee

CHEERY CHERRY SALAD

1 10-oz. jar maraschino cherries
2 3-oz. packages cream cheese, softened
1 8-oz. can crushed pineapple
1 c. miniature marshmallows
1/2 pt. whipping cream
1/4 c. sugar

Drain maraschino cherries, reserving juice. Add juice to cream cheese; blend well. Chop cherries. Combine cherries, cream cheese mixture, crushed pineapple and marshmallows in bowl; mix well. Whip cream until stiff, adding sugar gradually. Blend into fruit mixture. Place in serving bowl. Refrigerate until chilled.

Vicki R. Olson, Stillwater Sr. H.S.
Stillwater, Minnesota

CHRISTMAS GARLAND JELLY

1 3-oz. package red Jell-O
1 med. banana, sliced
1 14-oz. can pineapple tidbits
1 3-oz. package lime Jell-O
1 pkg. Dream Whip
1/2 c. milk
1/2 tsp. vanilla extract
Almonds
Maraschino cherries

Dissolve red Jell-O in 1 cup boiling water. Add 3/4 cup cold water. Chill until syrupy. Pour into 6-cup ring mold. Place banana slices vertically into Jell-O. Chill until almost firm. Drain

pineapple, reserving 3/4 cup juice. Dissolve lime Jell-O in 1 cup boiling water. Add pineapple juice. Chill 1/2 cup lime Jell-O until syrupy. Beat Dream Whip, milk and vanilla in small bowl until stiff. Fold 1 cup Dream Whip mixture into chilled lime Jell-O. Spoon over red Jell-O in mold. Chill until almost firm. Chill remaining lime Jell-O until partially set. Fold in pineapple. Spoon over Dream Whip layer. Chill until firm. Unmold onto serving plate. Fill center with remaining Dream Whip. Garnish with almonds and cherries.

Mrs. Elsie Fahlgren
John Taylor Collegiate School
Winnipeg, Manitoba, Canada

CHRISTMAS LIME SALAD

1 3-oz. package lime gelatin
1 c. miniature marshmallows
1/4 c. sugar
1 c. whipping cream, whipped
1 c. crushed drained pineapple
1 6-oz. package cream cheese, softened
1 c. chopped pecans

Combine first 3 ingredients with 1 cup boiling water. Stir until marshmallows dissolve. Refrigerate until partially congealed. Blend in whipped cream, pineapple, cream cheese and pecans. Chill until set.

Mrs. Nora Sweat, West Hardin H.S.
Stephensburg, Kentucky

CHRISTMAS SALAD

1 pkg. lime Jell-O
1 can pineapple chunks, drained
1 env. unflavored gelatin
1 c. pineapple juice
1/4 c. mayonnaise
1 4-oz. package cream cheese, softened
1/4 c. cream, whipped
1 pkg. red Jell-O

Dissolve lime Jell-O in 2 cups boiling water; add pineapple. Pour into large glass bowl. Chill until set. Soften gelatin in pineapple juice in saucepan. Heat until gelatin dissolves. Cool. Fold in mayonnaise, cream cheese and whipped cream. Pour over lime mixture. Chill until firm. Dissolve red Jell-O in 2 cups boiling water. Cool. Pour over cream cheese mixture. Chill until firm. Yield: 8 servings.

Mrs. Jean Head, Albertville H.S.
Albertville, Alabama

CINNAMON-APPLESAUCE SWIRL SALAD

1/3 c. red cinnamon candies
1 6-oz. package lemon gelatin
2 c. applesauce
6 oz. cream cheese, softened
1/4 c. cream
2 tbsp. mayonnaise

Dissolve candies and gelatin in 2 cups boiling water in bowl. Stir in applesauce. Chill until partially set. Pour into 8-inch square pan. Mix cream cheese, cream and mayonnaise in small bowl until smooth. Stir gently into applesauce mixture for swirled effect. Chill until firm. Cut into squares. Serve on crisp lettuce. Yield: 9-12 servings.

Elloise Reeves, Edgewood H.S.
Edgewood, Texas

CHRISTMAS CRANBERRY SALAD

1 3-oz. package raspberry gelatin
1 can cranberry sauce
1 sm. orange and rind, chopped
1/2 c. chopped nuts

Dissolve gelatin in 1 1/2 cups boiling water. Add cranberry sauce, stirring until well blended. Chill until partially set. Add orange and nuts; mix well. Pour into individual molds. Chill until set. Unmold on salad greens. Garnish with salad dressing.

Jeannette H. Mercer, Dublin H.S.
Dublin, Georgia

CRANBERRY-APPLE SALAD

1 pkg. red Jell-O
1 16-oz. can cranberry sauce, mashed
2 tart apples, grated
2 bananas, mashed
1/3 c. confectioners' sugar
1 tsp. vanilla extract.
1 c. whipping cream, whipped
1/2 c. chopped nuts

Dissolve Jell-O in 1 cup boiling water. Add next 3 ingredients; mix well. Pour into serving dish. Refrigerate until set. Add confectioners' sugar and vanilla to whipped cream. Spread over Jell-O. Sprinkle nuts over top.

Hazel Rogers, Van Buren H.S.
Van Buren, Arkansas

CONGEALED CRANBERRY SALAD

1 lb. fresh cranberries
1 orange, peeled, chopped
2 c. sugar
2 pkg. strawberry Jell-O
1 c. chopped nuts
1 c. chopped apple
1 lg. can crushed pineapple
2 lg. bananas, chopped
1 c. flaked coconut
Miniature marshmallows

Crush cranberries in blender. Combine cranberries, orange and sugar in large bowl. Let stand overnight. Dissolve Jell-O in 2 cups boiling water. Add Jell-O and remaining ingredients except marshmallows to cranberry mixture; mix well. Place in 9 x 13-inch dish. Chill until firm. Top with miniature marshmallows.

Deborah J.M. Escobar, Lanier H.S.
San Antonio, Texas

CRANBERRY-GELATIN SALAD

1 3-oz. package cherry gelatin
1 16-oz. can cranberry sauce, mashed
1/2 c. finely diced celery
1/4 c. chopped walnuts
1 c. sour cream

Dissolve gelatin in 1 cup boiling water. Chill until slightly thickened. Add next 3 ingredients; mix well. Fold in sour cream. Pour into 4-cup mold. Chill until firm. Yield: 4-6 servings.

Gena Kelly Basnett, Avalon H.S.
Avalon, Texas

CRANBERRY MOLD

1 sm. package raspberry Jell-O
1/2 tsp. salt
2 tsp. lemon juice
1 c. whole cranberry sauce, mashed
1/2 c. crushed pineapple, drained
1/2 c. diced celery
1/2 c. diced apple
1/4 c. chopped nuts

Dissolve Jell-O and salt in 1 cup boiling water in large bowl. Add 1/2 cup cold water and lemon juice. Chill until slightly thickened. Fold in remaining ingredients. Pour into mold. Chill until firm.

Linda Owens, Mt. Vernon H.S.
Mt. Vernon, Texas

CRANBERRY-LEMON SALAD

2 c. ground cranberries
2 c. sugar
2 pkg. lemon Jell-O
1 c. diced celery
1 c. chopped nuts
1 orange, ground

Combine cranberries and sugar in bowl. Let stand for several hours. Dissolve Jell-O in 1 1/2 cups boiling water in large bowl. Add 2 cups cold water. Chill until partially set. Stir in remaining ingredients with cranberry mixture. Chill until firm. Yield: 10-12 servings.

Carolyn Cotton, Bristow H.S.
Bristow, Oklahoma

CRANBERRY-ORANGE SALAD

1 3-oz. package orange gelatin
1 can whole cranberry sauce
1 8-oz. can crushed pineapple
1/2 c. chopped celery
1/2 c. chopped nuts

Dissolve gelatin in 1 1/2 cups boiling water. Add cranberry sauce; stir until dissolved. Add remaining ingredients; mix well. Pour into mold. Chill until set.

Naomi Austin, Gainesville H.S.
Gainesville, Texas

CRANBERRY-PECAN SALAD

1 lb. fresh cranberries
1 1/2 c. sugar
1 8-oz. package cream cheese, softened
1 8-oz. can crushed pineapple
1/2 c. pecans
1 c. Cool Whip

Wash cranberries. Place in blender container; chop. Add sugar; refrigerate overnight. Combine with cream cheese, pineapple, pecans and Cool Whip in large bowl; blend well. Place in serving dish. Refrigerate until serving time.

Carolyn Madewell, McKinney H.S.
McKinney, Texas

CRANBERRY-PINEAPPLE SALAD

2 sm. packages lemon Jell-O
2 c. sugar
1 1-lb. package fresh cranberries

Rind of 1 orange
1 c. chopped nuts
1 sm. can crushed pineapple, drained
2 oranges, peeled, chopped

Dissolve Jell-O in 2 cups boiling water. Add sugar, stirring until dissolved. Grind cranberries and orange rind in food chopper. Add to Jell-O mixture. Add nuts, pineapple and oranges. Pour into loaf pan. Chill until firm. Cut into squares to serve.

Ann B. Jones, Mountainburg Public Schools
Mountainburg, Arkansas

CRANBERRY-WALDORF SALAD

1/2 lb. cranberries
3/4 c. sugar
3 c. miniature marshmallows
2 c. chopped apples
1/2 c. seeded grapes
1/2 c. chopped nuts
1 c. whipping cream, whipped
1 8-oz. can chunk pineapple, drained

Chop cranberries coarsely in food processor. Mix with sugar. Let stand for 30 minutes. Add remaining ingredients; mix well. Chill thoroughly before serving. Yield: 10-12 servings.

Marihope Troutman, Bass H.S.
Atlanta, Georgia

MOLDED CRANBERRY SALAD

1 lb. cranberries
Rind of 1/2 orange
Juice of 2 oranges
2 c. sugar
2 env. unflavored gelatin
1 3-oz. package red Jell-O
Pinch of salt
2 stalks celery, finely chopped
1/2 c. nuts, chopped
2 apples, diced

Grind cranberries and orange rind in food grinder. Combine with orange juice and sugar in large bowl. Let stand for several hours. Soften unflavored gelatin in 1/2 cup cold water. Dissolve red Jell-O and gelatin in 2 1/4 cups boiling water. Add gelatin mixture and salt to cranberry mixture. Chill until partially set. Add celery, nuts and apples. Pour into mold. Chill until firm. Yield: 18-24 servings.

Sally A. Goode, Norwayne H.S.
Creston, Ohio

CRANBERRY CHECKERBOARD SALAD

    1   1-lb. can whole cranberry sauce
    2   3-oz. packages lemon gelatin
    1 tbsp. lemon juice
    1/4 tsp. salt
    1/2 c. mayonnaise
    1 apple, peeled and diced
    1/4 c. chopped walnuts

Heat cranberry sauce in saucepan. Strain, reserving cranberries. Mix liquid with 3 cups boiling water in bowl. Add gelatin; stir until completely dissolved. Add lemon juice and salt; mix well. Chill until thick. Reserve 1 1/2 cups thickened gelatin mixture. Pour remaining mixture into chilled 13 x 9 1/2 x 2-inch dish. Chill until firm. Add mayonnaise to reserved gelatin. Beat with rotary beater until light and fluffy. Fold in cranberries, apple and walnuts. Spoon evenly over first layer. Chill until firm. Cut into 12 squares; unmold. Arrange squares, inverting half, checkerboard-fashion on salad greens. Chill until ready to serve. Yield: 12 servings.

Photograph for this recipe above.

NOEL SALAD LOAF

1/2 c. cubed avocado
Lemon juice
1 8-oz. package cream cheese, softened
1/3 c. mayonnaise
1/2 c. chopped celery
1 9-oz. can crushed pineapple, drained
1/4 tsp. salt
1 c. sweetened whipped cream
Red food coloring
1 can jellied cranberry sauce

Coat avocado with lemon juice to prevent darkening. Set aside. Blend cheese and mayonnaise in bowl. Fold in celery and pineapple. Sprinkle with 1 teaspoon lemon juice and salt. Tint whipped cream pink. Fold avocado and whipped cream into cheese mixture. Cube 3/4 of the cranberry sauce. Fold into cheese mixture. Spoon into loaf pan. Freeze overnight. Unmold. Garnish with remaining cranberry sauce. Slice to serve.

Sue Dennis, Huntsville Sr. H.S.
Huntsville, Arkansas

FESTIVE GRAPEFRUIT SALAD

1/2 env. unflavored gelatin
Juice of 3 grapefruit
2 3-oz. packages lemon gelatin
1/4 tsp. cayenne pepper
3 grapefruit, sectioned
1 No. 303 can crushed pineapple,
   undrained
10 red maraschino cherries, quartered

Sprinkle unflavored gelatin over grapefruit juice. Let stand for 5 minutes. Stir lemon gelatin into 1 cup hot water until dissolved. Add grapefruit juice mixture; stir thoroughly. Stir in pepper, grapefruit sections, pineapple and cherries. Pour into mold. Refrigerate until set.

Marcia F. Swanson, Henry County Sr. H.S.
McDonough, Georgia

FROZEN CHRISTMAS SALAD

1 c. sour cream
1/2 2 1/4-oz. carton Cool Whip
1/2 c. sugar
2 tbsp. lemon juice
1 tsp. vanilla extract
2 med. bananas, diced
1 13-oz. can crushed pineapple, drained
1/2 c. red candied cherries, sliced
1/2 c. green candied cherries, sliced

1/2 c. chopped pecans
Lettuce leaves

Blend sour cream, Cool Whip, sugar, lemon juice and vanilla in mixing bowl. Fold in fruits and pecans. Turn into 4 1/2-cup ring mold. Freeze for several hours. Unmold onto lettuce bed; garnish with additional cherries. Let stand for 10 minutes before serving.

Jeretta Wilson, Moore, Central Mid H.S.
Moore, Oklahoma

HOLIDAY GELATIN SALAD

1 can crushed pineapple
2 3-oz. packages green gelatin
1 8-oz. package cream cheese, softened
1 c. pecans

Drain pineapple, reserving juice. Dissolve Jell-O in 2 cups boiling water. Cool for 20 minutes. Add enough water to reserved pineapple juice to measure 1 cup liquid. Stir liquid into cream cheese until smooth. Add cream cheese mixture to cooled Jell-O. Stir in pineapple and pecans; blend well. Pour into square dish. Chill until set. Cut into 2-inch squares. May serve on lettuce leaf garnished with whipped topping and maraschino cherries.

Katy Jo Powers, Haysi H.S.
Haysi, Virginia

LIME CONGEALED SALAD

1 sm. package lime gelatin
1 15 1/4-oz. can crushed pineapple
1 10 1/2-oz. package miniature
   marshmallows
1 c. chopped pecans
1 c. whipping cream, whipped
1 sm. carton small-curd cottage cheese

Dissolve gelatin in 2 cups boiling water in saucepan. Add pineapple. Bring to a boil. Remove from heat. Add marshmallows; stir until marshmallows dissolve. Chill until partially set. Add pecans, whipped cream and cottage cheese, stirring gently. Spoon into serving dish. Chill until firm.

Renee A. Jenkins, Glenmore Academy
Memphis, Tennessee

HOLIDAY PRETZEL SALAD

2 1/2 c. crushed pretzels
3/4 c. melted butter
Sugar

1 8-oz. package cream cheese, softened
2 c. whipped topping
1 6-oz. package raspberry Jell-O
2 10-oz. packages frozen raspberries

Mix pretzels, butter and 3 tablespoons sugar. Press into 9 x 13-inch baking dish. Bake at 375 degrees for 10 minutes. Cool completely. Combine cream cheese, whipped topping and 1 cup sugar in bowl; blend well. Spread over pretzel crust. Refrigerate for 4 to 6 hours or overnight. Dissolve Jell-O in 2 cups boiling water. Add raspberries; stir until raspberries separate and Jell-O is thickened. Pour over cream cheese layer. Chill for 2 to 3 hours.

Micki Jeffery, Center Jr. H.S.
Kansas City, Missouri

MANDARIN ORANGE MOLD

2 11-oz. cans mandarin oranges
1 3-oz. packages orange Jell-O
1 pt. orange sherbet
1 13 1/2-oz. can crushed pineapple

Drain oranges, reserving juice. Add enough water to juice to measure 1 1/2 cups liquid. Place in saucepan. Bring to a boil. Remove from heat. Add Jell-O, stirring until dissolved. Add sherbet, stirring until melted. Chill until thickened, about 5 to 10 minutes. Fold in oranges and pineapple. Pour into 2-quart mold. Chill for several hours or until firm. Unmold onto serving tray. Garnish with orange slices or whole strawberries.

Esther L. Moorhead, Berryhill H.S.
Tulsa, Oklahoma

MERRY CHRISTMAS SALAD

1 3-oz. package lime gelatin
10 marshmallows, quartered
1 8-oz. package cream cheese, softened
1 c. salad dressing
1/2 pt. whipping cream, whipped
1 No. 2 can crushed pineapple
1 6-oz. package raspberry gelatin
Lettuce leaves

Dissolve lime gelatin in 1 cup boiling water in large bowl. Add marshmallows; mix well. Whip cream cheese in bowl; blend in salad dressing. Fold whipped cream into cream cheese mixture. Add pineapple and cream cheese mixture to gelatin mixture; mix well. Pour into 2 rectangular dishes. Chill until firm. Dissolve raspberry gelatin in 4 cups boiling water. Cool.

Spoon over congealed lime gelatin. Cut in squares. Serve on lettuce leaves.

Mary Lou Young, Greenwood H.S.
Greenwood, Arkansas

PECAN SALAD

1 1/4 c. crushed pineapple
1/2 c. sugar
1 env. unflavored gelatin
2 c. whipping cream, whipped
1/2 c. chopped pecans
1 c. grated American cheese

Cook pineapple and sugar for 5 minutes over medium heat. Soften gelatin in 1/4 cup cold water. Add 3/4 cup boiling water; stir until dissolved. Mix with pineapple. Chill until slightly thickened. Fold in whipped cream, pecans and cheese. Pour into 8-inch square pan. Chill until set. Cut in squares. Serve on lettuce leaf.

Sharon Brozovsky
Scotus Central Catholic School
Columbus, Nebraska

PEAR-PECAN SALAD

1 No. 2 1/2 can pears
1 3-oz. package lemon gelatin
1 8-oz. package cream cheese, softened
1 c. chopped pecans
1 c. whipping cream, whipped

Drain juice from pears, reserving 1 cup liquid. Bring juice to a boil in saucepan. Add gelatin; stir until dissolved. Chill until partially set. Place pears and cream cheese in blender container; blend until creamy. Stir in gelatin mixture. Add pecans. Fold whipped cream into mixture. Pour into large mold or 16 individual molds. Chill until set. Serve on lettuce.

Dorothy Moore, Central Jr. H.S.
Sand Springs, Oklahoma

PINK DELIGHT

1 lg. can crushed pineapple
1 lg. package strawberry Jell-O
1 c. cottage cheese
1 sm. carton sour cream
1 lg. carton Cool Whip
1/2 c. chopped pecans
1/2 c. coconut

Place pineapple in large saucepan. Add Jell-O; heat until Jell-O dissolves. Remove from heat. Cool slightly. Add remaining ingredients; blend thoroughly. Pour into mold. Chill until firm.

Sara H. Cavanaugh, Wetumpka H.S.
Wetumpka, Alabama

PISTACHIO-COCONUT SURPRISE

2 c. sour cream
1 3-oz. package pistachio instant
   pudding mix
1 1/3 c. shredded coconut
1 sm. can crushed pineapple
1/4 to 1/2 c. chopped maraschino
   cherries (opt.)

Mix sour cream with pudding mix in bowl. Add coconut, pineapple and cherries; mix well. Spoon into loaf pan. Freeze for 3 hours or until firm. Slice and serve.

Jo Anne M. Stringer, Liberty H.S.
Youngstown, Ohio

YUMMY PISTACHIO SALAD

1 carton Cool Whip
1 med. carton cottage cheese
1 pkg. pistachio pudding mix
1 can fruit cocktail
1 can pineapple chunks

Combine Cool Whip with cottage cheese in bowl. Add pudding mix; mix well. Stir in fruit cocktail and pineapple. Place in serving dish. Chill until serving time.

Sherri Treible, Mesa Grande School
Calimesa, California

SNOW FLAKE SALAD

1 8-oz. package cream cheese, softened
1 9-oz. carton frozen whipped topping,
   thawed
2 16-oz. cans fruit cocktail, drained
1 16-oz. can chuck pineapple, drained
1 c. miniature marshmallows
1/2 c. diced red maraschino cherries
1 c. chopped pecans
1/2 c. shredded coconut
1/2 c. green maraschino cherries,
   sliced in halves (opt.)

Whip cream cheese in large bowl until fluffy. Add whipped topping; mix well. Fold in remaining ingredients except green cherries. Pour into serving dish. Refrigerate for 25 minutes. Garnish with green cherries. Yield: 10-12 servings.

Mrs. Evon F. McLendon
Montgomery County H.S.
Mt. Vernon, Georgia

STRAWBERRY-CREAM CHEESE SALAD

2 3-oz. packages strawberry Jell-O
2 bananas, mashed
2 10-oz. packages frozen strawberries
1/4 c. crushed pineapple, drained
1 c. confectioners' sugar
1 tsp. vanilla extract
1 8-oz. package cream cheese, softened
1/2 pt. whipping cream, whipped
1 c. chopped pecans or walnuts

Dissolve Jell-O in 2 cups boiling water. Reserve 1/4 cup mixture. Pour into serving dish. Add bananas, strawberries and pineapple to remaining Jell-O. Chill until set. Add confectioners' sugar and vanilla to cream cheese; mix until smooth. Add whipped cream to cream cheese mixture. Add reserved Jell-O; mix well. Spread over Jell-O layer. Sprinkle with nuts. Chill until set. Yield: 8-10 servings.

Pam Dangelmayr, Sacred Heart H.S.
Muenster, Texas

STRAWBERRY SALAD

1 4-oz. package strawberry Jell-O
1 10-oz. package frozen strawberries
1 can crushed pineapple
1 banana, mashed
1/2 c. chopped pecans
1 8-oz. carton sour cream

Dissolve Jell-O in 1 cup boiling water. Add frozen strawberries. Stir until thawed. Add remaining ingredients except sour cream. Spread 1/2 of the Jell-O mixture in serving dish. Chill until set. Spread sour cream over congealed Jell-O. Add remaining Jell-O mixture. Chill until set. Yield: 6 servings.

Lana Gates, Community School
Nevada, Texas

CHRISTMAS SALAD

1 lg. package strawberry gelatin
1 carton small-curd cottage cheese
1/2 c. chopped pecans
1/4 c. coconut
1/2 c. miniature marshmallows
1 8-oz. carton Cool Whip

Combine strawberry gelatin with cottage cheese; mix well. Reserve small amount pecans and coconut for garnish. Add remaining pecans and coconut. Stir in marshmallows and Cool

Whip. Chill for 30 minutes before serving. Garnish with reserved coconut and pecans.

Norita Cassity, Dawson Springs H.S.
Dawson Springs, Kentucky

STRAWBERRY JELL-O SALAD

2 sm. packages strawberry Jell-O
1 lg. package frozen strawberries
1 No. 2 can crushed pineapple
2 bananas, mashed
1 carton sour cream
1 c. chopped pecans

Dissolve Jell-O in 2 cups boiling water. Add next 3 ingredients; mix well. Pour half the Jell-O mixture into 9 x 13-inch dish. Chill until firm. Combine sour cream and pecans. Spread over congealed layer. Chill until set. Pour remaining Jell-O mixture over sour cream layer. Chill until firm. Cut into squares.

Mrs. Eloise Guerrant, Robert Lee H.S.
Robert Lee, Texas

HOLIDAY COTTAGE CHEESE SALAD

1 pkg. strawberry Jell-O
1 1-lb. carton small-curd cottage cheese
1 sm. can crushed pineapple, drained
1 sm. carton Cool Whip

Stir Jell-O into cottage cheese. Add pineapple and Cool Whip; mix well. Chill before serving.

Linda Albright, Panola School
Panola, Oklahoma

STRAWBERRY-NUT SALAD

2 3-oz. packages strawberry Jell-O
2 10-oz. packages frozen strawberries
1 1-lb. 4-oz. can crushed pineapple, drained
3 med bananas, mashed
1 c. chopped nuts
1 pt. sour cream

Dissolve Jell-O in 2 cups boiling water. Add frozen strawberries, pineapple, bananas and nuts. Stir until thoroughly mixed. Place half the Jell-O mixture in 12 x 8 x 3-inch serving dish. Refrigerate until firm. Spread sour cream over congealed Jell-O. Spoon remaining Jell-O mixture gently over sour cream. Refrigerate until set. Cut into squares. Place on crisp lettuce leaf for individual servings.

Sister Julie Budai, Providence H.S.
San Antonio, Texas

TRI-LEVEL CHRISTMAS JELL-O

1 6-oz. package each lemon, lime and raspberry Jell-O
1 c. miniature marshmallows
2 3-oz. packages cream cheese, softened
1 c. crushed drained pineapple
1 c. whipping cream, whipped, sweetened

Dissolve each package Jell-O separately in 2 cups boiling water. Stir marshmallows into lemon Jell-O. Set aside. Add 1 1/2 cups cold water to lime Jell-O. Pour into 12 x 16-inch pan. Chill until firm. Add 1 1/2 cups cold water to raspberry Jell-O. Add cream cheese to lemon mixture; beat until blended. Chill until slightly thickened. Fold in pineapple and whipped cream. Spread lemon mixture over congealed lime Jell-O. Chill until partially set. Chill raspberry Jell-O until partially set. Spoon over lemon layer. Chill until firm.

Karen Robinson, Alta H.S.
Sandy, Utah

YUM-YUM SALAD

1 3-oz. package lime Jell-O
1/2 c. salad dressing
1/2 c. whipping cream, whipped
1 c. crushed pineapple
12 marshmallows, chopped
Chopped pecans (opt.)
Chopped maraschino cherries (opt.)

Dissolve Jell-O in 1/2 cup boiling water. Chill until partially set. Fold in remaining ingredients. Chill until firm.

Jo Etta Penn, Howe H.S.
Howe, Texas

PASTA SALAD

1 pkg. vermicelli
1 bunch celery, chopped
1 lg. can pimentos, chopped
4 jalapeno peppers or to taste
1 sm. green pepper, chopped (opt.)
1 med. onion, grated
2 to 3 c. Kraft Miracle Whip Dressing
Salt and pepper to taste

Cook vermicelli using package directions. Drain; cool. Combine celery, pimentos, peppers and onion in serving bowl. Add vermicelli; mix well. Add salad dressing, salt and pepper. Cover. Refrigerate for 24 hours. Keeps well for 4 or 5 days.

Bonnie N. Prewitt, Swartz Jr. H.S.
Swartz, Louisiana

RICE SALAD

5 chicken bouillon cubes
1/4 c. margarine
Salt to taste
4 1/2 c. Minute Rice
1 c. each chopped green peppers, celery
and green onions
1 lg. jar chopped pimentos
1 bottle of Creamy Italian dressing

Combine first 3 ingredients in saucepan. Add 4 1/2 cups water. Bring to a boil, stirring well. Add rice. Remove from heat; cover. Allow to fluff. Add remaining ingredients; mix well. Refrigerate. Keeps well for several days. Yield: 10-12 servings.

Glynda Hooper, Marlow H.S.
Marlow, Oklahoma

CHICKEN SALAD

3 c. diced cooked chicken
1 1/2 c. chopped celery -
2 tbsp. chopped parsley
1 tsp. salt
1/2 tsp. pepper
1/2 c. heavy cream, whipped
1 c. mayonnaise
2 tbsp. lemon juice
1/2 c. coarsely chopped toasted almonds

Combine chicken with celery, parsley, salt and pepper in large bowl; toss to mix. Fold in whipped cream, mayonnaise, lemon juice and almonds gently. Refrigerate until well chilled, about 1 hour.

Jane Clark, Avery County H.S.
Newland, North Carolina

CHICKEN-FRUIT SALAD

1 16-oz. can pineapple chunks
1 apple, sliced
1 c. seedless grapes
3 c. diced cooked chicken
3 tbsp. butter
3 tbsp. flour
1/4 c. sugar
1 tsp. salt
1/3 c. lemon juice
3 egg yolks, beaten
1/2 c. whipping cream, whipped
Lettuce
1/3 c. toasted slivered almonds

Drain pineapple chunks, reserving juice. Dip apple slices in reserved pineapple juice. Combine fruit and chicken. Chill. Melt butter in small saucepan over low heat; blend in flour. Add sugar, salt, lemon juice and 1/3 cup pineapple juice. Cook until thickened, stirring constantly. Stir small amount of hot mixture into egg yolks; stir egg yolks into hot mixture. Cook about 2 minutes, stirring constantly. Chill. Fold in whipped cream. Add to chicken mixture; toss lightly. Serve on lettuce topped with almonds. Yield: 6-8 servings.

Naomi Mayes, Warren East H.S.
Bowling Green, Kentucky

HOT CHICKEN SALAD RING

1 1/2 c. diced cooked chicken
1 8-oz. can pineapple tidbits, drained
1/3 c. mayonnaise
1/4 c. diced celery
1/4 c. chopped almonds
1/4 c. diced green pepper
Salt and pepper to taste
1 can refrigerator crescent rolls
1 egg, beaten

Combine first 7 ingredients in bowl; toss lightly. Set aside. Separate rolls into 8 triangles. Arrange triangles on greased cookie sheet in circle with bases overlapping and tips pointing outward. Spoon chicken salad in ring around bases of triangles, packing firmly to insure ring shape. Fold triangle tips over filling and tuck under bases. Brush with egg. Bake at 350 degrees for 25 to 30 minutes or until golden. Serve hot.

Deborah E. Foust, Southeast H.S.
Greensboro, North Carolina

NEW YEAR'S HAM SALAD

1 1-lb. can diced beets, drained
1/2 c. finely chopped celery
2 tbsp. chopped cucumber pickle chips
2 med. apples, peeled, chopped
2 hard-boiled eggs, chopped
1 to 2 c. cooked ham, cubed
1 to 2 tbsp. sugar
1/2 c. mayonnaise
1/2 c. sour cream

Combine first 7 ingredients in large bowl. Mix mayonnaise and sour cream. Stir into ham mixture. Refrigerate for several hours. Serve on buttered hard rolls.

Marthanne Argyle, Spanish Fork H.S.
Spanish Fork, Utah

TURKEY SALAD

2 c. chopped turkey breast
1 c. bite-sized orange segments
1 c. pineapple chunks
1/2 c. chopped pecans
1/2 c. chopped apple
1 tbsp. lemon juice
1/2 tsp. curry powder
3/4 c. mayonnaise
Apple slices

Combine first 5 ingredients in large bowl. Combine lemon juice, curry powder and mayonnaise in small bowl; mix well. Add to salad ingredients; toss to mix. Garnish with apple slices.

Betty H. Knight, West Wilkes H.S.
Millers Creek, North Carolina

SUPER EASY TURKEY SALAD

4 c. diced turkey
1 1/2 c. chopped celery
1 1/2 c. mayonnaise
1 tbsp. soy sauce
1 tsp. curry powder
Salt and pepper to taste
1 20-oz. can pineapple chunks, drained
2/3 c. sliced almonds, toasted

Combine turkey, celery, mayonnaise, soy sauce, curry, salt and pepper; mix well. Refrigerate. Top with pineapple and almonds just before serving. Yield: 6 servings.

Linda B. Smith, Avery H.S.
Newland, North Carolina

TIERED PARTY SALAD MOLD

3 env. unflavored gelatin
3 c. consomme
1/4 tsp. pepper
1 tsp. salt
1/8 tsp. paprika
4 c. chopped cooked turkey
1 sm. green pepper, chopped
1 tbsp. minced chives (opt.)
1 c. celery, chopped
1 c. chopped cucumber
1 7-oz. jar pimento, chopped
1 tbsp. lemon juice
1 3-oz. package cream cheese, softened
1 1/2 c. mayonnaise

Soften gelatin in cold consomme in saucepan. Heat until gelatin dissolves. Remove from heat. Add pepper, salt and paprika. Set aside. Combine turkey with remaining ingredients; mix well. Add gelatin mixture; blend thoroughly.

Divide salad mixture among 3 oiled small, medium and large cake pans. Chill until firm. Unmold largest pan onto serving plate. Unmold medium pan on top of large layer. Top with small layer. Yield: 12-15 servings.

Doris Wren, Lexington H.S.
Lexington, Texas

MACARONI-TURKEY SALAD

1 8-oz. package elbow macaroni
1 tbsp. salt
1 c. sour cream
1/3 c. mayonnaise
1/4 c. lemon juice
1 tsp. seasoned salt
1/2 tsp. dillweed
1/4 tsp. white pepper
2 c. julienne-cut cooked turkey
1 c. cut green beans, cooked
1/4 c. chopped sweet onion
1 4-oz. can pimentos, drained and halved
1 6-oz. jar marinated artichoke
*   hearts, drained*
Salad greens

Prepare macaroni according to package directions, using 1 tablespoon salt. Pour into colander. Rinse with cold water; drain. Set aside. Combine sour cream, mayonnaise, lemon juice, seasoned salt, dillweed and pepper in large bowl; mix well. Add macaroni; toss to coat. Arrange turkey, green beans, onion, pimentos and artichoke hearts over macaroni; chill. Toss together before serving. Serve on salad greens. Yield: 4-6 servings.

Photograph for this recipe on page 46.

SHRIMP MOLD

1 can tomato soup
1 6-oz. package cream cheese, softened
2 tbsp. unflavored gelatin
1 c. mayonnaise
1/2 c. diced green pepper
1/2 c. diced celery
1 sm. onion, grated
2 c. shrimp, cooked, chopped

Heat soup and cream cheese over low heat in saucepan until cheese melts, stirring occasionally. Soften gelatin in 1/2 cup cold water; add to hot mixture, stirring until dissolved. Remove from heat. Add remaining ingredients. Pour into oiled mold. Chill until firm. Serve with crackers.

Nancy Newell Stiles, West H.S.
Iowa City, Iowa

asparagus with tips down along sides of mold. Chill until thick. Spoon in remaining gelatin mixture. Chill until firm. Unmold to serve. Garnish with salad greens and whole pitted ripe olives if desired. Yield: 8-10 servings.

Photograph for this recipe on this page.

TACO SALAD

    1 lb. ground beef
    1 pkg. onion soup mix
    1 can pinto beans, drained
    2 or 3 tomatoes, quartered
    1 head of lettuce, chopped
    4 oz. grated Cheddar cheese
    3/4 bag taco chips
    1 lg. bottle of Catalina dressing

Brown ground beef with onion soup mix in frypan. Drain. Cool. Place in bowl. Add beans, tomatoes, lettuce and cheese. Add taco chips and dressing just before serving.

Diane Lindsey, Claymont H.S.
Uhrichsville, Ohio

ONION-ORANGE SALAD

    1 qt. mixed salad greens
    1 11-oz. can mandarin oranges
    1/2 c. roasted cocktail peanuts
    1/2 c. sliced Bermuda onions, separated
       into rings
    1/3 c. sugar
    1/3 c. vinegar
    1 tsp. dry mustard
    1 tsp. salt
    1 tbsp. celery seed
    1 sm. onion

Combine first 4 ingredients in serving bowl; toss well. Set aside. Place next 6 ingredients in blender container. Blend until smooth; pour over salad. Toss lightly. Let stand to allow flavors to blend.

Ruth Beebe, Mauldin H.S.
Mauldin, South Carolina

BEET SALAD

    1 c. beet juice
    1 3-oz. package lemon Jell-O
    1 c. julienne beets
    1 tbsp. horseradish
    2 tbsp. vinegar
    2 tsp. chopped onion

ELEGANT OLIVE-CRAB MOUSSE

    2 10-oz. packages frozen asparagus
       spears
    2 env. unflavored gelatin
    1/2 c. mayonnaise
    2 tbsp. lemon juice
    1/2 tsp. salt
    1/2 tsp. Worcestershire sauce
    Several drops of liquid red pepper
       seasoning
    1/4 c. catsup
    1 c. canned pitted ripe olives, sliced
    2 c. sour cream
    1 7 1/2-oz. can crab meat, drained,
       flaked

Cook asparagus according to package directions in saucepan; drain. Slice asparagus, reserving enough white spears for garnish. Soften gelatin in 3/4 cup cold water in saucepan. Cook over low heat until dissolved, stirring constantly. Add to mayonnaise in bowl, beating with wire whisk. Stir in seasonings and catsup; mix well. Fold in olives, reserving several slices for garnish. Fold in sour cream and crab meat. Chill until partially congealed. Place reserved olives in bottom of 6-cup mold. Spoon in a small amount of gelatin mixture to cover. Arrange

3/4 c. chopped celery
1/2 tsp. salt
Sour cream

Bring beet juice to a boil in saucepan. Add Jell-O, stirring to dissolve. Combine remaining ingredients in bowl. Pour Jell-O into bowl; mix well. Pour into mold. Chill until set. Serve with dollops of sour cream.

Kathleen Omalley, North Arlington H.S.
North Arlington, New Jersey

COBB SALAD

1/4 c. vinegar
1/2 c. salad oil
1 tsp. lemon juice
1 clove of garlic, chopped
1/2 tsp. salt
Dash of pepper
1 head romaine, finely chopped
8 slices crisp bacon, crumbled
1/4 lb. Roquefort cheese, crumbled
3 tomatoes, diced fine
2 avocados, peeled, diced
2 hard-boiled eggs, chopped fine
4 strips pimento, chopped

Combine first 6 ingredients; mix well. Toss remaining ingredients together. Add dressing; toss well.

Nancy L. Myers, Pine Tree H.S.
Longview, Texas

BROCCOLI SALAD

1 bunch broccoli, cut into flowerets
1 can mushroom pieces, drained
1 can ripe olives, drained, sliced
1 can water chestnuts, drained, sliced
1 bottle of Zesty Italian dressing

Combine first 4 ingredients. Add dressing. Marinate 6 to 8 hours, stirring occasionally.

Faye H. Lynch, Hichman County H.S.
Centerville, Tennessee

SUPER BOWL SALAD

1/2 head cabbage, shredded
1/2 bag spinach, shredded
1/2 head lettuce, shredded
1 lb. bacon, fried, crumbled
6 hard-boiled eggs, chopped
1 bunch green onions, chopped

1 pkg. Ranch-style dressing mix
1 c. sour cream
2 c. mayonnaise
2 c. shredded Swiss or Longhorn cheese

Layer first 3 ingredients in large bowl. Add layers of bacon, eggs and green onions. Combine dressing mix and sour cream in bowl. Add mayonnaise; blend thoroughly. Spread dressing mixture over salad, spreading to side of bowl. Top with cheese. Seal tightly. Refrigerate for 24 hours before serving. Yield: 12 servings.

Diana K. Dukes, Marion H.S.
Marion, Texas

SPINACH SALAD

1/2 lb. fresh spinach
1 No. 2 can bean sprouts, drained
8 slices crisp bacon, crumbled
3 hard-boiled eggs, chopped
1/2 c. Crisco salad oil
3/4 c. sugar
1/3 c. catsup
1/4 c. vinegar
1 tsp. Worcestershire sauce
1 sm. onion, grated

Wash spinach thoroughly. Drain; tear into bite-sized pieces. Combine with bean sprouts, bacon and eggs in salad bowl. Combine remaining ingredients; mix well. Toss with spinach just before serving.

Frances Baker Bishop, Denton Sr. H.S.
Denton, Texas

KATIE'S SPINACH SALAD

2/3 c. salad oil
1/4 c. wine vinegar
2 tbsp. white wine
2 tsp. soy sauce
1 tsp. each sugar, dry mustard
1/2 tsp. each curry powder, salt and
*   garlic salt*
3 bunches of spinach
1 lb. bacon, fried and crumbled
3 hard-boiled eggs, grated

Combine first 9 ingredients in glass jar. Shake well. Chill. Wash spinach thoroughly. Tear into bite-sized pieces. Place spinach in large bowl; add bacon and eggs. Top with dressing; toss well.

Katie Johnston, Mohave H.S.
Scottsdale, Arizona

Party-Time Main Dishes

The door bell rings; friends come in smiling; the aroma of the main dish you're preparing drifts through the air. A few final touches, and you're ready — confident that this holiday dinner will be the best ever.

When entertaining, select your main dish first — but carefully. It's the part of the menu around which everything else revolves.

Busy holiday times often require plenty of planning ahead. That's why this chapter is full of one-dish delicious meals. Casseroles and quiches of chicken, ground beef, seafood and ham that you can fix ahead, saving valuable last minute time. Recipes also range from the traditional holiday ham to foreign dish favorites. Shish kabobs, crepes and Italian specialties such as manicotti, and cannelloni abound! And there are so many variations on preparing your holiday turkey, your family will never tire of trying new ways!

For those lazy mornings that seem to come most frequently around the holidays, there are special breakfast dishes included too.

Plan ahead with these time-honored recipes so you can enjoy your family and friends.

BARBECUED BRISKET OF BEEF

*Celery salt, onion salt and garlic salt
   to taste*
1 5-lb. brisket
1 3-oz. bottle of liquid smoke
*Salt, pepper and Worcestershire
   sauce to taste*
3/4 c. barbecue sauce
2 tbsp. flour

Sprinkle celery, onion and garlic salts on both sides of brisket. Marinate overnight in liquid smoke. Sprinkle salt, pepper and Worcestershire sauce on both sides of brisket. Place in large pan; cover tightly. Bake at 275 degrees for 5 hours. Add barbecue sauce to brisket. Bake for 1 hour longer. Let stand for 1 hour before slicing. May mix flour, 1/2 cup water and pan drippings for sauce.

*Darrelynn Barnett, Ore City H.S.
Ore City, Texas*

BEST-EVER BRISKET

1/2 bottle of liquid smoke
8 tbsp. Worcestershire sauce
*1 tsp. each garlic salt, onion salt and
   celery salt*
1 8 to 10-lb. brisket
1 med. onion, chopped
1/2 stick margarine
1/4 c. (firmly packed) brown sugar
1/2 bottle of catsup

Combine liquid smoke, 4 tablespoons Worcestershire sauce, garlic, onion and celery salts together in bowl. Place brisket on large heavy foil in baking dish. Pour marinade over brisket. Seal foil. Refrigerate overnight. Bake at 225 degrees for 1 hour per pound of brisket. Slice brisket; place in casserole. Saute onion in skillet with margarine. Add brown sugar, 4 tablespoons Worcestershire sauce and catsup; mix well. Pour sauce over meat. Bake at 250 degrees for 1 hour.

*Linda Richardson, R.L. Turner H.S.
Carrollton, Texas*

HOLIDAY SWISS STEAK

1/3 c. flour
2 tsp. salt
1/4 tsp. pepper
*1 2 to 2 1/2-lb. round or chuck steak,
   1 in. thick*
3 tbsp. shortening
1 c. seasoned tomato sauce
1 1/3 c. pizza sauce
1 med. onion, sliced
1 med. green pepper, sliced

Combine flour, salt and pepper; pound into steak. Brown steak slowly on both sides in Dutch oven with shortening. Pour tomato sauce and pizza sauce over steak. Top with onion slices. Simmer, uncovered, for 10 minutes. Cover. Bake at 350 degrees for 1 hour or longer, until steak is fork-tender. Place steak on serving platter. Garnish with green pepper slices.

*Melba M. Sanders, Pike County H.S.
Brundidge, Alabama*

PERFECT FILET

1 1/2 c. salad oil
3/4 c. soy sauce
1/4 c. Worcestershire sauce
2 tbsp. dry mustard
2 to 3 tsp. salt
1/4 tsp. pepper
1/2 c. white vinegar
1/3 c. lemon juice
1 tbsp. chopped parsley
1 tbsp. garlic powder
1 2 1/2 to 3-lb. beef tenderloin
1/4 lb. butter

Combine first 10 ingredients in small bowl; mix well. Pour over tenderloin in shallow dish. Refrigerate for 24 hours. Remove tenderloin from marinade. Pat dry with paper towels. Place in jelly roll pan. Arrange thin slices of butter over top. Bake at 450 degrees for 15 minutes. Reduce temperature to 350 degrees. Bake for 15 to 30 minutes longer. Test for doneness by cutting through center; ends will be well done, interior medium rare.

*Nancy T. Hagerty, Central-Lanier H.S.
Macon, Georgia*

MEXICALI CHILI

2 lb. beef chuck, cut in 1/2-in. cubes
Flour
1/4 c. salad oil
2 c. sliced onion
1 c. chopped green pepper
1 clove of garlic, crushed
2 1-lb. cans tomatoes, drained
1 6-oz. can tomato paste
2 tbsp. chili powder
1 tbsp. sugar
3 tsp. salt
1/4 tsp. pepper

1/8 tsp. paprika
2 bay leaves
1 tsp. cumin
1 tsp. dried basil leaves
2 cans kidney beans, drained
1/2 to 1 c. grated Cheddar cheese
Cooked rice

Coat beef cubes with flour. Brown in salad oil in large saucepan. Drain. Add remaining ingredients except beans, cheese and rice. Simmer for 1 hour. Add beans; heat thoroughly. Layer rice, meat mixture and cheese in large casserole. Bake at 350 degrees until cheese is melted.

Johnsie Walker Reglin
Marengo Community H.S.
Marengo, Illinois

SHISH KABOBS

4 steaks, cut in 1-in. cubes
Cherry tomatoes
Green peppers, cut in chunks
Onions, cut in chunks
1 lg. bottle of Catalina salad dressing
Fresh mushrooms

Place first 4 ingredients in large flat dish. Cover with Catalina dressing. Marinate for 4 hours in refrigerator. Place mushrooms in marinade 1 hour before grilling. Place all ingredients on skewers. Grill over hot coals. Yield: 5-6 servings.

Joyce R. Roberts, El Reno H.S.
El Reno, Oklahoma

CHICKEN SUPREME

8 chicken breasts
Salt and pepper to taste
1 can cream of mushroom soup
1 can cream of celery soup
1 env. Lipton onion soup mix
1/2 to 1 c. wine (opt.)

Place chicken breasts in 9 x 12-inch baking dish. Sprinkle with salt and pepper. Mix canned soups in small bowl; pour over chicken. Spread to cover. Sprinkle onion soup mix over all. Add wine; cover. Bake at 350 degrees for 1 hour and 30 minutes to 2 hours.

Camille M. Yates, Lee Academy
Clarksdale, Mississippi

TOUCHDOWN CURRY

1 30-oz. can apricot halves
1 15 1/4-oz. can pineapple chunks

6 lg. chicken breast halves, skinned
   and boned
3 tbsp. cornstarch
1/4 c. butter or margarine
3 med. onions, sliced
3 to 4 tsp. curry powder
1 10 3/4-oz. can chicken broth,
   undiluted
1 1/2 tsp. salt
1/4 tsp. ginger
3 c. hot cooked rice
Condiments, if desired (chutney, dark
   and white raisins, toasted almonds,
   toasted coconut)

Drain apricots and pineapple, reserving 1/2 cup each apricot liquid and pineapple liquid. Slice chicken crosswise into chunks. Coat chicken with cornstarch. Melt butter in large skillet. Add chicken, onions and curry powder. Cook over medium heat, stirring occasionally, until onions are tender, about 10 minutes. Stir in reserved fruit liquids, chicken broth, salt and ginger. Cook until mixture thickens and begins to boil. Pour into 2-quart baking dish. Add apricots and pineapple chunks. Cover baking dish with plastic wrap or foil; refrigerate. Bake, uncovered, in 350-degree oven for 45 minutes until hot and bubbly. Serve with hot, cooked rice and assortment of condiments, if desired. Yield: 4 servings.

Photograph for this recipe below.

APRICOT CHICKEN

5 lb. chicken pieces
1 pkg. dry onion soup mix
1/4 c. mayonnaise
1/2 c. Russian dressing
1 c. apricot preserves

Place chicken in baking dish; cover with waxed paper. Microwave on High for 10 minutes; turn. Continue cooking for 10 minutes longer. Combine remaining ingredients in small bowl; blend well. Pour sauce over chicken. Microwave for 2 minutes longer. Serve over rice. May be prepared in conventional oven by covering chicken with sauce and baking at 350 degrees for 1 hour or until chicken is tender.

Sister Julie Budai, Providence H.S.
San Antonio, Texas

CHICKEN AND ALMOND CASSEROLE

1/2 c. chopped onions
1 c. chopped celery
3/4 c. margarine
2 cans cream of mushroom soup
2 cans cream of chicken soup
1 1/2 c. evaporated milk
1 lg. can chow mein noodles
1 3 to 4-lb. cooked chicken, deboned
2 c. Pepperidge Farm herb stuffing mix
1 1/2 c. chopped almonds

Saute onions and celery in 1/4 cup margarine in large skillet. Add next 4 ingredients; mix well. Add chicken and stuffing mix; mix well. Place in 9 x 14-inch greased baking dish. Saute almonds in 1/2 cup margarine. Sprinkle over top of casserole. Bake at 350 degrees for 20 to 30 minutes. Yield: 6 servings.

Kathy Fulmer, Cale H.S.
Cale, Arkansas

CHICKEN CASSEROLE

2 c. chopped cooked chicken
1 c. chopped celery
1 c. cooked rice
3/4 c. mayonnaise
1 tsp. onion
1 tsp. lemon juice
1 tsp. salt
1 can water chestnuts, sliced
1 can cream of chicken soup
3 hard-boiled eggs, sliced

1/4 lb. butter, melted
Potato chips, crushed
1 pkg. sliced almonds

Combine first 10 ingredients in 2-quart casserole. Cover with melted butter, crushed potato chips and almonds. Bake at 350 degrees for 35 to 40 minutes. Yield: 4-6 servings.

Christine J. Anders, New Haven H.S.
New Haven, Indiana

PARTY-TIME CHICKEN

4 slices bacon
1 frying chicken, cut up
1 3/4-oz. envelope French's Au Jus Gravy Mix
1/2 c. chopped onion
1/4 c. chopped green pepper
1 8-oz. can tomato sauce
Cooked rice

Fry bacon in skillet until crisp. Drain on absorbent paper, reserving drippings. Crumble. Set aside. Roll chicken pieces in gravy mix to coat. Brown chicken, onion and pepper in bacon drippings. Stir in tomato sauce and any remaining gravy mix; cover. Cook for 45 minutes over medium heat. Stir in bacon. Cook for 15 minutes longer, uncovered. Serve over cooked rice. Yield: 4 servings.

Photograph for this recipe on page 62.

CHICKEN AND DRESSING CASSEROLE

Chopped onions and celery to taste
1 pkg. Pepperidge Farm stuffing mix
Sage to taste (opt.)
Chicken broth
Chicken, cooked, cut into pieces
1 can cream of chicken soup
1 sm. can evaporated milk

Saute onions and celery in skillet. Add to stuffing mix in large bowl. Add sage; mix well. Add enough chicken broth for desired consistency. Place chicken in bottom of casserole. Mix soup and milk; pour over chicken. Cover with stuffing mixture. Bake at 350 degrees for 30 minutes.

Norma Jean King, Sevier Co. Vocational Center
Sevierville, Tennessee

CHICKEN-SAUSAGE CASSEROLE

1 lg. fryer
1 stalk celery
1 bay leaf
Salt
1 med. package Uncle Ben's Wild Rice
1 lb. hot sausage
2 med. onions, chopped
2 cans cream of mushroom soup
1/2 to 3/4 pkg. Pepperidge Farm herb
*   stuffing mix*
1/2 to 3/4 c. butter, melted

Boil fryer with celery and bay leaf in salted water to cover until tender. Bone chicken. Reserve chicken stock. Cook rice by package directions using chicken stock instead of water. Brown sausage in skillet. Drain; crumble. Cook onions in sausage drippings. Add soup and sausage to onions; mix well. Place in greased 2-quart casserole. Combine chicken and rice; place over sausage mixture in casserole. Bake at 350 degrees for 15 minutes. Mix stuffing and butter. Place over casserole. Bake for 15 minutes longer.

Margaret Ann Larson
Paul Revere Middle School
Houston, Texas

CHICKEN TETRAZZINI

8 oz. spaghetti
1 tbsp. vegetable oil
2 tbsp. chopped onion
3 tbsp. butter
1 tbsp. flour
1 c. chicken broth
1 tsp. salt
1 c. milk
1 can mushroom soup
1 c. shredded sharp cheese
3 tbsp. chopped pimento
2 tbsp. parsley
2 1/2 to 3 c. diced cooked chicken
1/2 c. slivered almonds
1/4 c. Sherry
1 c. buttered cracker crumbs

Cook spaghetti in boiling salted water for 8 to 10 minutes. Stir in oil; drain. Saute onion in butter in saucepan until tender. Blend in flour. Add broth gradually, stirring constantly until thickened. Add next 4 ingredients. Heat until

cheese melts. Combine with spaghetti and remaining ingredients except crumbs. Place in large shallow baking dish. Cover with buttered crumbs. Bake at 350 degrees for 45 minutes or until heated through and crumbs are golden brown.

Marie Jones, Osage City H.S.
Osage City, Kansas

SESAME SEED CHICKEN

1 1/2 c. mayonnaise
1 tsp. dry mustard
1 tsp. instant minced onions
1/2 c. fine dry bread crumbs
1/4 c. sesame seed
2 lb. chicken, cut into 2-in. strips
3 tbsp. honey
1/2 tsp. chopped parsley

Mix 1/2 cup mayonnaise, mustard and onions; set aside. Mix bread crumbs and sesame seed; set aside. Dip chicken into mayonnaise mixture; roll in bread crumb mixture. Place on baking sheet. Bake at 375 degrees about 15 minutes or until brown. Mix 1 cup mayonnaise with honey and parsley for dip. Serve chicken hot with dip. Yield: 6-10 servings.

Judy Greene, Lloyd C. Bird H.S.
Chesterfield, Virginia

SUPREME CHICKEN CASSEROLE

1 box crackers, crushed
6 cooked chicken breasts, cut in
*   bite-sized pieces*
1 can water chestnuts, sliced
1 can cream of mushroom soup
1 can cream of chicken soup
8 oz. sour cream
1 stick margarine

Place half the cracker crumbs on bottom of baking dish. Mix chicken with water chestnuts, soups and sour cream in bowl. Pour into baking dish. Top with remaining cracker crumbs. Dot with margarine. Bake at 350 degrees for 25 to 30 minutes.

Mrs. Peggy White, Califf Middle Grades
Gray, Georgia

PARTY CHICKEN

1 sm. jar dried beef
6 whole chicken breasts, skinned, boned
6 slices bacon
1 can cream of mushroom soup
1 c. sour cream

Line 2-quart greased baking dish with dried beef. Wrap each chicken breast with bacon. Place on dried beef. Combine soup and sour cream. Pour over chicken breasts. Bake at 350 degrees for 1 hour and 30 minutes. Serve with wild rice.

Viola B. Farner, Central H.S.
Louisville, Kentucky

ROLLED CHICKEN BREAST

1/2 c. finely chopped mushrooms
2 tbsp. butter
1/2 c. light cream
Salt
Dash of cayenne pepper
Flour
1 1/4 c. shredded sharp cheese
6 boned whole chicken breasts
6 thin slices boiled ham
2 eggs, slightly beaten
3/4 c. fine bread crumbs

Saute mushrooms in butter about 5 minutes. Blend in cream. Add 1/4 teaspoon salt, cayenne pepper and 2 tablespoons flour. Cook, stirring constantly, until mixture becomes very thick. Stir in cheese. Cook over low heat until cheese is melted. Turn mixture into pie plate. Cover; chill thoroughly, about 1 hour. Remove skins from chicken breasts. Place each piece, bone side up between 2 pieces of Saran Wrap; overlap meat where chicken breast is split. Working out from center, pound with mallet to form 1/4-inch thick cutlets. Sprinkle chicken with salt. Cut cheese mixture into 6 equal portions. Shape into short sticks. Place 1 ham slice and 1 cheese stick in center of each cutlet. Tuck in sides; roll up. Dust with flour; dip in eggs. Roll in bread crumbs. Chill about 1 hour. Fry rolls in deep hot fat, 375 degrees for 5 minutes; drain. Place rolls in shallow baking dish. Bake in 325-degree oven about 30 to 45 minutes. Yield: 6 servings.

Joan W. Harmon, Bleckley County H.S.
Cochran, Georgia

THOUSAND DOLLAR CHICKEN

6 chicken breasts, skinned
Salt, pepper and paprika to taste
1 stick butter, melted
1/4 tsp. basil
1/4 tsp. rosemary
1/2 c. chopped onions
1 c. sliced mushrooms
1/2 c. slivered almonds
1/4 c. cooking Sherry
Juice of 1/2 lemon
1 can cream of mushroom soup
Cooked rice

Place chicken in baking dish. Sprinkle with salt, pepper and paprika. Combine all remaining ingredients except rice. Pour over chicken. Bake at 350 degrees for 1 hour and 15 minutes. Arrange chicken breasts around rice on serving platter. Serve pan drippings over rice.

Judy Fine, Science Hill H.S.
Johnson City, Tennessee

CANNELLONI

12 manicotti shells
1 lb. ground beef
1/4 lb. sausage
3 tbsp. butter
3 eggs
1 tsp. oregano
1 tsp. onion powder
8 tbsp. Parmesan cheese
Bread crumbs
1/2 c. chopped onion
6 tbsp. tomato paste
2 tbsp. basil
1 tsp. salt
1/8 tsp. pepper
4 c. tomato sauce

Cook manicotti shells using package directions for 12 minutes. Drain; cool. Brown ground beef and sausage in skillet until crumbly. Add butter. Remove from heat. Add next 3 ingredients with 5 tablespoons Parmesan cheese and enough bread crumbs to absorb moisture. Stuff meat mixture into manicotti shells; place in baking dish. Combine last 6 ingredients with 2 cups water in saucepan. Simmer for 30 minutes. Pour sauce over stuffed shells. Top with 3 tablespoons Parmesan cheese. Bake at 350 degrees for 30 minutes. Serve hot.

Kay F. Poole, Friendly Sr. H.S.
Silver Spring, Maryland

BARBECUED MEATBALLS

2 lb. ground beef
1 pkg. dry onion soup mix
2 eggs
1 c. seasoned dry bread crumbs
1 c. barbecue sauce
1/4 c. honey
4 drops of Tabasco sauce

Mix ground beef, onion soup mix, eggs and bread crumbs. Shape into small balls. Place balls in shallow baking pan. Bake in 350-degree oven for 20 to 30 minutes or until brown. Drain; place in chafing dish. Mix barbecue sauce, honey and Tabasco sauce. Pour over meatballs. Yield: 36 meatballs.

Miriam G. Fuller, Jefferson City H.S.
Jefferson City, Missouri

MEAT ROLL FOR FIFTY

10 c. flour
Salt
6 tbsp. baking powder
1 lb. shortening
3 1/2 c. milk
1 1/2 c. finely chopped onions
1 1/2 c. melted butter
6 qt. ground cooked meat
6 qt. gravy
1 c. chili sauce

Sift flour, 3 tablespoons salt and baking powder into large bowl. Cut in shortening until crumbly. Stir in milk; blend well. Turn onto lightly floured board; knead 4 or 5 times. Roll into 1/4-inch thick rectangles, 10 inches wide. Saute onions in 1/2 cup butter in large pan until golden brown. Add meat, gravy, chili sauce and 1 teaspoon salt; mix well. Brush dough with melted butter. Spread meat mixture over dough. Roll from long side as for jelly roll. Seal edges. Cut into 1-inch slices. Place cut-side down on shallow greased baking sheets. Brush with additional butter. Bake at 425 degrees for 20 to 30 minutes. Serve hot with hot gravy, mushroom or tomato sauce.

Doreen Kerner, Senator Gershaw H.S.
Bow Island, Alberta, Canada

HAMBURGER QUICHE

1/2 lb. ground beef
1/2 c. mayonnaise
1/2 c. milk
2 eggs
1 tbsp. cornstarch
1 1/2 c. Cheddar cheese, grated
1/3 c. chopped green onion
Dash of pepper
1 9-in. pie shell, unbaked

Brown ground beef in skillet; drain. Blend mayonnaise, milk, eggs and cornstarch in bowl until smooth. Stir in ground beef and remaining ingredients. Pour mixture into pie shell. Bake at 350 degrees for 25 to 40 minutes or until golden brown and knife inserted in center comes out clean. Yield: 6-8 servings.

Barbara Porter, Horizon H.S.
Scottsdale, Arizona

STUFFED BREAD

1 lb. ground beef
1 med. onion, chopped
1 tsp. garlic salt
1/4 c. chopped bell pepper
1 4 1/2-oz. can chopped olives
1 8-oz. can tomato sauce
1 tbsp. vinegar
1/2 lb. Cheddar cheese, shredded
1 pkg. sourdough French rolls

Brown ground beef in large skillet until crumbly. Add next 6 ingredients; mix well. Simmer for 30 minutes. Remove from heat. Stir in cheese. Spoon into sliced rolls. Wrap in foil. Bake at 400 degrees for 30 minutes.

Marianne Traw, Ball Jr. H.S.
Anaheim, California

SWEET AND SOUR MEATBALLS

2 lb. ground beef
1 tbsp. minced onion
2 eggs
1/4 c. milk
Salt and pepper to taste
Oatmeal
2 10-oz. jars grape jelly
2 10-oz. bottles of chili sauce

Combine first 5 ingredients with enough oatmeal to make firm mixture. Form into 1/2-inch balls. Freeze on cookie sheet. Store frozen until needed. Combine jelly and chili sauce in large pan. Warm over low heat, stirring occasionally until smooth and well blended. Add meatballs. Cook over low heat, stirring occasionally, for 30 minutes or until meatballs are thoroughly cooked. Serve in chafing dish with toothpicks.

Rita Hall, Flour Bluff H.S.
Corpus Christi, Texas

MEATBALL CASSEROLE

1 lb. ground beef
1/2 lb. pork sausage
1/2 c. cracker crumbs
1 tbsp. minced onion
Chili powder
2 eggs
1 can cream of celery soup
1 can cream of mushroom soup
1 1/2 c. flour
1 tbsp. baking powder
1/4 tsp. salt
1/3 c. milk
1/3 c. salad oil
1 c. shredded American cheese

Mix ground beef, sausage, cracker crumbs, onion, 1 tablespoon chili powder and 1 egg. Shape by tablespoonfuls into meatballs. Place in greased 2-quart casserole. Bake, uncovered, at 425 degrees for 20 minutes. Remove from oven; drain. Add soups. Combine dry ingredients with 1 teaspoon chili powder. Blend milk, oil and 1 egg. Add to dry ingredients; mix well. Knead lightly on floured surface. Roll out to 12-inch square. Sprinkle with cheese. Roll up; seal edges. Cut into 12 slices. Place biscuits over meat mixture, cut-side up. Bake at 425 degrees for 30 minutes.

Robin Weynand, Bangs H.S.
Bangs, Texas

WYOMING STRAW HATS

1 c. chopped onions
2/3 c. chopped celery
2/3 c. chopped green pepper
3 tbsp. shortening
2 lb. ground beef
2 to 3 tsp. chili powder
1/2 tsp. thyme
2 6-oz. cans tomato paste
Dash of Tabasco sauce
2 tsp. salt
1/4 tsp. pepper
1/2 c. catsup
2 tbsp. Worcestershire sauce
1 10-oz. package corn chips
2 c. shredded sharp cheese

Cook onions, celery and green pepper in hot shortening in large skillet until tender but not brown. Add ground beef. Brown lightly. Add remaining ingredients except corn chips and cheese. Simmer, uncovered, for 1 hour, stirring occasionally. Serve meat sauce over corn chips. Top with shredded cheese.

Kathy Callahan, East H.S.
Cheyenne, Wyoming

EASY HAM AND CHEESE SOUFFLE

1 10 3/4-oz. can Cheddar cheese soup
6 eggs, separated
1 6 3/4-oz. can chunk-style ham,
    drained

Melt soup over low heat in saucepan, stirring occasionally. Remove from heat. Beat egg yolks until thick and lemon colored. Stir in soup and ham gradually. Beat egg whites in large bowl until stiff peaks form. Fold in soup mixture. Pour into ungreased 2-quart casserole. Bake at 300 degrees for 1 hour or until souffle is brown. Serve immediately. Yield: 4-6 servings.

Mary Ann Purdham, Gasconade R-2 Jr. H.S.
Owensville, Missouri

HAM AND CHEESE CASSEROLE

1 c. finely chopped onions
1 c. chopped celery
2 tbsp. butter
6 eggs, well beaten
1 1/3 c. cracker crumbs
3 c. milk
1/4 tsp. pepper
4 c. finely chopped cooked ham
3 c. grated sharp Cheddar cheese

Saute onions and celery in butter in large skillet until soft. Remove from heat; stir in remaining ingredients. Line two 10 x 6 x 1 1/2-inch baking pans with heavy-duty foil. Grease foil generously. Divide mixture evenly between 2 pans. Bake at 350 degrees for 45 to 50 minutes, or until brown and firm in center. May be frozen before baking.

Darlene Clevenger, Madison-Grant H.S.
Fairmount, Indiana

HAM POCKETS

1 c. (scant) flour
1/2 c. butter
1/4 lb. cottage cheese, drained
1/4 tsp. salt
2 c. coarsely ground ham
1 egg, lightly beaten

Place flour in bowl; cut in butter until crumbly. Stir in cheese and salt. Knead dough on floured board until smooth. Roll out dough paper thin. Cut into 3 1/2 or 4-inch squares. Place mound of ham in center of each square. Bring corners of square toward center. Pinch seams closed.

Place on ungreased baking sheet. Brush with beaten egg. Bake at 400 degrees about 20 minutes.

Helen B. Boots,
Lakeland Village, Medical Lake School Dist.
Cheney, Washington

HAM AND POTATO CASSEROLE

2 c. diced cooked potatoes
2 c. diced cooked ham
4 tbsp. butter
4 tbsp. flour
1 1/2 tsp. salt
2 c. milk
1/2 c. shredded cheese
1 tsp. prepared mustard
1 tbsp. grated onion

Arrange potatoes in 2-quart casserole. Sprinkle ham over potatoes. Melt butter in medium saucepan. Blend in flour and 1 teaspoon salt until smooth. Add milk gradually, stirring constantly. Cook until white sauce is medium thick. Add cheese, mustard, 1/2 teaspoon salt and onion. Pour over ham and potatoes. Bake at 350 degrees for 30 minutes or until bubbly.

Adrian M. Croutch, N. Gulfport School
N. Gulfport, Mississippi

HAM-STUFFED MANICOTTI

8 manicotti shells
1/4 c. chopped onion
2 tbsp. cooking oil
3 c. ground ham
1 4-oz. can mushrooms, drained
3 tbsp. grated Parmesan cheese
1/4 c. chopped green pepper
3 tbsp. butter
3 tbsp. flour
2 c. milk
1 c. shredded Swiss cheese
Paprika

Cook manicotti shells using package directions. Drain, rinse and cool. Saute onion in oil in skillet until tender. Add ham and mushrooms. Cool. Stir in Parmesan cheese. Saute green pepper in butter in saucepan until tender. Blend in flour; add milk. Cook, stirring constantly until thickened. Add Swiss cheese; stir until melted. Mix 1/4 cup cheese sauce into ham mixture. Fill each shell with 1/3 cup ham mixture. Arrange in shallow greased baking dish. Top with remaining cheese sauce. Sprinkle with paprika. Cover. Bake at 350 degrees for 30 minutes. Yield: 4 servings.

Sandra J. Lau, Lockport Sr. H.S.
Lockport, New York

HOLIDAY HAM

1 boneless ham
Whole cloves
1 lg. can crushed pineapple with syrup
1 1/2 c. white wine

Stud ham with cloves. Combine pineapple and wine in blender container. Blend well. Place ham on large sheet of heavy foil in baking dish. Pour pineapple mixture over ham. Seal tightly. Marinate at least 24 hours in refrigerator. Bake in 320-degree oven until heated through. Let stand, still wrapped for at least 1 hour before slicing.

Margaret D. Randall, Tallulah H. S.
Tallulah, Louisiana

SAUSAGE CREPES

3 eggs, beaten
Milk
1 tbsp. cooking oil
1 c. sifted flour
1/2 tsp. salt
1 lb. pork sausage
1/4 c. chopped onion
1/2 c. shredded American cheese
1 3-oz. package cream cheese, softened
1/4 tsp. celery salt
1/4 tsp. marjoram
1 c. sour cream
4 tbsp. softened butter

Combine eggs, 1 cup milk and oil in bowl. Add flour and salt; beat well. Pour 2 tablespoons batter into hot greased 6-inch skillet; tilt to cover bottom. Cook until brown; flip. Brown second side. Invert on paper towel. Cook sausage and onion in large skillet until brown and crumbly. Stir in American cheese, cream cheese, celery salt and marjoram. Remove from heat. Stir in 3/4 cup sour cream and 1 tablespoon milk. Place 2 tablespoons mixture in center of each crepe; roll. Arrange in 11 3/4 x 7 1/2 x 1 3/4-inch baking dish. Combine butter and 1/4 cup sour cream; dot on crepes. Cover. Bake at 375 degrees for 20 minutes. Crepes may be made in advance and frozen. Yield: 16 crepes.

Jenney L. Kubal, Eisenhower H.S.
Houston, Texas

ZESTY SAUSAGE SQUARES

1 c. Bisquick
1/3 c. milk
4 tbsp. mayonnaise
1 lb. hot sausage
1/2 c. chopped onions
1 egg
2 c. Cheddar cheese
2 4-oz. cans chopped green chilies

Combine Bisquick, milk and 2 tablespoons mayonnaise in small bowl; mix well. Pat into well-greased 9 x 13-inch casserole. Saute sausage and onions. Drain on paper towels. Spread on Bisquick mixture. Beat egg with remaining mayonnaise, Cheddar cheese and green chilies. Spread over meat layer. Bake at 375 degrees for 25 minutes. Cut into squares.

Mary Garnett Richey
Allen County-Scottsville H.S.
Scottsville, Kentucky

STUFFED PORK TENDERLOIN

1 whole pork tenderloin
Salt and pepper to taste
1/4 c. chopped celery
2 tbsp. chopped onion
1 c. fresh mushrooms
2 tbsp. butter
4 c. dry bread cubes
1/2 tsp. each poultry seasoning, sage
2 tbsp. chicken broth
4 slices bacon

Split tenderloin lengthwise. Season with salt and pepper. Saute celery, onion and mushrooms in butter in large frypan. Add 1/4 teaspoon each salt and pepper. Add remaining ingredients except bacon; mix well. Place half the tenderloin on rack in baking dish, cut-side up. Spread stuffing over tenderloin. Top with remaining half tenderloin, cut-side down. Secure with string. Wrap with bacon. Bake at 325 degrees for 1 hour and 30 minutes. Yield: 8 servings.

Kathy Komishke, Wm. F. Hay Composite H.S.
Stettler, Alberta, Canada

HOLIDAY SHRIMP AND RICE CASSEROLE

12 oz. frozen peeled shrimp
1/4 c. butter

1/2 c. flour
2 c. half and half
1/2 c. dry Sherry
1/4 c. tomato paste
2 tsp. salt
1 tsp. dillweed
1/2 tsp. onion powder
1/4 tsp. pepper
1 tbsp. lemon juice
1 4-oz. can sliced mushrooms, drained
1 1/2 c. drained cooked green peas
3 c. cooked rice

Cut shrimp in half lengthwise. Melt butter in saucepan. Stir in flour until smooth. Blend in half and half gradually. Simmer about 5 minutes, stirring constantly. Stir in Sherry, tomato paste, seasonings, lemon juice, mushrooms, peas, shrimp and rice. Turn into greased shallow 2 1/2-quart baking dish. Bake at 350 degrees for 25 to 30 minutes. Yield: 6-8 servings.

Betty Bullock Pitts, Sierra Vista Jr. H.S.
Canyon Country, California

SEAFOOD GUMBO

1 1-lb. can tomatoes
2 tbsp. flour
12 oysters in liquor
1 c. chopped onions
2 10-oz. packages frozen cut okra,
   partially thawed
2 cloves of garlic, crushed
3 tbsp. Planters Peanut Oil
4 tsp. salt
1/4 tsp. cayenne pepper
1 lb. medium shrimp, shelled, deveined
1 7-oz. can crab meat

2 tsp. Worcestershire sauce
1 1/4 c. hot cooked rice

Drain tomatoes, reserving liquid. Add tomato liquid to flour gradually, stirring until smooth; set aside. Drain oysters, reserving liquor. Add water to liquor to measure 5 cups; set aside. Saute onions, okra and garlic in 3 tablespoons oil in Dutch oven until onion is transparent. Stir in drained tomatoes, tomato liquid, oyster liquor, salt and cayenne pepper. Cook over medium heat until mixture comes to a boil, stirring constantly. Reduce heat. Simmer for 1 hour. Stir in shrimp and oysters. Cook for 4 minutes or until shrimp turns pink. Add crab meat and Worcestershire sauce; heat through. Ladle 1 cup hot gumbo over 2 tablespoons cooked rice in soup bowl to serve. Yield: 10 servings.

Photograph for this recipe on page 74.

FESTIVE SHRIMP AND RICE

    2   8-oz. cans pizza sauce
    2   8-oz. cans tomato sauce with onions
    1 c. chopped celery
    1 c. chopped green pepper
    2 tsp. chili powder
    1 tsp. basil leaves
    1 tsp. garlic salt
    2 lb. shrimp, cooked
    1/2 lb. sliced mushrooms
    3/4 c. butter
    6 c. hot cooked rice
    Chopped parsley

Combine 1/2 cup water and first 7 ingredients in covered 3-quart saucepan; mix well. Bring to a boil. Reduce heat; simmer for 15 to 20 minutes, stirring occasionally. Add shrimp to sauce. Heat, covered, to serving temperature. Saute mushrooms in melted butter in saucepan. Combine with cooked rice. Spoon onto serving platter. Top with shrimp mixture. Sprinkle with parsley. Yield: 8-10 servings.

Photograph for this recipe on page 15.

SEAFOOD QUICHE

    2 eggs, beaten
    1/2 c. mayonnaise
    1 tbsp. flour
    1/4 c. white wine

    1   6-oz. can crab meat
    1   4 1/2-oz. can shrimp
    6 oz. Swiss cheese, shredded
    1/4 c. diced celery
    1/4 c. chopped green onion
    1   9-in. unbaked pastry shell

Combine first 4 ingredients in bowl. Beat until fluffy. Fold in next 5 ingredients. Pour into pastry shell. Bake at 400 degrees for 10 minutes. Reduce temperature to 350 degrees. Bake for 30 to 35 minutes longer or until quiche tests done. Yield: 5-6 servings.

Betty Mitchell, Portage Collegiate School
Portage LaPrairie, Manitoba, Canada

SHRIMP QUICHE

    8 oz. Swiss cheese, grated
    2 tbsp. flour
    1 lb. small frozen shrimp, peeled,
        deveined
    2 tbsp. Sherry
    1/2 c. mayonnaise
    1/4 c. milk
    2 eggs
    1/2 tsp. salt
    2 green onions, chopped
    1   9-in. pie shell

Toss cheese with flour in large bowl. Cook shrimp using package directions; rinse. Combine next 6 ingredients; add to cheese. Fold in shrimp. Pour into pie shell. Bake at 350 degrees for 45 minutes.

Claudia Triolo, Dayton Avenue School
Manorville, New York

SHRIMP SCAMPI

    1/2 c. butter
    1/2 c. oil
    1/4 c. chopped onion
    2 to 3 cloves of garlic, minced
    1 tbsp. lemon juice
    1/4 c. white wine
    4 tbsp. chopped parsley
    1 lb. shrimp, shelled, deveined

Melt butter and oil over low heat in skillet. Add onion and garlic cloves; saute. Add lemon juice, white wine and parsley. Place shrimp in single layer in bottom of broiling pan. Pour wine mixture over shrimp; turn shrimp to coat evenly. Broil for 5 to 8 minutes until shrimp are pink.

Sue L. Fry, Atlantic H.S.
Delray Beach, Florida

FESTIVE CURRIED TURKEY

1 sm. onion, finely chopped
1 tart apple, unpared, chopped
1/4 c. butter
1/4 c. flour
1 tsp. (or less) curry powder
Salt and pepper to taste
1/4 tsp. ginger
1 c. turkey broth
1 c. milk
3 c. coarsely chopped cooked turkey
1 tbsp. lemon juice
Sliced water chestnuts (opt.)
Sliced toasted almonds (opt.)
3 c. cooked rice
Orange slices
White grapes

Saute onion and apple in butter in large skillet until transparent. Blend in flour and spices. Add broth and milk. Cook, stirring constantly, until thickened. Simmer for 5 minutes. Add turkey and remaining ingredients except rice and fruits; mix well. Heat thoroughly. Serve over rice. Garnish with fruits.

Mary Ellen Benedict, Palatka H.S.
Palatka, Florida

TURKEY LASAGNE

1/2 c. chopped onions
1/2 c. chopped green pepper
3 tbsp. butter
1 4-oz. can mushrooms, drained
1/4 c. chopped pimentos
1 10 1/2-oz. can cream of chicken soup
1/3 c. milk
1/2 tsp. basil
8 oz. lasagne noodles, cooked, drained
1 1/2 c. cottage cheese
3 c. cubed cooked turkey
2 c. shredded Cheddar cheese
1/2 c. grated Parmesan cheese

Saute onions and green pepper in butter in 2-quart saucepan until tender. Stir in mushrooms, pimentos, soup, milk and basil. Heat well. Arrange one-half the noodles in greased 13 x 9 x 2-inch baking dish. Layer one-half the sauce, one-half the cottage cheese, one-half the turkey, one-half the Cheddar cheese and one-half the Parmesan cheese. Repeat layers, ending with Parmesan cheese. Bake at 350 degrees for 45 minutes or until hot and bubbly. Yield: 6-8 servings.

Linda Burlingame, Maries County R-II School
Belle, Missouri

LEFTOVER TURKEY PASTRY

1/2 c. minced onion
1/2 c. coarsely cut celery
1/2 c. chopped pecans
6 tbsp. butter
3 c. coarsely cut turkey
1 1/2 tsp. caraway seed
1/2 tsp. salt
1 recipe pie pastry
1/4 c. Parmesan cheese, grated
1 c. Cheez Whiz
1/4 c. sliced pimento (opt.)
1/4 lb. mushrooms, sliced

Saute onion, celery and pecans in butter in skillet until golden brown. Add turkey, caraway seed and salt; mix well. Cool. Roll out pastry on floured surface. Sprinkle with Parmesan cheese. Roll to press cheese into pastry. Cut pastry into squares. Fill half the square with turkey mixture. Fold; seal into triangle with fork. Bake at 350 degrees until lightly browned. Combine Cheez Whiz, pimento and mushrooms in saucepan. Heat and serve over pastries.

Faye I. Purdy, Kaysville Jr. H.S.
Kaysville, Utah

ORIENTAL TURKEY

1 onion, sliced
1 4-oz. can mushrooms, drained
1/8 tsp. ground ginger
1 tsp. salad oil
1 10 1/2-oz. can cream of celery soup
1 c. diced cooked turkey
1 5-oz. can water chestnuts, drained,
   sliced
1/3 c. cooked chopped spinach
1 tbsp. soy sauce

Saute onion, mushrooms and ginger in oil in skillet until onion is tender. Stir in soup, 2/3 cup water, turkey, water chestnuts, spinach and soy sauce. Cook over low heat for 10 minutes, stirring often. Serve with rice or noodles. Yield: 4 servings.

Mary Jean Earl, Meritt Hutton Jr. H.S.
Thornton, Colorado

TURKEY AND DRESSING CASSEROLE

4 c. dressing
5 c. diced turkey
4 c. chicken broth
1/2 c. butter
1/2 c. flour

1/2 tsp. salt
1/4 tsp. pepper

Place dressing in 9 x 13-inch cake pan. Spread to cover bottom of pan. Top with turkey. Place broth, butter, flour, salt and pepper in blender container. Blend well. Pour liquid mixture over turkey and dressing. Cover pan with foil. Bake at 350 degrees for 45 to 60 minutes. Yield: 9-12 servings.

Beth Viland, Kindred H.S.
Kindred, North Dakota

TURKEY ENCHILADAS

1/2 onion, chopped
1 tbsp. margarine
2 c. cream of chicken soup
1 lg. can evaporated milk
Diced chili peppers
12 corn tortillas
2 c. grated cheese
2 1/2 c. cooked turkey

Saute onion in margarine in saucepan. Add soup, milk and chilies. Warm tortillas to soften. Place cheese and turkey on tortillas. Roll; place folded-side down in baking pan. Pour chili sauce over tortillas. Bake at 350 degrees for 30 to 40 minutes. May substitute cream of mushroom soup for chicken soup.

Jan Cable, Arcadia H.S.
Phoenix, Arizona

TURKEY PIE

2 c. buttermilk biscuit mix
1/4 c. sliced green onions
1/2 tsp. poultry seasoning
2 2/3 c. milk
1/2 c. shredded Cheddar cheese
1/4 c. chopped green pepper
1/4 c. butter
1/2 c. chopped celery
1/4 c. all-purpose flour
1 tsp. Worcestershire sauce
1/2 tsp. dry mustard
2 c. diced cooked turkey
1 10-oz. package frozen mixed
    vegetables, cooked, drained

Combine biscuit mix, green onions and poultry seasoning in small bowl. Stir in 2/3 cup milk until dry ingredients are moistened. Pat dough into buttered 9-inch pie plate. Bake at 400 degrees for 20 to 30 minutes. Remove from oven. Sprinkle with cheese and green pepper.

Return to oven until cheese is melted. Melt butter in skillet. Saute celery until tender, about 3 minutes. Stir in flour, Worcestershire sauce and mustard until smooth. Stir in remaining 2 cups milk gradually. Heat to boiling point; stir for 1 minute. Stir in turkey and vegetables. Heat to serving temperature. Cut cheese bread into wedges. Spoon sauce over bread. Yield: 6 servings.

Phyllis Smith, Taylor County H.S.
Butler, Georgia

TROPICAL RICE STUFFING

1 13 1/2-oz. can pineapple tidbits
1 10 1/2-oz. can chicken consomme
1 c. rice
1 5-oz. can water chestnuts, drained
    and sliced
1/4 c. butter
1/2 c. chopped green onion
1/2 c. thinly sliced celery
1 tbsp. soy sauce

Drain syrup from pineapple; combine with consomme. Add water to measure 2 cups; pour into saucepan. Stir in rice; bring to a boil. Reduce heat; cover. Cook for 15 minutes or until liquid is absorbed. Mix in pineapple, water chestnuts and remaining ingredients; stir until butter is melted. Yield: 5 cups.

Photograph for this recipe below.

TURKEY ROLL

1 3-oz. package cream cheese, softened
1 3-oz. package cream cheese with
   chives, softened
2 c. cubed cooked turkey
1 4-oz. can mushrooms with stems
1/2 c. margarine
2 cans crescent dinner rolls
2/3 c. seasoned stuffing mix, crushed
1/2 c. chopped walnuts
1 can cream of chicken soup
1 can cream of mushroom soup
1 soup can milk

Blend cream cheese, turkey, mushrooms and 1/4 cup margarine together. Open dinner rolls. Separate rolls and lay out flat. Place 1/4 cup turkey mixture in each roll. Fold 2 corners together; roll up toward third. Seal. Dip into 1/4 cup melted margarine. Roll in mixture of crushed stuffing and chopped walnuts. Place on ungreased cookie sheet. Bake at 325 degrees for 30 minutes. Mix soups with 1 soup can milk in saucepan. Cook until piping hot; pour over baked turkey rolls.

Connie Harmon, Grantsville H.S.
Grantsville, Utah

TURKEY STROGANOFF SANDWICH

6 slices white bread, toasted
Butter
18 thin slices cooked turkey
12 slices tomato
1 can mushroom soup
1 2 1/2-oz. jar mushrooms, drained
1 c. sour cream
2 tbsp. chopped fresh parsley
French-fried onion rings

Brush toast with butter. Alternate 3 slices turkey and 2 slices tomato on each slice of bread. Place on baking sheet. Cover with foil. Bake at 400 degrees for 10 to 15 minutes or until heated through. Combine soup and mushrooms in saucepan. Bring to a boil. Stir in sour cream and parsley. Heat; do not boil. Spoon sauce over sandwiches. Garnish with onion rings.

Brandy Harris, Texas City H.S.
Texas City, Texas

GINGERED DUCKLING WITH ORANGE RICE

2 ducklings, quartered
Butter
2 c. thinly sliced celery

6 to 8 c. cooked rice
Pepper to taste
1 1/4 tsp. salt
1 c. mandarin oranges, drained
1/3 c. (firmly packed) brown sugar
1/4 c. sugar
1 tbsp. cornstarch
1 c. orange juice
1/4 tsp. ground ginger

Place ducklings, skin-side down, in broiler pan. Broil for 8 to 10 minutes, basting with melted butter. Turn; broil until golden brown. Saute celery in 1/4 cup butter until tender-crisp. Add hot rice, pepper and 1 teaspoon salt. Toss to blend. Add orange sections. Set aside; keep hot. Combine sugars and cornstarch in saucepan. Add orange juice, 1/4 teaspoon salt and ginger. Stir over low heat until sugar dissolves. Simmer until clear and thickened, about 3 minutes. Serve over duckling and rice. Yield: 8 servings.

Alice P. Schleg, Grayslake Community H.S.
Grayslake, Illinois

SHERRY AND SPICE GAME HENS

1/2 c. olive oil
1/2 c. Sherry
1 med. onion, grated
2 tbsp. Worcestershire sauce
1 tbsp. dry mustard
1 tsp. marjoram
1/2 tsp. oregano
1/2 tsp. garlic salt
1/2 tsp. salt
1/2 tsp. freshly ground pepper
4 1-lb. Cornish game hens

Combine all ingredients except game hens in jar. Shake well. Place game hens in dish. Add marinade. Marinate for 2 hours, spooning mixture over game hens every 15 minutes. Rotisserie-cook over medium to low heat for 50 to 60 minutes, basting with marinade during final 20 minutes. Heat remaining marinade to serve as sauce. Yield: 4 servings.

Peggy R. Cruth, Huron Jr. H.S.
Denver, Colorado

BRAISED PHEASANT

1 pheasant, cut into pieces
1 med. onion, chopped
2 stalks celery, chopped
2 to 3 tsp. cornstarch
Salt and pepper to taste
Butter

2 oz. Brandy
1/2 c. white wine
1 tbsp. sweet cream

Combine pheasant neck, wings, liver and back in saucepan with onion, celery and enough water to cover. Cook until tender. Remove meat from bones; return to broth. Mix cornstarch with small amount cold water. Add to broth. Cook, stirring constantly until thickened. Season to taste. Brush remaining pheasant pieces with butter; brown in skillet. Pour warm Brandy over pheasant; ignite. Place pheasant in casserole. Add sauce to skillet; simmer for 2 to 3 minutes. Add 1/2 cup white wine. Pour over pheasant. Bake at 325 degrees for 35 to 40 minutes, adding additional wine if necessary. Blend 1 tablespoon cream into sauce just before serving.

Rose Marie Tondl, East H.S.
Lincoln, Nebraska

HOT DOGS WITH CONEY ISLAND SAUCE

1/2 lb. ground beef
1 1/2 c. chopped onions
1/4 c. chopped celery
1/4 c. butter
4 8-oz. cans tomato sauce
3 tbsp. lemon juice
4 tbsp. brown sugar
1 1/2 tbsp. Worcestershire sauce
2 tsp. chili powder
1 tsp. salt
1 tsp. prepared mustard

Saute first 3 ingredients in butter in large skillet for 10 minutes. Add remaining ingredients; mix well. Cover. Simmer for 20 minutes to blend flavors. Serve over hot dogs.

Beth Hilty, Jonathan Alder H.S.
Plain City, Ohio

HOMEMADE PIZZA

1/2 pkg. dry yeast
1 tsp. sugar
2 c. flour
3 tsp. baking powder
1 tsp. salt
1/3 c. shortening
Tomato sauce
Oregano
Garlic salt
Grated cheese
Salami

Combine yeast, sugar and 3/4 cup warm water in small bowl. Sift dry ingredients into large bowl. Cut in shortening until crumbly. Add yeast mixture; mix well. Knead on lightly floured surface until smooth. Spread on baking sheet. Spread tomato sauce over dough. Sprinkle with spices. Add cheese and salami. Bake at 375 degrees until crust is golden and topping bubbly.

Marisa Gonzalez, El Rancho Verde School
Union City, California

BAKED EGGS AND SAUSAGE

6 eggs, slightly beaten
2 c. milk
1 c. grated Cheddar cheese
6 slices white bread, cubed
1 tsp. each salt, pepper
1 tsp. Worcestershire sauce
1 tsp. dry mustard
1 lb. pork sausage, browned, drained
Dash of Tabasco sauce

Combine eggs and milk in bowl; beat well. Add remaining ingredients; mix well. Pour into greased 9 x 13-inch baking pan. Cover. Refrigerate overnight. Bake, uncovered, in 350-degree oven for 35 minutes or until set. Yield: 12-15 servings.

Florence Benson, Westfield H.S.
Westfield, Indiana

BREAKFAST EGGS

1 10-oz. package frozen chopped broccoli
10 slices white sandwich bread
3/4 lb. Olde English cheese slices
2 c. diced cooked ham
8 eggs
3 c. milk
2 tsp. minced onion
1/2 tsp. Tabasco
1/2 tsp. each salt, dry mustard

Cook broccoli using package directions. Drain well. Cut crusts and 1-inch diameter holes from bread slices. Place crusts and holes in bottom of greased 9 x 12-inch baking dish. Place half the cheese slices over bread. Add layers of ham, broccoli and bread slices. Combine remaining ingredients except cheese in bowl; beat well. Pour over bread. Top with remaining cheese slices. Cover. Refrigerate overnight. Bake, uncovered, at 325 degrees for 1 hour. Let stand for 10 minutes before serving.

Jan Moeller, Thomas Jefferson Sr. H.S.
Cedar Rapids, Iowa

CHRISTMAS MORNING EGGS

8 slices white bread
8 eggs, beaten
4 c. milk
1 lb. Cheddar cheese, grated
Salt and pepper to taste
1 lb. bacon, crisp-fried, crumbled

Remove crusts from bread; cut bread into cubes. Spread in 9 x 13-inch buttered baking dish. Combine eggs and milk in large bowl; mix well. Pour over bread cubes. Sprinkle with cheese and seasoning. Cover. Refrigerate overnight. Sprinkle with crumbled bacon. Bake at 350 degrees for 1 hour. Serve immediately.

Marie L. Bristol, Park Sr. H.S.
Cottage Grove, Minnesota

EGG STRATA

1 lb. sausage
6 slices bread, cubed
5 to 8 oz. grated Cheddar cheese
5 eggs
2 c. half and half
1 tsp. each salt, dry mustard

Brown sausage in skillet, stirring until crumbly. Drain well. Layer bread cubes, sausage and cheese in greased 2-quart casserole. Combine remaining ingredients in mixer bowl; beat well. Pour over cheese. Let stand for 10 minutes. Bake at 350 degrees for 1 hour. May be made ahead and frozen. Yield: 6-8 servings.

Mary Broadway, Midway H.S.
Waco, Texas

HOLIDAY EGGS MORNAY

Butter
3/4 c. flour
1 1/2 tsp. salt
3 c. cream
2 oz. Swiss cheese, grated
6 tbsp. grated Parmesan cheese
12 hard-boiled eggs
1/2 lb. mushrooms, minced
2 tbsp. finely chopped parsley
1/2 tsp. tarragon
1 c. fresh bread crumbs

Melt 3/4 cup butter in saucepan over low heat. Add flour and salt, blending until smooth. Cook for about 1 minute; do not brown. Remove from heat. Add cream gradually, stirring constantly. Return to heat; cook just until bubbly, stirring constantly. Add Swiss cheese and 4 tablespoons Parmesan cheese; stir until melted. Remove from heat. Cover. Set aside.

Slice eggs in half lengthwise. Separate yolks; mash in small bowl. Saute mushrooms in small amount of butter in skillet. Add parsley and tarragon. Combine mushroom mixture, egg yolks and 1/2 cup cream sauce; mix well. Fill egg white cavities with mushroom mixture. Arrange in 9 x 13-inch buttered casserole. Spoon remaining sauce over eggs. Toss bread crumbs with 2 tablespoons melted butter and 2 tablespoons Parmesan cheese; sprinkle over top. Bake at 350 degrees for 30 minutes. May be made ahead and refrigerated. Yield: 12 servings.

Gerald A. Hils, Keene H.S.
Keene, New Hampshire

HASHED-BROWN OMELET

4 slices bacon
2 c. cooked shredded potatoes
1/4 c. chopped onions
1/4 c. chopped bell pepper
4 eggs
1/4 c. milk
1/2 tsp. salt
Dash of pepper
1 c. shredded American cheese

Cook bacon in large skillet until crisp. Drain bacon on paper towels; crumble. Set aside. Combine potatoes, onions and bell pepper in bowl; mix well. Pat potato mixture into hot skillet with bacon drippings. Cook over low heat without turning or stirring until underside is crisp and brown. Combine eggs, milk and seasonings in bowl; blend thoroughly. Pour over potatoes. Top with cheese and crumbled bacon. Cover. Cook over low heat until eggs are done.

Carline Cuttrell, West Lamar H.S.
Petty, Texas

CHRISTMAS MORNING PINEAPPLE QUICHE

1 10-oz. package pastry mix
1 13 1/4-oz. can crushed pineapple
3 eggs, lightly beaten
1 3/4 c. half and half
1 1/4 tsp. salt
1/8 tsp. white pepper
4 drops of liquid red pepper seasoning
2 c. grated process Swiss cheese
6 slices crisp cooked bacon, crumbled

Prepare pastry mix according to package directions. Divide into 4 portions. Roll each to 7 1/2-inch circle; fit into four 6-inch quiche pans. Drain pineapple thoroughly, pressing out excess syrup. Combine eggs with half and half,

2 tbsp. finely chopped onion
Milk
1/2 c. whipping cream
3 tbsp. cornstarch
3 eggs
1/8 tsp. nutmeg
1/2 tsp. salt
Dash of pepper
1 1/2 c. shredded Swiss cheese
1   9-in. pastry shell

Saute bacon in skillet with butter until crisp. Add onion; cook until transparent. Set aside. Heat 1 cup milk and cream over low heat in saucepan. Mix cornstarch with 3 tablespoons milk; stir into milk-cream mixture. Cook, stirring constantly, until sauce is smooth and thick. Remove from heat; cool slightly. Beat eggs until light and fluffy. Mix nutmeg, salt, pepper, cheese and cooled cream sauce into eggs. Stir in bacon and onion. Place in pastry shell. Bake in 400-degree oven about 35 minutes. Yield: 6-8 servings.

Roberta Manfredo, Mineola H.S.
Garden City Park, New York

SPINACH-MUSHROOM QUICHE

1 pkg. pie crust mix
1 lb. fresh mushrooms, thinly sliced
1/4 c. chopped onions
Butter
2   10-oz. packages frozen chopped
*   spinach, thawed, drained*
6 eggs
1 1/2 c. heavy cream
1 c. milk
2 tbsp. flour
1 tsp. salt
1/8 tsp. each cayenne pepper, nutmeg
1/2 lb. Swiss cheese, shredded

Prepare pie crust mix using package directions. Roll dough into 15 x 17-inch rectangle on lightly floured surface. Line 9 x 13-inch baking dish with pastry. Crimp edges with fork; cover. Refrigerate until needed. Saute mushrooms and onions in 2 tablespoons butter in skillet until tender. Remove from heat; stir in spinach. Beat next 4 ingredients with seasonings and 1/4 cup melted butter in bowl. Spoon spinach mixture into crust. Sprinkle with cheese. Pour egg mixture over spinach. Bake at 425 degrees for 15 minutes. Reduce temperature to 325 degrees. Bake for 40 minutes longer or until knife inserted in center comes out clean.

Cindy L. Benting, Lower Lake H.S.
Lower Lake, California

salt, pepper, pepper seasoning, drained pineapple and cheese. Turn into pastry-lined pans. Top with bacon. Bake at 425 degrees about 25 minutes or until set in center. Garnish with pineapple slice and sprig of holly. Yield: 4 servings.

Photograph for this recipe above.

QUICHE LORRAINE

12 slices crisp-fried bacon, crumbled
1 c. shredded Swiss cheese
1/3 c. finely chopped onion
1   9-in. unbaked pie shell
4 eggs
2 c. half and half
3/4 tsp. salt
1/4 tsp. pepper
1/8 tsp. cayenne pepper

Sprinkle bacon, cheese and onion in pie shell. Beat eggs in bowl; beat in remaining ingredients. Pour egg mixture into pie shell. Bake at 425 degrees for 15 minutes. Reduce oven temperature to 300 degrees. Bake about 30 minutes longer or until quiche tests done. Let stand 10 minutes before cutting. Yield: 6 servings.

Carole Fisher, Martinsville H.S.
Martinsville, Indiana

SIMPLE SIMON CHEESE PIE

2 slices bacon, chopped
1 tsp. butter

Harvest-Time Vegetables and Side Dishes

Although the holiday season falls in mid-winter when there's not an abundant supply of fresh vegetables available, there is a surprising variety that is less expensive now than at other times.

Broccoli, Chinese cabbage and Brussels sprouts add a fresh green touch to your holiday meals without straining your budget. Squash is still plentiful. Be sure and select holiday recipes using root vegetables too — carrots, sweet potatoes, turnips, rutabagas and Jerusalem artichokes are all in good supply now. And, as you'll soon discover from this chapter, there are so many delightful ways to prepare them!

Delicious vegetable casseroles and souffles . . . fresh ways to bake vegetables . . . fry them . . . mix them . . . even roll them in balls! And many recipes are do-ahead dishes that freeze well. Use later for your own entertaining or help another hostess by offering to bring a vegetable casserole to her holiday meal.

Home Economic teachers are aware of the vital part vegetables should play in our menus, especially when so many goodies are around. So these recipes are not only nutritious, but so good that every member of your family, as well as guests, are sure to ask for seconds.

ASPARAGUS MOLD

1 14 1/2-oz. can cut asparagus
3 env. unflavored gelatin
3/4 c. asparagus liquid
3 c. cottage cheese
1/2 c. buttermilk
1 c. finely chopped celery
1 or 2 tbsp. minced onion
1/2 tsp. salt

Puree asparagus; set aside. Soften gelatin in asparagus liquid in saucepan; cook over low heat until dissolved, stirring occasionally. Beat cottage cheese until smooth in small mixing bowl. Add buttermilk and dissolved gelatin, mixing well. Fold in celery, onion and salt. Mix 2 cups cottage cheese mixture and pureed asparagus in bowl. Spoon into 7-cup salad mold. Chill until set. Pour reserved cottage cheese mixture over asparagus layer. Chill until firm. Unmold to serve. Garnish with pimento, carrot curls and ripe olives if desired. Yield: 8-10 servings.

Photograph for this recipe on page 15.

SCALLOPED ASPARAGUS

2 tbsp. butter
2 tbsp. flour
1/2 tsp. salt
1 can asparagus
Milk
1 c. grated Cheddar cheese
3 hard-boiled eggs, sliced
1/3 c. chopped nuts
1 c. coarsely crushed potato chips
1/2 tsp. paprika

Melt butter in saucepan; blend in flour and salt. Drain asparagus reserving liquid. Add enough milk to liquid to measure 1 cup. Pour into flour mixture; cook until thickened, stirring frequently. Remove from heat. Add cheese; stir until melted. Layer asparagus, eggs, cheese sauce and nuts in greased 2-quart casserole. Sprinkle with potato chips and paprika. Bake at 350 degrees for 30 minutes.

Marilyn L. Burrows, Putnum City North H.S.
Oklahoma City, Oklahoma

CHEESY ITALIAN GREEN BEANS

1 env. instant beef broth
1 pkg. frozen green beans
3 med. tomatoes, peeled, sliced
1 tsp. instant minced onion
1/2 tsp. salt

1 tsp. oregano
2 oz. mozzarella cheese

Dissolve broth in 1/2 cup boiling water in medium saucepan. Add green beans. Cook for 3 minutes. Drain. Pour into baking dish. Top with tomato slices, minced onion, salt, oregano and cheese. Bake at 325 degrees for 30 minutes. Yield: 6 servings.

Gloria Gauthier, F.J. Brennan H.S.
Windsor, Ontario, Canada

COMPANY GREEN BEANS

1 lb. green beans
1 tbsp. instant minced onion
2 tsp. dry mustard
1 1/2 tsp. salt
3 tbsp. butter
1/2 c. chopped walnuts, toasted
1/2 c. coarsely grated radish (opt.)

Cut green beans into thin diagonal slices. Place in large skillet. Add 2/3 cup water, onion, mustard and salt; cover. Cook over medium heat until tender-crisp. Melt butter; stir in walnuts. Add to cooked green beans; mix well. Spoon into serving dish; top with grated radish. Yield: 6 servings.

Photograph for this recipe on page 85.

BROCCOLI PUFF

1 10-oz. package frozen chopped broccoli
1/2 c. chopped onions
2 tbsp. butter
1 10 3/4-oz. can cream of mushroom soup
2 c. cooked rice
1 tsp. Worcestershire sauce
1/4 tsp. thyme
4 eggs, separated
2 c. grated Cheddar cheese

Cook broccoli using package directions. Drain. Saute onions in butter in skillet until tender. Stir in soup, rice, broccoli and seasonings. Turn into greased shallow 2-quart casserole. Bake at 400 degrees for 20 minutes. Beat egg yolks in large bowl until thick and lemon-colored. Stir in cheese. Beat egg whites until soft peaks form. Fold into egg yolk mixture. Remove casserole from oven; stir. Spread egg mixture over top. Bake for 15 minutes longer or until golden brown. Yield: 4 servings.

Deborah J. Risch, Beaufort Jr. H.S.
Beaufort, South Carolina

BROCCOLI SPECIAL

2 lb. fresh broccoli
1 stick butter
1/2 c. flour
2 c. milk
1 c. mayonnaise
1 tsp. salt
6 hard-boiled eggs, chopped
6 oz. grated American cheese

Cut broccoli into bite-sized pieces. Steam broccoli until tender-crisp. Melt butter in saucepan; blend in flour. Add milk gradually. Cook until thickened, stirring constantly. Add mayonnaise and salt; blend well. Stir in eggs. Place 1/3 of the broccoli in 3-quart casserole. Add layer of sauce and layer of cheese. Repeat until all ingredients are used, ending with cheese. Bake at 350 degrees for 25 to 30 minutes. Yield: 8 servings.

M. V. "Lynne" Fielding, Jordan H.S.
Long Beach, California

SCALLOPED CORN

1 to 1 1/2 c. crushed crackers
1 can whole kernel corn, drained
1 can cream-style corn
1 c. milk
Salt and pepper to taste
1/4 c. each chopped onion, chopped green
*   pepper*
1/4 c. margarine

Crush crackers; place in casserole. Add corns, milk, seasoning, onion and green pepper. Mix well. Dot with margarine. Bake at 350 degrees for 45 minutes or until tests done. Serve hot.

Cheryl Moffat Bargman, Piedmont H.S.
Piedmont, Oklahoma

CINNAMON-GLAZED CARROTS

2 lb. carrots, peeled
2 tbsp. butter
1 1/2 tsp. salt
1/4 tsp. cinnamon
2 tbsp. honey
2 tsp. lemon juice
1/2 c. chopped walnuts, toasted

Cut carrots into 3-inch strips. Place in large skillet. Add 1/2 cup water, butter and salt; cover. Cook until tender-crisp. Stir in cinnamon, honey and lemon juice; simmer for several minutes, stirring constantly. Add walnuts. Heat for 1 minute longer. Yield: 6-8 servings.

Photograph for this recipe on page 85.

COPPER CARROTS

2 lb. carrots, pared, sliced
1 onion, sliced
1/2 c. chopped green pepper
2/3 c. sugar
1/2 c. oil
1 tbsp. mustard
1/4 tbsp. freshly ground pepper (opt.)
1 can condensed tomato soup
1 c. wine vinegar
1 tbsp. Worcestershire sauce
Dash of Tabasco sauce

Cook carrots in boiling water until tender-crisp. Drain. Cool. Combine with onion and green pepper in large bowl. Add remaining ingredients. Stir well. Cover. Let marinate in refrigerator for 2 days. Yield: 8 servings.

Marcia Barkemeyer, Granger H.S.
Granger, Texas

FAR-EAST CELERY

2 c. celery, sliced
1/2 tsp. salt
1 can water chestnuts, sliced
1 can cream of mushroom soup
Buttered bread crumbs

Cook celery in 2 cups salted water until tender; drain. Add water chestnuts and soup; mix well. Pour into well-greased casserole. Top with buttered crumbs. Bake at 350 degrees for 30 minutes. Yield: 6 servings.

Mary H. McMillin, Ripley H.S.
Ripley, Mississippi

CELERY EN CASSEROLE

4 c. diagonally sliced celery
1 5-oz. can water chestnuts, drained,
    sliced
1/4 c. diced pimento
1/4 c. slivered almonds
1 can condensed cream of chicken soup
1/2 c. bread crumbs
4 tbsp. butter, melted

Cook celery in small amount of boiling water
for 4 minutes or until tender-crisp. Drain well.
Combine celery with next 4 ingredients. Pour
into greased 1 1/2-quart casserole. Combine
bread crumbs and butter; spread over top. Bake
in 350-degree oven for 25 minutes or until
crumbs are brown.

Betty Kennedy, Northwest H.S.
McDermott, Ohio

PERKY POTATO SALAD MOLD

6 med. potatoes, cooked, diced
4 hard-boiled eggs, chopped
1 sm. green pepper, sliced in thin strips
1 sm. onion, finely chopped
1/3 c. chopped sweet pickles
1/3 c. mayonnaise
1/3 c. sour cream
Juice and grated rind of 1 lemon
2 tbsp. chopped canned pimento
1 tbsp. sugar
1 tsp. salt
1/2 tsp. celery seed
1/4 tsp. pepper

Combine potatoes and remaining ingredients in
large bowl; mix well. Press mixture firmly into
oiled 6-cup ring mold. Chill for several hours.
Run knife around insides of mold; invert onto
serving dish. May garnish with lemon twists,
carrot curls and parsley if desired. Yield: 6-8
servings.

Photograph for this recipe below.

LEMONY ONION POTATOES

1/4 c. butter
1 tsp. grated lemon rind
2 tbsp. lemon juice

1/2 tsp. salt
Pinch of pepper
2 lb. potatoes, cooked, peeled, sliced
2 tbsp. chopped green onion

Melt butter in large skillet; add lemon rind, lemon juice, salt and pepper, mixing well. Add potatoes; stir to coat. Cook over medium heat until heated through. Stir in green onion. Yield: 4-6 servings.

Photograph for this recipe on page 86.

LEMON-SOUR CREAM SAUCE FOR BAKED POTATOES

1 c. sour cream
Juice and grated rind of 1/2 lemon
2 tbsp. chopped green onion
2 tbsp. chopped parsley
1/2 tsp. seasoned salt
6 potatoes, baked

Combine sour cream, lemon rind and lemon juice, green onion, parsley and seasoned salt in small bowl. Chill for several hours. Spoon over baked potatoes. Yield: 1 cup.

Photograph for this recipe on page 86.

GOURMET POTATOES

6 med. potatoes
2 c. shredded Cheddar cheese
Butter
8 oz. sour cream
3 green onions, chopped
1 tsp. salt
1/4 tsp. pepper

Cover potatoes with salted water; bring to a boil. Reduce heat; cook about 30 minutes. Cool slightly. Peel and coarsely shred potatoes. Set aside. Combine cheese and 1/4 cup butter in saucepan. Cook over low heat until cheese melts. Combine potatoes, cheese mixture, sour cream, onions, salt and pepper. Spoon into shallow 2-quart casserole. Dot with 2 tablespoons butter. Cover. Bake at 300 degrees for 25 minutes. Yield: 6-8 servings.

Mrs. Pam Miller, Bradley Jr. H.S.
Cleveland, Tennessee

POTATO KUGEL

1 lg. onion, minced
1/4 c. butter
2 eggs, beaten
2 c. grated, raw potatoes, drained
1/2 c. flour

1/2 tsp. baking powder
1 1/2 tsp. salt
Pepper to taste

Saute onion in butter in skillet until lightly browned. Combine eggs and potatoes in bowl. Sift dry ingredients together; add to potato mixture. Stir in onions. Pour into well-greased 1-quart casserole. Bake at 350 degrees for about 1 hour or until edges are crisp. Yield: 6 servings.

Anita Weintraub, Aberdeen Middle School
Aberdeen, Maryland

CREAMY SCALLOPED POTATOES

6 to 9 med. potatoes
Butter, melted
1 can cream of chicken soup
1 pt. sour cream
1 1/2 c. grated Cheddar cheese
1/4 to 1/3 c. chopped green onions
1 1/2 c. crushed corn flakes or potato chips

Boil potatoes in skins until half done. Peel and grate coarsely. Combine 1 stick melted butter, soup, sour cream, cheese and onions; mix well. Stir in potatoes. Pour into 9 x 13-inch baking dish. Top with 1/4 cup melted butter and corn flakes. Bake at 350 degrees for 40 minutes.

Marthanne Argyle, Spanish Fork H.S.
Spanish Fork, Utah

SPINACH BALLS

2 10-oz. packages frozen spinach
3 c. herb stuffing mix
1 lg. onion, chopped fine
6 eggs, well beaten
3/4 c. melted margarine
1/2 c. grated Parmesan cheese
1 tbsp. pepper
1 1/2 tsp. garlic salt
1/2 tsp. thyme

Cook spinach using package directions. Drain, squeezing out excess liquid. Combine spinach with remaining ingredients in large bowl; mix well. Shape into 3/4-inch balls. Place on lightly greased baking sheet. Bake at 325 degrees for 15 minutes. May be frozen and baked 20 minutes for party. Yield: 10 dozen balls.

Evelyn Kearns Harris
Southwestern Randolph H.S.
Asheboro, North Carolina

SPINACH-NOODLE RING

1 8-oz. package med. egg noodles,
broken
Salt
1 10-oz. package frozen chopped spinach
2 tbsp. chopped onion
1/2 c. butter
4 c. milk
1 c. soft bread crumbs
2 c. shredded process American cheese
4 eggs, slightly beaten
1/4 c. flour
1 1/2 tbsp. prepared mustard
1 tsp. horseradish

Cook noodles and 1 tablespoon salt in saucepan according to package directions; drain. Cook spinach in saucepan according to package directions; drain well. Saute onion in 1/4 cup butter in skillet until tender-crisp. Combine noodles, spinach, 2 cups milk, bread crumbs, cheese, eggs and 1 1/2 teaspoons salt. Spoon into well-buttered 2-quart ring mold. Place mold in pan of hot water. Bake at 350 degrees for 45 to 60 minutes or until mold tests done. Remove from water; let stand for 5 minutes. Unmold. Melt 1/4 cup butter in saucepan. Blend in flour, mustard, horseradish and 1 1/4 teaspoons salt. Stir in 2 cups milk gradually. Bring to a boil. Boil for 1 minute, stirring constantly. Serve over noodle ring. Yield: 6 servings.

Photograph for this recipe on page 82.

SPINACH TORTA

2 1-lb. packages frozen leaf spinach
2 med. onions, chopped
1 clove of garlic, minced
1/3 c. vegetable oil
2 tbsp. butter
7 eggs
1/2 c. milk
1/2 c. fine bread crumbs
1/2 c. grated Parmesan cheese
Salt and pepper to taste

Cook spinach using package directions. Drain, squeezing out excess moisture. Chop fine; set aside. Saute onions and garlic in oil until transparent. Remove from heat; add butter, stirring until melted. Set aside. Beat eggs in large bowl. Add remaining ingredients; mix well. Stir in sauteed vegetables and spinach, blending thoroughly. Pour into well-greased 8 x 15-inch pan. Bake at 325 degrees for 15 to 20 minutes or until firm in center. Pierce bubbles with fork. Allow to cool for 5 minutes before cutting into

2-inch squares. May be served warm as a side dish or cold as an appetizer.

Diane Duke, Sweet Home Jr. H.S.
Sweet Home, Oregon

FRIED SAUERKRAUT BALLS

1/4 lb. lean ham
1/4 lb. lean pork
1/4 lb. corned beef
2 tbsp. chopped onion
1 tbsp. chopped parsley
2 tbsp. shortening
Flour
1 c. milk
1/2 tsp. dry mustard
1/2 tsp. salt
1 1-lb. can sauerkraut, drained
1 egg, beaten
Fine dry bread crumbs

Put meats and onion through medium blade of food chopper. Add parsley; mix well. Panfry in shortening until brown. Blend in 1 cup flour. Stir in milk slowly; add seasonings. Cook, stirring constantly until mixture thickens and becomes light and fluffy. Cool. Mix in sauerkraut. Put through food chopper again. Return mixture to skillet. Cook, stirring constantly, until thickened. Cool. Shape into walnut-sized balls. Dredge in flour; dip in egg. Roll in bread crumbs. Fry in deep fat at 375 degrees until golden brown. Serve hot. Yield: 40-45 balls.

Mrs. William Demens, Milwee Middle School
Longwood, Florida

GLORIFIED SQUASH

2 c. cooked squash
3 tbsp. butter
1/3 c. milk
2 tbsp. each grated onion, bell pepper
and pimento
1 tsp. Worcestershire sauce
2 tbsp. catsup
Salt and pepper to taste
3/4 c. grated cheese
2 eggs
3/4 c. bread crumbs

Mash squash in bowl. Add 2 tablespoons butter and remaining ingredients except bread crumbs; mix well. Pour into greased baking dish. Combine 1 tablespoon butter with bread crumbs in skillet. Stir over low heat until bread crumbs are well coated. Sprinkle over squash mixture.

Bake at 350 degrees for 30 minutes or until firm.

Rebecca S. Hughes, J.C. Booth Jr. H.S.
Peachtree City, Georgia

SQUASH FRITTERS

Salt and pepper to taste
3 c. grated squash
1 egg
2 tbsp. sugar
6 tbsp. flour
2 tbsp. minced onion
Oil for frying

Salt squash; let drain in colander. Squeeze moisture from squash. Combine all ingredients except oil in large bowl; mix well. Fry a small amount at a time in deep fat until brown on both sides. Serve hot.

Patricia Ann Ervin, Kempsville Jr. H.S.
Virginia Beach, Virginia

JO'S SWEET POTATO CASSEROLE

3 c. cooked mashed sweet potatoes
1/2 c. sugar
2 eggs
1/2 c. milk
1 tsp. vanilla extract
Butter
1 c. (firmly packed) brown sugar
1/2 c. flour
1 c. chopped nuts

Combine sweet potatoes, sugar, eggs, milk, vanilla and 1/4 cup butter in large bowl; mix well. Place in buttered casserole. Mix brown sugar with flour. Cut in 1/2 stick butter until crumbly. Stir in nuts. Sprinkle over top of casserole. Bake at 350 degrees for 30 minutes.

Jo Burroughs, Trinity H.S.
Trinity, North Carolina

FRENCH-FRIED SWEET POTATOES

Sweet potatoes
Oil for frying
Salt or sugar to taste

Peel potatoes; cut into thin strips. Fry in hot fat until crisp and brown outside and tender on inside. Drain on paper towels. Serve hot. Serve plain or sprinkled with salt or sugar. May be served as a substitute for hashed brown potatoes with breakfast.

Rosemary Houchins, Wedgewood Middle School
Columbus, Ohio

AMBROSIA SWEET POTATOES

1/2 lemon, thinly sliced
1/2 orange, thinly sliced
6 to 7 c. cooked sweet potatoes
1 9-oz. can crushed pineapple
1/2 c. (firmly packed) brown sugar
2 tbsp. melted butter
1/2 tsp. salt
1/2 c. shredded coconut
Green or red stemmed cherries

Arrange lemon and orange slices alternately with sweet potatoes in shallow baking dish. Combine next 4 ingredients in bowl; mix well. Pour over sweet potatoes. Sprinkle with coconut. Top with cherries. Bake at 350 degrees for 30 minutes or until bubbly.

Mary Jo Lyle, Gatewood School
Eatonton, Georgia

THANKSGIVING YAMS WITH TOPPING

4 or 5 med. yams
1 c. pineapple juice
1 c. orange juice
1/4 c. butter
1 egg, slightly beaten
1 tsp. salt
1/4 tsp. cinnamon
3 tbsp. brown sugar
1/3 c. cream

Peel yams; cut into large chunks. Place in saucepan; add fruit juices. Cook about 20 minutes, or until tender. Mash yams well. Add butter, egg, salt, cinnamon, brown sugar and cream. Beat until creamy, adding additional cream or juice if needed. Spoon into well-greased baking dish.

Topping

1/4 c. sifted flour
3 tbsp. brown sugar
1/2 tsp. cinnamon
1/4 tsp. salt
3 tbsp. butter
1/4 c. chopped nuts
1 c. miniature marshmallows

Combine flour, brown sugar, cinnamon and salt. Cut butter into mixture until resembles coarse crumbs. Stir in nuts; sprinkle mixture over yam mixture. Press marshmallows lightly into top. Bake at 350 degrees for 25 minutes. Yield: 6 servings.

Katy Smith, Morristown-Hamblen West H.S.
Morristown, Tennessee

HELEN'S SWEET POTATO CASEROLE

3 to 6 c. sweet potatoes, drained, mashed
Margarine, melted
2 eggs
1 c. sugar
1 tbsp. vanilla extract
1 c. (firmly packed) brown sugar
1/3 c. flour
1 c. chopped nuts

Mix sweet potatoes, 1/2 cup melted margarine, eggs, sugar and vanilla together in bowl. Pour into buttered casserole. Mix remaining ingredients with 1/3 cup margarine. Sprinkle over potato mixture. Bake at 350 degrees for 20 minutes.

Mrs. Helen Walker, Champaign Central H.S.
Champaign, Illinois

SWEET POTATO BALLS

1/4 c. butter, softened
3/4 c. (firmly packed) brown sugar
2 tbsp. milk
1/4 tsp. salt
1/2 tsp. grated orange rind
Chopped nuts (opt.)
3 c. cooked mashed sweet potatoes
8 marshmallows
1 c. crushed corn flakes

Add butter, sugar, milk, salt, orange rind and nuts to sweet potatoes; mix well. Shape 1/4 cup mixture around each marshmallow, using more potatoes as needed, to make ball. Roll each ball in corn flakes. Place on buttered baking dish. Cover with foil; freeze until needed. Bake at 325 degrees about 20 minutes. Yield: 8 servings.

Judy Doughty, Zanesville H.S.
Zanesville, Ohio

SWEET POTATO PUDDING

2 eggs, beaten
3/4 c. sugar
Dash of salt
1 tsp. vanilla extract
1 c. milk
2 c. grated raw sweet potato
Dash of cinnamon
Sprinkle of nutmeg
1 tbsp. butter
Marshmallows

Combine eggs, sugar, salt and vanilla. Stir in milk and sweet potatoes. Pour into buttered

casserole. Sprinkle with spices. Dot with butter. Bake at 350 degrees for 30 minutes. Press marshmallows lightly into top of casserole. Bake for 10 minutes longer.

Janet Chapman, Woodstock H.S.
Woodstock, Illinois

OLD-FASHIONED SWEET POTATO PUDDING

4 eggs, beaten
2 c. sugar
3 c. sweet potatoes, grated
1 c. butter, softened
1 c. milk
1 tsp. cinnamon
1 tsp. orange peel (opt.)
1 tsp. vanilla extract (opt.)

Combine eggs and sugar in mixing bowl; mix well. Stir in sweet potatoes; mix well. Add butter, milk, cinnamon, peel and flavoring. Pour into deep baking dish. Bake at 300 degrees for 45 minutes to 1 hour, stirring brown crust under occasionally until mixture thickens.

Mary Mast, Hibriten H.S.
Lenoir, North Carolina

SWEET POTATO SOUFFLE

4 or 5 sweet potatoes, cooked, mashed
1/2 c. sugar
1/2 tsp. salt
2 eggs, beaten
Margarine
1/2 c. milk
1/2 c. (firmly packed) brown sugar
1/3 c. flour
1 c. chopped nuts

Combine mashed sweet potatoes with sugar, salt, eggs, 3 tablespoons margarine and milk. Pour into greased 1 1/2-quart baking dish. Mix remaining ingredients with 5 tablespoons margarine; spread over potatoes. Bake at 350 degrees for 35 minutes. May make a day ahead.

Carol Huffstetler, Boca Raton H.S.
Boca Raton, Florida

CRANBERRY-SWEET POTATO BAKE

4 med. sweet potatoes, cooked, peeled,
  halved
1/2 c. whole cranberry sauce
3 tbsp. lemon juice

1/3 c. honey
1 tbsp. melted margarine

Place potatoes in shallow buttered baking dish. Combine cranberry sauce and lemon juice in small bowl; mix well. Spread cranberry mixture over potatoes. Combine honey and margarine. Pour over sweet potatoes. Bake at 350 degrees for 25 minutes, basting occasionally.

Marjorie Yandell, Caldwell County H.S.
Princeton, Kentucky

APPLE AND SWEET POTATO CASSEROLE

    3 med. sweet potatoes, peeled, sliced
    2 c. sliced peeled apples
    3 c. miniature marshmallows
    1 c. sugar
    1 tsp. salt
    1 tsp. cinnamon
    Chopped nuts (opt.)
    2 tbsp. cornstarch
    1 tbsp. butter

Place sweet potatoes in buttered baking dish. Add apples; layer with marshmallows. Mix sugar, salt, cinnamon and nuts. Sprinkle over marshmallows. Mix cornstarch with 1/2 cup water until smooth; pour over all. Dot with butter. Cover. May make several days ahead; cover tightly and refrigerate. Bake at 350 degrees for 1 hour. Yield: 6 servings.

Kathleen Ann McConkie, Southwest Jr. H.S.
Hot Springs, Arkansas

MARY JO'S SWEET POTATO CASSEROLE

    3 c. mashed sweet potatoes
    1/2 c. sugar
    2 eggs
    1 tbsp. vanilla extract
    1/2 c. raisins
    Margarine
    1 c. (firmly packed) brown sugar
    1 c. chopped pecans
    1/3 c. flour

Combine first 5 ingredients with 1/2 cup melted margarine in bowl; mix well. Pour into buttered casserole. Combine brown sugar, pecans, flour and 1/3 cup melted margarine in small bowl. Mix until crumbly. Sprinkle over

sweet potato mixture. Bake at 325 degrees for 25 minutes.

Mary Jo Campbell, Liberty H.S.
Liberty, Mississippi

PAM'S SWEET POTATO CASSEROLE

    3 c. cooked, mashed sweet potatoes
    1 c. sugar
    2 eggs, beaten
    1 tsp. vanilla extract
    1/3 c. milk
    Melted butter
    1/2 c. (firmly packed) brown sugar
    1/4 c. flour
    1/2 c. chopped nuts

Combine first 5 ingredients with 1/2 cup butter in mixing bowl; mix well. Pour into 2-quart casserole. Combine brown sugar, flour, 2 1/2 tablespoons butter and nuts in small mixing bowl; mix well. Sprinkle topping over potato mixture. Bake at 350 degrees for 30 to 40 minutes. Yield: 8-10 servings.

Pam Dangelmayr, Sacred Heart H.S.
Muenster, Texas

SOUR CREAM-NOODLE BAKE

    16 oz. medium egg noodles
    2 tbsp. butter
    1 lb. ground beef
    1 15-oz. can tomato sauce
    1 tsp. salt
    1/4 tsp. garlic salt
    1/8 tsp. pepper
    1 c. cottage cheese
    1 c. sour cream
    1/2 c. chopped green onions
    3/4 c. shredded Cheddar cheese

Cook noodles according to package directions. Rinse and drain. Melt butter in skillet. Add ground beef; cook, stirring occasionally, over moderate heat until beef loses pink color. Stir in tomato sauce, salt, garlic salt and pepper; cover. Simmer for 5 minutes. Fold together noodles, cottage cheese, sour cream and onions. Spoon half the noodle mixture into 3 1/2-quart casserole. Cover with half the meat mixture. Repeat layers. Sprinkle cheese over top. Bake at 350 degrees for 25 to 30 minutes until mixture is thoroughly heated and cheese is melted. Yield: 6-8 servings.

Mrs. Mary F. Yost, Cairo-Durham H.S.
Cairo, New York

HOLIDAY VEGETABLE MEDLEY

    1 9-oz. package frozen whole green
       beans
    1 15 1/2-oz. can small whole peeled
       onions
    1/2 c. slim milk
    4 tsp. cornstarch
    1/4 tsp. ground nutmeg
    1/2 lb. fresh mushrooms, sliced

Prepare green beans in saucepan according to
package directions. Drain onions, reserving
liquid. Combine onion liquid, skim milk, cornstarch and nutmeg in saucepan; mix well. Bring
to a boil, stirring constantly. Reduce heat; add
mushrooms and onions. Simmer for 4 to 5 minutes, stirring occasionally. Spoon into serving
dish, reserving 1/4 cup sauce. Surround with
green beans. Spoon reserved sauce over green
beans. Yield: 6 servings.

Photograph for this recipe above.

ITALIAN DRESSING

    1 1/2 to 2 lb. pork sausage
    1 lg. onion, chopped
    1/2 stalk celery, finely chopped
    1 c. chopped pecans
    1 pkg. Pepperidge Farm herb-seasoned
       stuffing mix

Brown sausage in skillet, stirring until crumbly;
drain. Add onion, celery and pecans. Simmer
for 10 to 15 minutes. Prepare stuffing mix
using package directions, substituting 1/3 cup
additional water instead of egg. Combine meat
mixture with stuffing; mix thoroughly. Place a
portion of stuffing inside turkey. Place remaining stuffing in baking dish. Sprinkle water over
dressing before cooking. Bake at 350 degrees
for 1 hour.

Diana Watson, Paoli H.S.
Paoli, Oklahoma

SAUSAGE-MUSHROOM STUFFING

    1/2 lb. bulk sausage
    Butter
    1 lb. fresh mushrooms, thickly sliced
    1/2 c. chopped onion
    1/2 c. chopped celery
    4 c. soft bread crumbs
    1/4 tsp. thyme
    1/2 tsp. marjoram
    Salt and pepper to taste
    Turkey broth

Saute sausage in skillet until well browned and crumbly. Remove from pan. Add butter to pan drippings to measure 1/2 cup. Saute mushrooms, onion and celery for 4 to 5 minutes in drippings. Mix in bread crumbs, seasonings and sausage. Moisten with broth. Place in casserole. Refrigerate, covered, until ready to use. Bake at 350 degrees for 30 minutes or use to stuff turkey. Yield: 6-7 cups.

Mary L. Hartle, Bloomington H.S. North
Bloomington, Indiana

POTATO DRESSING

    3 lb. potatoes, boiled, mashed
    4 to 6 slices bread, cubed
    1 med. onion, chopped
    2 c. chopped celery
    Salt and pepper to taste

Combine all ingredients in large bowl; mix well. Place in casserole; cover. Bake at 350 degrees for 1 hour. May also be used to stuff turkey or round steak.

Joan A. Brislen, Perry Middle School
Carpentersville, Illinois

SQUASH DRESSING

    3 c. cooked drained squash
    3 c. crumbled corn bread
    3 eggs
    1 med. onion, chopped
    1 stick margarine
    1 can cream of chicken soup

Mix all ingredients together in casserole. Bake at 350 degrees for 30 to 45 minutes or until golden brown.

Becki Scott, Wheeler H.S.
Wheeler, Mississippi

GRITS CASSEROLE

    2 tsp. salt
    1 1/2 c. grits
    1 lb. Velveeta cheese, grated
    1 1/2 sticks margarine
    3 tsp. savory salt
    3 or 4 dashes of Tabasco sauce
    3 eggs, well beaten

Bring 6 cups water to a boil with salt in saucepan. Stir in grits; cook until done. Add remaining ingredients; mix well. Pour into two 11 x 17 x 2-inch casseroles. Bake at 250 degrees for 1 hour.

Linda Winget Kittelson, Holmes H.S.
San Antonio, Texas

RICE-MUSHROOM CASSEROLE

    1/2 lb. ground beef
    1 lg. onion, chopped
    1 c. diced celery
    1 green pepper, chopped
    Salt and pepper to taste
    2 c. cooked rice
    2 cans tomato soup
    2 cans whole mushrooms

Combine first 5 ingredients in skillet. Cook until browned, stirring occasionally. Add remaining ingredients; mix well. Place in casserole. Bake at 300 degrees for 1 hour. Yield: 6 servings.

Janet K. Alvord, Gilmanton H.S.
Gilmanton, Wisconsin

WILD RICE CASSEROLE

    1 pkg. wild rice mix
    1/2 c. chopped onion
    1/2 c. margarine
    3 c. chopped cooked chicken
    1 c. cream of chicken soup
    1 6-oz. can sliced mushrooms
    1/4 c. chopped pimento
    1 tsp. salt
    1/4 tsp. pepper
    1/2 c. chopped pecans

Cook rice using package directions. Saute onion in margarine. Add remaining ingredients; mix well. Pour into buttered 2-quart casserole. Bake at 350 degrees for 25 to 30 minutes. Freezes well.

Mrs. Retha Henderson, Heritage Academy H.S.
Columbus, Mississippi

RICE-MUSHROOM MEDLEY

    1 6-oz. package Uncle Ben's long grain
    *   and wild rice mix*
    6 oz. beef bouillon
    1 sm. onion, chopped
    1/2 c. chopped celery
    4 tbsp. butter
    1 3-oz. can sliced mushrooms, drained

Prepare rice using package directions, substituting bouillon and 1 1/4 cups water for liquid. Saute onion and celery in butter in skillet until tender. Stir onion mixture and mushrooms into rice 5 minutes before end of cooking time. Continue cooking until all liquid is absorbed. Yield: 6-8 servings.

Jo Etta Penn, Howe H.S.
Howe, Texas

Treasured Holiday Breads

Nothing impresses your guests more than adding homemade bread to the menu. Piping hot biscuits, steaming loaves, nutty fruit bread — all fresh from the oven — never fail to bring smiles of delight. But homemade breads aren't just for good impressions; they're wholesome, nutritious and economical additions to your family's diet.

Baking good homemade bread is as simple as following any other recipe, so don't be afraid to try. These recipes are all tried-and-true favorites that are sure to make you a proud hostess.

Coffee cakes are ideal for long weekends during the holidays or that special brunch you're planning. Here are several recipes using everything from cherries to blueberries to sour cream for a flavorful variety. Many foreign breads are included too.

And if you like having holiday breads handy, ready to slice for unexpected company, you'll love these unusual recipes using strawberry preserves, pumpkin, apple or zuchinni. How your guests will too! For dinner time, here's a bountiful selection of all kinds of breads. Remember, fresh baked goods make beautiful Christmas and hostess gifts too.

ANGEL BISCUITS

1 pkg. yeast
2 c. flour
2 1/2 tsp. baking powder
1 tsp. salt
1/4 tsp. soda
2 tbsp. sugar
1/2 c. shortening
3/4 c. buttermilk

Dissolve yeast in 2 tablespoons lukewarm water. Let stand for 5 minutes. Sift dry ingredients together in bowl. Cut in shortening with pastry blender until crumbly. Add yeast to buttermilk; mix well. Add liquid ingredients to flour mixture, stirring slowly with fork. Turn dough onto lightly floured surface. Knead several times. Roll on floured surface to 1/2-inch thickness. Cut with biscuit cutter. Place on ungreased cookie sheet. Bake at 450 degrees for 10 to 12 minutes. Yield: 2 dozen biscuits.

Gloria Bland Byrd, Baker H.S.
Mobile, Alabama

NEVER FAIL BISCUITS

1 c. milk
2 tbsp. mayonnaise
2 c. self-rising flour

Stir ingredients together in medium bowl; blend well. Spoon into muffin pan. Bake at 400 degrees until golden brown. Yield: 6 biscuits.

Ann Dyess, Elba H.S.
Elba, Alabama

DINNER CHEESE BISCUITS

6 c. self-rising flour
2 sticks margarine, softened
3 c. buttermilk
1/2 c. grated sharp cheese

Place flour in bowl; cut in margarine with pastry blender until crumbly. Add buttermilk; mix well. Stir in cheese; mix well. Spoon onto baking sheet. Bake at 450 degrees for 8 to 10 minutes. May bake partially and freeze.

Linda P. Yates, Pisgah Sr. H.S.
Canton, North Carolina

BREAD STICKS

1 cake compressed yeast
5 tbsp. oil
3 1/8 c. flour
Butter
Coarse salt

Dissolve yeast in 1 cup warm water in large bowl. Add oil. Stir in flour gradually, mixing thoroughly. Cover. Let rise in warm place until doubled in bulk. Roll out dough into pencil-thin strips; cut into sticks. Melt butter in saucepan. Dip sticks in butter; place on cookie sheets. Sprinkle with coarse salt. Let rise in warm place until light. Bake at 400 degrees until golden. Garlic or onion salt may be used to season.

Nancy C. Cruise, Loomis Public School
Loomis, Nebraska

COFFEE CAN CHEESE BREAD

1/2 c. milk
1/4 c. sugar
1/2 c. vegetable oil
1 tsp. salt
3 1/2 c. flour
1 pkg. dry yeast
2 eggs
6 oz. sharp cheese, grated
1/2 tsp. pepper

Combine milk, 1/2 cup water, sugar, vegetable oil and salt in saucepan. Heat over low heat until blended. Combine 1 1/2 cups flour and yeast in large mixing bowl. Add liquid mixture to flour; beat until smooth. Blend in eggs, cheese and pepper. Stir in 2 cups flour to make a stiff batter. Beat until smooth and elastic. Spoon into 2 greased 1-pound coffee cans. Cover with plastic lids. Let rise in warm place for 1 hour or until light and bubbly. Batter should be 1/2 inch below can cover. Remove lids. Bake at 375 degrees for 30 to 35 minutes. Cool for 15 minutes. Remove from cans. Cool on wire rack. Yield: 2 loaves.

Kathy Brown, R.L. Turner H.S.
Carrollton, Texas

CANDY CANE COFFEE CAKES

2 c. sour cream
2 pkg. dry yeast
1/4 c. margarine, softened
2 tsp. salt
2 eggs
Sugar
6 c. flour
4 1/2 c. chopped apples
1 c. raisins
Cinnamon to taste
2 c. confectioners' sugar

Heat sour cream in saucepan over low heat until lukewarm. Dissolve yeast in 1/2 cup warm water in large bowl. Stir in sour cream, next 3 ingredients, 1/3 cup sugar and 2 cups flour; beat until smooth. Mix in enough remaining flour to make dough easy to handle. Turn dough onto floured board. Knead until smooth, about 10 minutes. Place in greased bowl, turning to grease surface. Cover. Let rise in warm place until doubled in bulk, about 1 hour. Punch down dough. Divide into 3 portions. Roll each portion into 15 x 6-inch rectangles. Place on greased cookie sheet. Make 2-inch cuts at 1/2-inch intervals on long sides of rectangles. Combine fruit with 1/2 cup sugar and cinnamon. Spread down center of rectangle. Crisscross strips to cover fruit. Stretch and curve to form candy cane. Bake at 375 degrees for 15 to 20 minutes or until golden brown. Brush with butter while warm. Combine confectioners' sugar and 2 tablespoons water; mix well. Drizzle over warm bread. Garnish with candied cherries to resemble holly clusters.

Mary W. Dick, John Rolfe Middle School
Richmond, Virginia

CHERRY COFFEE CAKE

    3 c. flour
    2 c. sugar
    1 tsp. baking powder
    1/2 lb. margarine, softened
    1 egg
    3/4 c. milk
    1 can cherry pie filling
    1/2 c. butter, softened

Sift together 2 cups flour, 1 cup sugar and baking powder into bowl. Cut in margarine with pastry blender until crumbly. Add egg and milk; mix well. Pour into greased jelly roll pan. Spoon pie filling over top. Combine 1 cup flour, 1 cup sugar and butter; mix well. Sprinkle over pie filling. Bake at 400 degrees for 30 to 35 minutes or until golden brown.

Karen Anding Crook, Schaumburg H.S.
Schaumburg, Illinois

BLUEBERRY HOLIDAY RING

    4 c. biscuit mix
    1 1/3 c. milk
    1/2 c. butter
    3/4 c. dry bread crumbs
    1/2 c. coarsely chopped nuts
    1/4 c. sugar
    1/2 tsp. cinnamon
    1 tsp. grated orange rind
    Dash of Angostura aromatic bitters

    1 can blueberries, well drained
    1 c. confectioners' sugar
    2 tbsp. orange juice

Combine biscuit mix with milk in bowl. Prepare dough according to package directions for rolled biscuits. Turn onto lightly floured board; knead several times. Roll out into 10 x 14-inch rectangle. Melt butter in small saucepan. Stir in bread crumbs, nuts, sugar, cinnamon, orange rind and bitters. Saute together until lightly browned. Stir in drained blueberries, reserving several for garnish. Spread blueberry filling evenly over dough. Roll as for jelly roll, starting at wide end. Place dough in buttered 6-quart ring mold, joining ends to form ring. Bake at 375 degrees for 30 to 35 minutes or until golden brown. Turn out onto serving plate. Combine confectioners' sugar and orange juice in small bowl, stirring until smooth. Spread over top of warm ring to glaze. Garnish with maraschino cherry stars and reserved whole blueberries. Serve warm. Yield: 8-10 servings.

Photograph for this recipe on page 94.

NEW YORK POLISH CHEESE COFFEE CAKE

    1 pkg. dry yeast
    1/4 c. evaporated milk, warmed
    Sugar
    2 1/2 c. sifted flour
    1/2 tsp. salt
    1 c. butter, softened
    4 egg yolks, slightly beaten
    1 lb. cream cheese, softened
    1 egg, separated
    1 tsp. vanilla extract
    1/2 c. chopped nuts
    Confectioners' sugar

Dissolve yeast in evaporated milk; add 1 tablespoon sugar. Combine flour and salt in bowl. Cut in butter with pastry blender until crumbly. Add egg yolks and yeast; mix well. Divide dough into halves. Roll each half to fit 13 x 9 x 2-inch pan. Place half in bottom of pan. Beat cream cheese, egg yolk, 1 cup sugar and vanilla in bowl until light and fluffy. Spread over dough. Place remaining half dough over cheese mixture. Brush top with slightly beaten egg white. Sprinkle with nuts. Cover. Let rise in warm place until doubled in bulk, about 2 hours. Bake at 350 degrees for 30 minutes. Cool. Sprinkle with confectioners' sugar.

Daryl Carothers, New Diana H.S.
Diana, Texas

GERMAN CHRISTMAS STOLLEN

1 1/2 c. scalded milk
2 pkg. dry yeast
3/4 c. sugar
2 tsp. salt
2 eggs
Soft shortening
7 3/4 c. (about) all-purpose flour
3/4 c. chopped blanched almonds
1 lb. candied mixed fruit
1/2 c. golden raisins
1/2 c. raisins
1 tbsp. grated lemon rind
1 c. confectioners' sugar
1/2 tsp. vanilla extract
2 tbsp. milk

Cool milk to lukewarm. Dissolve yeast in 1/2 cup warm water in large bowl. Add lukewarm milk, 1/2 cup sugar, salt, eggs, 1/2 cup shortening and 3 1/2 cups flour. Mix until smooth. Add almonds, fruit, raisins and lemon rind. Add 3 1/2 to 4 cups flour to handle easily. Turn onto floured board. Knead until smooth. Place in greased bowl, turning dough to grease surface. Cover. Let rise until doubled in bulk, about 1 hour and 30 minutes. Punch down. Let rise again until doubled in bulk, about 30 minutes. Divide dough in half. Divide each half into thirds. Roll each portion into long ropes. Braid 3 ropes together. Place each loaf on greased baking sheet. Cut 2 tablespoons shortening into 1/4 cup flour and 1/4 cup sugar in small bowl until mixture is crumbly. Sprinkle on top of loaves. Let rise for 45 minutes. Bake at 375 degrees for 30 to 35 minutes. Mix confectioners' sugar, vanilla and 2 tablespoons milk until smooth in small bowl. Drizzle over warm stollen. Serve thinly sliced spread with butter.

Deborah Warren, James Bowie H.S.
Simms, Texas

KRINGLERS

Butter
2 c. flour
3 eggs
Almond extract
1 c. confectioners' sugar
1 tbsp. milk

Cut 1/2 cup butter into 1 cup flour in bowl until crumbly. Add 1 tablespoon water; stir until dough leaves side of bowl. Pat into two 3-inch wide strips on ungreased cookie sheet, leaving space between strips. Bring 1 cup water to boil. Remove from heat. Add 1 cup flour;

beat well. Add eggs, one at a time, beating well after each addition. Add 1/2 teaspoon almond flavoring. Spread over each strip. Bake at 375 degrees for 45 minutes. Cool. Combine confectioners' sugar, 1 tablespoon butter, milk and 1 tablespoon almond extract; beat until smooth. Frost Kringlers.

Deb Bach, Bridgewater H.S.
Bridgewater, South Dakota

SOUR CREAM COFFEE CAKE

1 box Duncan Hines Butter Recipe Golden
*   Cake Mix*
1/2 c. sugar
3/4 c. oil
1 8-oz. carton sour cream
1 tsp. vanilla extract
1 tsp. butter flavoring
4 eggs
4 tbsp. (firmly packed) brown sugar
3 tsp. cinnamon
1/2 c. chopped nuts
2 tbsp. melted margarine
3 tbsp. milk
1 c. confectioners' sugar

Combine first 4 ingredients in large bowl; mix well. Add flavorings. Add eggs one at a time, beating well after each addition. Pour half the batter into greased and floured bundt pan. Combine brown sugar, cinnamon and nuts in small bowl; mix well. Sprinkle over batter. Spoon in remaining batter. Bake in preheated 350-degree oven for 1 hour. Cool thoroughly. Remove from pan. Mix remaining ingredients in small bowl until smooth. Drizzle over cake.

Vivian Bowden, Ariton H.S.
Ariton, Alabama

CHRISTMAS TOWERS

2 pkg. dry yeast
6 c. sifted all-purpose flour
1/2 c. butter, softened
1 c. crunchy peanut butter
Sugar
1 tsp. salt
4 eggs
1 egg, separated
1 4-oz. jar cut citron
1 c. light raisins
1/3 c. chopped candied cherries

Sprinkle yeast over 1 cup warm water in large mixing bowl; stir until dissolved. Add 3 cups

flour, butter, peanut butter, 3/4 cup sugar, salt, eggs and egg yolk. Blend together on low speed of electric mixer until smooth. Beat on medium speed for 2 minutes. Add remaining flour and fruit; beat with wooden spoon. Turn onto floured board; knead until smooth. Place in lightly greased bowl; turn to grease surface. Cover. Let rise in warm place until doubled in bulk, about 2 hours. Punch down; knead until smooth. Divide into thirds. Place into 3 greased and floured 1-pound coffee cans. Let rise until doubled in bulk, about 30 to 45 minutes. Bake at 350 degrees for 45 minutes. Brush with egg white; sprinkle with additional sugar. Bake for 45 minutes longer or until bread tests done. Yield: 3 loaves.

Photograph for this recipe above.

BRAN MUFFINS

3 c. All-Bran
1/2 c. oil
2 1/2 c. all-purpose flour
1 tsp. salt
1 1/2 c. sugar
2 1/2 tsp. soda
2 eggs, beaten
2 c. buttermilk
1 c. raisins

Combine All-Bran, oil and 1 cup boiling water in bowl; set aside. Combine dry ingredients in mixing bowl. Add eggs and buttermilk, stirring until ingredients are moistened. Add All-Bran mixture and raisins; mix well. Fill greased muffin tins 2/3 full. Bake at 400 degrees for 15 to 20 minutes. Store batter in refrigerator up to 2 weeks to use when needed.

Patsy C. Gaines, Daleville H.S.
Daleville, Alabama

ORANGE STREUSEL MUFFINS

1 egg
1/2 c. orange juice
1/2 c. orange marmalade
1/4 c. milk
1/4. vegetable oil
2 c. all-purpose flour
1 tbsp. baking powder
1 tsp. salt
Sugar
1/2 tsp. cinnamon
1/4 tsp. nutmeg

Grease bottoms only of 12 muffin cups. Beat egg in large bowl. Stir in next 4 ingredients. Add flour, baking powder, salt and 1/3 cup sugar. Stir only until moistened. Fill muffin cups 2/3 full. Mix 1/4 cup sugar with cinnamon and nutmeg. Sprinkle over batter. Bake at 400 degrees for 20 to 25 minutes. Yield: 12 muffins.

Mary Ann McDevitt, Crawfordsville H.S.
Crawfordsville, Indiana

REFRIGERATOR MUFFINS

1 c. oil
3 c. sugar
4 eggs, slightly beaten
5 c. flour
3 tsp. baking powder
2 tsp. salt
1 qt. buttermilk
1 10-oz. package raisin-bran cereal

Combine oil and sugar in bowl; mix well. Add eggs; mix well. Sift dry ingredients together; add to sugar mixture alternately with buttermilk, mixing well after each addition. Stir in cereal. Spoon batter into greased muffin cups. Bake at 400 degrees for 15 to 20 minutes. Remaining batter can be stored in refrigerator for 6 weeks. Recipe may be made day ahead of serving time.

Deborah Frizzell, Fordsville Jr. H.S.
Fordsville, Kentucky

UH-OH MUFFINS

2 c. Bisquick
2/3 c. milk
1 8-oz. package cream cheese, softened
1/2 c. sugar
1/2 tsp. vanilla extract
1/2 c. chopped nuts
1/2 c. raisins
Honey

Combine all ingredients except honey in large bowl. Beat at low speed of electric mixer. Fill baking cup-lined muffin tins 1/2 full. Bake at 350 degrees for 10 minutes. Drizzle with honey. May add cherries for color. Yield: 18 muffins.

Debra Bowen, East Surry H.S.
Pilot Mountain, North Carolina

NORWEGIAN FLATBROD

1/4 c. shortening
2 c. flour
2 c. whole wheat flour
1/2 c. sugar
1 tbsp. salt

Cut shortening into flours, sugar and salt in large bowl until crumbly. Add 2 cups plus 2 tablespoons warm water; mix well. Roll out small egg-sized portion dough on floured surface. Roll very thin into 16 to 18-inch circle. Bake on ungreased griddle or lefse iron at 375 degrees until lightly browned on both sides. Cool. Store in airtight container. Serve spread with butter. Yield: 30 servings.

Margo Van Dan, Alden-Hebron H.S.
Hebron, Illinois

BUTTER ROLLS

4 c. flour
1/2 c. sugar
1/2 tsp. salt
1 c. shortening
1 yeast cake
1 c. milk, warmed
2 eggs, beaten

Combine flour, sugar and salt in bowl; cut in shortening with pastry blender until crumbly. Dissolve yeast cake in a small amount of warm milk. Add remaining milk and eggs. Add liquid ingredients to dry ingredients; mix well. Refrigerate overnight. Divide dough into 5 parts. Roll each portion on floured surface to 9 x 1/2-inch circle. Brush with melted butter. Cut into 8 wedges. Roll up each wedge, starting with wide end. Place on greased pan; cover. Let rise for 1 hour until doubled in bulk. Bake at 400 degrees for 17 minutes. May be frosted, if desired. Yield: 40 rolls.

Joy L. Manson, Miami H.S.
Miami, Arizona

ANNA'S YEAST ROLLS

1 pkg. yeast
4 c. self-rising flour
1 1/2 sticks margarine, melted
1/4 c. sugar

Dissolve yeast in 2 cups warm water in large bowl. Add remaining ingredients; mix well. Cover bowl tightly. Refrigerate. Spoon dough into greased muffin pans. Bake at 350 degrees for 15 to 20 minutes. May be stored in refrigerator for 3 or 4 days. Yield: 2 dozen rolls.

Anna Wright, Heath H.S.
West Paducah, Kentucky

COTTAGE CHEESE ROLLS

1 pkg. yeast
2 1/2 c. flour
1 1/4 tsp. salt
1 c. creamed cottage cheese
1/4 c. sugar
1 egg
3/4 c. margarine, softened
3/4 c. (firmly packed) brown sugar
1/2 tsp. vanilla extract
2/3 c. chopped nuts
Confectioners' sugar glaze

Dissolve yeast in 1/4 cup warm water. Sift flour with 1 teaspoon salt into large bowl. Add cottage cheese, sugar, egg, 1/2 cup margarine and yeast; mix well. Roll out dough onto lightly floured surface. Combine 4 tablespoons margarine and 1/4 teaspoon salt with remaining ingredients in bowl; mix well. Spread over dough. Roll as for jelly roll; slice. Place in greased baking pan. Cover. Let rise in warm place until doubled in bulk. Bake at 400 degrees for 10 to 15 minutes. Spread with a confectioners' sugar glaze when cool. Yield: 18 rolls.

Cynthia J. Singley, West Fork School
West Fork, Arkansas

PULL-APART BREAKFAST ROLLS

1 pkg. frozen rolls
1 pkg. butterscotch pudding mix
3/4 c. (firmly packed) brown sugar
1 stick margarine
1/2 c. chopped nuts (opt.)

Layer frozen rolls in greased tube cake pan. Sprinkle pudding mix and brown sugar over rolls. Slice margarine over rolls. Sprinkle with nuts. Cover with cloth. Let stand overnight. Bake at 350 degrees for 25 to 30 minutes. Let stand for 5 minutes. Turn out on serving plate.

Petrena Forsythe, Fredonia Sr. H.S.
Fredonia, Kansas

FLAVORFUL TOMATO BREAD

2 c. tomato juice
2 tbsp. butter
3 tbsp. honey
1 tsp. salt
1/4 c. tomato catsup
1 pkg. active dry yeast
6 1/2 c. all-purpose flour

Heat tomato juice and butter together in saucepan until butter is melted. Add honey, salt and catsup; stir to blend. Cool until lukewarm. Measure 1/4 cup warm water into large mixing bowl. Sprinkle yeast over water, stirring to dissolve. Add tomato mixture and 3 cups flour. Beat for 2 minutes at medium speed of electric mixer, scraping bottom and side of bowl. Mix in enough remaining flour to make dough easy to handle. Turn onto lightly floured board. Knead until smooth and elastic, about 8 to 10 minutes. Place in greased bowl; turn to grease surface. Cover. Let rise in warm place until doubled in bulk, 1 hour to 1 hour and 30 minutes. Punch down; divide into halves. Cover; let rest for 10 minutes. Shape into 2 loaves. Place into 2 greased 9 x 5 x 3-inch loaf pans. Cover. Let rise until almost doubled in bulk, about 1 hour. Bake at 425 degrees for 25 minutes or until loaves test done. Remove from pans. Cool on wire racks. Bread freezes well.

Photograph for this recipe on this page.

DANISH PUFFS

2 c. sifted flour
1 1/3 c. butter, softened
1 tsp. almond extract
3 eggs
3 c. sifted confectioners' sugar
3 tbsp. cream
1 1/2 tsp. vanilla extract
Chopped nuts

Combine 1 cup flour with 1/2 cup butter; mix well. Add up to 3 tablespoons water to form dough. Divide dough in half. Pat each portion into 3 x 12-inch strip in shallow baking pan. Place 1/2 cup butter and 1 cup water in saucepan. Bring to a rolling boil. Add almond extract and 1 cup flour; mix well. Remove from heat. Add eggs one at a time, beating well after each addition. Cool. Spoon over pastry strips, spreading to cover. Bake at 350 degrees for 40 to 45 minutes. Cool slightly on rack. Blend 1/3 cup butter with confectioners' sugar in bowl. Stir in cream and vanilla until smooth. Spread half the icing over 2 warm Danish Puffs. Sprinkle with nuts.

Martha Dunlap, Corsicana H.S.
Corsicana, Texas

FREEZER KOLACHES

5 1/4 to 6 1/4 c. flour
Sugar
1 tsp. salt
Grated lemon rind
2 pkg. active dry yeast
1 c. margarine, softened
2 eggs
2 8-oz. packages cream cheese
2 egg whites
Confectioners' sugar

Combine 1 1/2 cups flour, 1/3 cup sugar, salt 1/2 teaspoon lemon rind and yeast in large bowl. Add margarine and 1 1/3 cups warm water. Beat with electric mixer for 2 minutes. Add eggs and 1/2 cup flour. Beat for 2 minutes longer. Stir in enough additional flour to make soft dough. Cover. Let rest for 20 minutes. Divide dough into 3 equal portions onto well-floured board. Roll each portion into 8-inch square. Cut into 1-inch strips. Twist each strip; coil into circle. Seal ends underneath. Place on greased baking sheets. Press centers of each to make wide indentation. Combine cream cheese,

1/2 cup sugar, 1 tablespoon grated lemon rind and 2 egg whites in bowl; blend well. Place 2 tablespoons filling in each indentation. Freeze. Place in plastic bags. Freeze up to 4 weeks. Remove from freezer. Place on ungreased baking sheet. Cover loosely with plastic wrap. Let stand until fully thawed, about 1 hour and 45 minutes. Let rise about 45 minutes in warm place until doubled in bulk. Bake at 375 degrees for 15 to 20 minutes or until evenly browned. Cool on wire rack. Sprinkle with confectioners' sugar. Yield: 2 dozen rolls.

Mrs. Lillian M. Kwas, Warren Township H.S.
Gurnee, Illinois

BRAN BROWN BREAD

2 c. bran
2 c. sour milk
1 tbsp. molasses
1 c. sugar
2 c. flour
2 tsp. soda
1 tsp. salt
1 c. raisins, washed

Combine first 4 ingredients in large bowl; mix well. Sift flour, soda and salt. Beat into bran mixture. Stir in raisins. Pour into greased loaf pan. Bake at 375 degrees for 1 hour.

Margaret Sloan, Devon H.S.
Devon, Alberta, Canada

BISHOP'S BREAD

2 c. all-purpose flour
2 tsp. baking powder
1 tsp. salt
2 c. chopped nuts
1 c. chopped pitted dates
1 c. sliced maraschino cherries
1 c. semisweet chocolate pieces
4 eggs, beaten
1 c. sugar

Mix first 3 ingredients in large bowl. Add nuts, fruit and chocolate; mix lightly. Beat eggs and sugar together; stir into first mixture. Line 9 x 5 x 3-inch loaf pan with brown paper; butter paper. Pour mixture into pan. Bake at 325 degrees about 1 hour and 15 minutes. Turn onto rack to cool. Wrap cooled bread; store for 1 to 2 days before slicing.

Pat Kuiper, Wheaton North H.S.
Wheaton, Illinois

ANISE BREAD

1 tbsp. salt
1/2 lb. margarine
1 c. sugar
1 pkg. yeast
6 eggs
3/4 c. white cooking wine
2 to 3 tbsp. aniseed
5 lb. (or less) bread flour

Heat first 3 ingredients with 2 cups water in saucepan until margarine melts and sugar dissolves. Cool. Dissolve yeast in 1/3 cup warm water in large bowl. Add eggs, wine and aniseed; mix well. Add cooled sugar-water. Stir in flour gradually, mixing until dough forms ball and pulls away from side of bowl. Turn onto floured surface. Knead until smooth. Let rise until doubled in bulk. Knead again. Shape into 4 loaves. Place in greased loaf pans. Let rise until doubled in bulk. Bake in 300-degree oven for about 1 hour or until bread tests done. Remove from pans. Cool on rack. Rub tops with margarine while warm. Cool thoroughly. Store in plastic bags in refrigerator.

Helen Kelley, Lockhart Jr. H.S.
Orlando, Florida

CRANBERRY-ORANGE BREAD

2 c. flour
1 c. sugar
1 1/2 tsp. baking powder
1/2 tsp. soda
1 tsp. salt
Juice and grated rind of 1 orange
1 egg, beaten
2 tbsp. oil
1/2 c. chopped nuts
2 c. cranberries, halved

Sift dry ingredients into large bowl. Combine orange juice and rind with enough water to measure 3/4 cup. Add egg and oil; mix well. Pour over dry ingredients, mixing until moistened. Add nuts and cranberries; mix well. Pour into greased loaf pan. Bake at 325 degrees for 50 to 60 minutes. Cool before slicing.

Jan Sellars, Harry F. Byrd Middle School
Richmond, Virginia

CHERRY-NUT BREAD

1 10-oz. jar maraschino cherries
2 c. flour

1 tsp. soda
1/2 tsp. salt
3/4 c. sugar
1/2 c. margarine
2 eggs
1 tsp. vanilla extract
1 c. buttermilk
1 c. chopped pecans
1 c. confectioners' sugar

Drain and chop cherries, reserving juice. Mix next 3 ingredients in bowl. Cream sugar, margarine, eggs and vanilla in large bowl. Add dry ingredients alternately with buttermilk, beating well after each addition. Fold in cherries and pecans. Pour into greased 9 x 5 x 3-inch loaf pan. Bake at 350 degrees for 30 minutes or until bread tests done. Mix confectioners' sugar with enough reserved cherry juice to form glaze. Pour over slightly warm bread.

Durene French, Cameron H.S.
Cameron, Oklahoma

DELICIOUS MONKEY BREAD

2/3 c. sugar
2/3 c. Crisco
1 c. milk
1 1/2 tsp. salt
1 c. mashed potatoes
1 pkg. yeast
2 eggs, slightly beaten
Flour
3 sticks margarine

Combine first 4 ingredients in large saucepan. Heat until shortening melts. Remove from heat. Add next 3 ingredients and 1/2 cup warm water; mix well. Add 6 cups flour; blend thoroughly. Place in greased bowl. Turn to grease surface. Let rise until doubled in bulk. Punch down. Divide in half. Knead each half several times on floured surface. Roll out to 1/4-inch thick. Cut into 1 x 4-inch strips. Melt 1 stick margarine in cake pan. Dip 1 strip dough in margarine. Coil around finger; place in center of pan. Dip next strip in margarine; coil around first rolled strip. Repeat coils continuously until pan is filled. Let rise until doubled in bulk. Bake at 350 degrees until golden brown. May be sprinkled with sugar and cinnamon before coiling. Yield: 3 loaves.

Pam V. Chaney, Teague H.S.
Teague, Texas

CRANBERRY-ORANGE-NUT BREAD

1 c. whole wheat flour
1 c. all-purpose flour
1 1/2 tsp. baking powder
1/2 tsp. soda
1 c. sugar
Juice of 1 orange
2 tbsp. butter
1 egg, well beaten
1 c. chopped cranberries
1 c. chopped walnuts

Combine flours, baking powder, soda and sugar in bowl; set aside. Add enough boiling water to orange juice to measure 3/4 cup liquid. Add butter, stirring until melted. Stir into dry ingredients; mix well. Add egg, beating until smooth. Fold in cranberries and walnuts. Spoon batter into greased and floured 9 x 5 x 3-inch loaf pan. Bake at 350 degrees for 50 to 55 minutes or until bread tests done. Yield: 1 loaf.

Bobbie Vinson, Wilburton H.S.
Wilburton, Oklahoma

GUMDROP BREAD

3 c. applesauce
1 c. shortening
2 c. sugar
5 c. flour
4 tsp. soda
1 tsp. each nutmeg, allspice and salt
2 1/2 tsp. cinnamon
1/2 tsp. cloves
3 pkg. small gumdrops, no black ones
1 1/2 c. raisins

Heat applesauce in saucepan. Add shortening and sugar; mix well. Cover. Let stand overnight. Combine dry ingredients in large bowl; mix thoroughly. Blend in applesauce mixture. Stir gumdrops and raisins into mixture. Pour into greased and floured loaf pans. Bake at 250 degrees for 2 hours.

Sandy Nelson, Cavalier H.S.
Cavalier, North Dakota

GREEK HOLIDAY BREAD

2 cinnamon sticks
1 lb. butter, softened
3 c. sugar
12 eggs, beaten
4 cakes yeast
1 c. milk
1 tsp. baking powder
3 mashed potatoes

Flour
1 egg yolk, beaten
Walnuts

Boil 1 cup water with cinnamon sticks for 5 minutes. Set aside. Cream butter and sugar in large bowl. Add eggs; blend thoroughly. Dissolve yeast in milk. Add to egg mixture; mix well. Remove cinnamon sticks from water. Blend cinnamon water, baking powder and potatoes into egg mixture. Stir in enough flour to make soft dough. Knead on floured surface until smooth and elastic. Divide into 4 portions. Place in 4 greased loaf pans. Cover. Let rise in warm place until doubled in bulk. Brush tops of loaves with egg yolk. Garnish with walnuts. Bake at 350 degrees for 1 hour. Remove from pan. Cool on racks. Yield: 4 loaves.

Hazel C. Tassis, Imperial H.S.
Imperial, California

HOLIDAY FRUIT BREAD

1/2 c. shortening
2/3 c. sugar
2 tsp. salt
1/4 tsp. cardamom seed
2 c. milk, scalded
2 yeast cakes
2 eggs
8 c. flour
1 c. raisins
1 c. mixed fruit

Combine shortening, sugar, salt, cardamom seed and milk in bowl; mix well. Cool to lukewarm. Dissolve yeast in 1/2 cup lukewarm water. Add to milk mixture. Add eggs; beat well. Add 4 cups flour, blending thoroughly. Add fruit and remaining flour. Turn out on lightly floured surface. Knead thoroughly until smooth and elastic. Shape into 2 loaves. Place in greased loaf pans. Let rise until doubled in bulk. Bake at 350 degrees for 45 minutes.

Nancy M. Riley, Waterford H.S.
Waterford, Ohio

ARNIECE'S NUT LOAF

1 lb. butter, softened
1 c. sugar
1 lb. light brown sugar
6 eggs
1 tsp. vanilla extract
4 c. flour
Pinch of salt
1 tsp. baking powder

1 1/2 qt. pecans
1 lb. raisins
1 c. Mogan David Grape Wine

Cream butter and sugars in large mixer bowl until fluffy. Add eggs one at a time, beating well after each addition. Add vanilla; mix well. Sift dry ingredients together. Place pecans and raisins in large bowl; coat well with 1/4 cup flour mixture. Set aside. Add flour mixture to creamed mixture, 1/2 cup at a time, alternately with wine, mixing well, at low speed of mixer, after each addition. Stir in pecans and raisins. Pour into greased and floured tube pan. Bake at 300 degrees for 2 hours. Store wrapped in wine-dampened cheesecloth in airtight container. May substitute 1/2 cup milk for half the wine.

Marguerite Y. Anderson, Ouachita Jr. H.S.
Monroe, Louisiana

PUMPKIN BREAD

1 c. sugar
1/2 c. (firmly packed) brown sugar
1 c. canned pumpkin
1/2 c. oil
2 eggs
2 c. flour
1 tsp. soda
1/2 tsp. each salt, nutmeg and cinnamon
1/4 tsp. ginger
1/2 c. chopped nuts

Combine sugars, pumpkin, oil and eggs in bowl; beat well. Sift dry ingredients together. Add to pumpkin mixture, mixing well. Stir in nuts and 1/4 cup water. Pour into well-greased 9 x 5 x 3-inch loaf pan. Bake at 350 degrees for 1 hour to 1 hour and 15 minutes or until bread tests done. Yield: 1 loaf.

Cheryle A. Smith, Nevada Girls Training Center
Caliente, Nevada

JEAN'S PUMPKIN BREAD

2/3 c. shortening
1 2/3 c. sugar
4 eggs
1 16-oz. can pumpkin
3 1/3 c. flour
2 tsp. soda
1 1/2 tsp. salt
1/2 tsp. baking powder
1 tsp. each cinnamon, cloves
2/3 c. each nuts, raisins

Cream shortening and sugar until fluffy in large bowl. Beat in eggs, pumpkin and 2/3 cup water.

Blend in dry ingredients, mixing thoroughly. Stir in nuts and raisins. Pour into 2 greased 9 x 5 x 3-inch loaf pans. Bake at 350 degrees for 60 minutes or until bread tests done.

Jean Johnson, Conway Jr. H.S.
Orlando, Florida

STRAWBERRY BREAD

1/2 c. margarine, softened
1/2 c. sugar
1 tsp. vanilla extract
2 eggs
2 c. sifted flour
1/2 tsp. salt
1/4 tsp. soda
1 c. strawberry preserves
1/2 c. buttermilk
1/2 c. chopped nuts

Cream margarine in large bowl. Add sugar and vanilla; beat until fluffy. Add eggs one at a time, beating well after each addition. Sift dry ingredients together. Combine preserves and buttermilk in small bowl. Add dry ingredients alternately with preserves mixture to eggs mixture. Beat only until well blended. Stir in nuts. Pour into greased 8 1/2 x 4 1/2-inch loaf pan. Bake at 325 degrees for 1 hour and 30 minutes. Cool in pan for 15 minutes. Turn out onto wire rack to cool completely. Wrap loaf. Store overnight in cool place for easier slicing. Yield: 1 loaf.

Lana J. Crawford, Tarkington H.S.
Cleveland, Texas

ZUCCHINI BREAD

3 eggs
1 c. oil
2 1/2 c. sugar
2 c. grated zucchini
2 1/2 tsp. vanilla extract
3 c. flour
1 tsp. salt
1 tsp. soda
1/2 tsp. baking powder
3 tsp. cinnamon
1/2 c. chopped nuts

Beat eggs in large bowl. Add oil, sugar, zucchini and vanilla. Combine dry ingredients. Add to egg mixture; blend well. Stir in nuts. Pour into 2 greased loaf pans. Bake at 350 degrees for 1 hour. Yield: 2 loaves.

Sandra Souza, El Rancho Verde H.S.
Hayward, California

BASIC SWEET DOUGH

5 to 6 c. flour
2 pkg. instant-blend dry yeast
1 1/2 c. milk
1/2 c. butter
1/2 c. sugar
1 1/2 tsp. salt
2 eggs

Combine 2 cups flour and yeast in large mixing bowl. Combine milk, butter, sugar and salt in 1-quart saucepan. Heat until warm. Add to flour; add eggs. Beat for 1/2 minute at low speed of electric mixer, scraping side of bowl constantly. Beat for 3 minutes at high speed. Add 1 cup flour; beat for 1 minute. Stir in enough remaining flour to make soft dough. Turn onto lightly floured surface. Knead for 5 to 10 minutes or until smooth and elastic. Place in greased bowl; turn to grease surface. Cover. Place on rack over hot water. Let rise until doubled in bulk. Shape as desired.

Photograph for this recipe on page 109.

GOLDEN APPLE SWIRL

1 recipe Basic Sweet Dough
1 c. almond paste
2 1/2 c. peeled, chopped apples
1 c. chopped dates
1 tbsp. lemon juice
1 c. confectioners' sugar
4 tsp. milk
1/2 tsp. vanilla extract
Yellow food coloring

Punch dough down; divide into halves. Roll out into 27 x 6-inch rectangle. Spread 1/2 cup almond paste to within 1 inch of edges. Combine apples, dates and lemon juice in bowl. Sprinkle half the apple-date mixture evenly over dough. Roll up, jelly roll fashion from long sides. Cut 3-inch length from end. Pinch ends to seal. Shape roll into apple design on greased baking sheet. Shape 3-inch piece for apple stem; pinch into place. Repeat process. Cover. Let rise until doubled in bulk. Bake at 350 degrees for 25 to 30 minutes. Cool on wire rack. Combine confectioners' sugar, milk, vanilla and food coloring. Ice coffee cakes. Yield: 2 coffee cakes.

Photograph for this recipe on page 109.

WINTER WREATH

1 recipe Basic Sweet Dough
1 c. confectioners' sugar
1 1/2 tbsp. milk
Candied cherries
Tinted sugar

Punch dough down; divide into halves. Divide each part into 3 equal portions. Shape each portion into 24-inch long roll. Braid 3 rolls loosely together. Place on greased baking sheets. Form into circles, sealing ends together. Cover. Let rise until doubled in bulk. Bake at 350 degrees for 25 to 30 minutes. Cool on wire rack. Combine confectioners' sugar and milk in small bowl. Ice wreaths. Garnish with cherries and tinted sugar.

Photograph for this recipe on page 109.

GOLDEN JEWELED TREE

1 recipe Basic Sweet Dough
1 1/2 c. confectioners' sugar
1 1/2 to 2 tbsp. milk
1/2 tsp. vanilla extract
Green food coloring
1/2 c. sugar
1/2 tsp. almond extract
2 apples, thinly sliced
Sliced almonds
Candied cherries
Mixed candied fruits

Punch dough down; divide into halves. Divide each part into 11 equal portions. Shape into smooth balls. Place 10 balls on buttered baking sheet in four rows to form tree. Shape remaining ball for tree trunk; pinch into place. Repeat process with second half dough. Cover. Let rise in warm place until doubled in bulk. Bake at 350 degrees for 25 to 30 minutes or until golden brown. Cool on wire rack. Combine confectioners' sugar, milk, vanilla and food coloring in bowl. Spread on coffee cakes. Boil sugar and 1 cup water in saucepan for 5 minutes. Add almond flavoring and apple slices; cover. Poach until apples are tender but retain shape. Drain. Cool. Decorate glazed trees with apple slices, almonds, cherries and fruit "ornaments." Yield: 2 coffee cakes.

Photograph for this recipe on page 109.

Traditional Holiday Desserts

How we all look forward to dessert! It's the final glory of every good meal, but seems to be extra special around the holidays. Maybe it's because there are so many kinds of desserts in imaginative shapes and delectable flavors. Scrumptious cakes with melt-in-your-mouth frostings — creamy, smooth puddings . . . cookies with surprise fillings . . . candies . . . flavored nuts . . . fancy tortes . . . the variety is endless!

Every cook has her traditional baked good recipes saved especially for the holidays. That's what makes this chapter so exciting. It's as good as paying a visit to Home Economics teachers around the country, nibbling on their favorite holiday treats all along the way. So tempting, these recipes are sure to become a part of your own family traditions.

But don't hide that pretty dessert in the kitchen. Use your creation as a festive centerpiece. That way your guests will enjoy your handiwork, while anticipating the delights to come.

CHRISTMAS AMBROSIA

6 oranges, peeled and sectioned
1 1/2 c. sugar
1/2 c. freshly grated coconut
1/2 c. Sherry
Maraschino cherries

Alternate layers of orange sections, sugar and coconut in serving dish until all ingredients are used. Pour Sherry over fruit. Garnish with maraschino cherries. Chill until serving time.

Frances Morton, Tallulah H.S.
Tallulah, Louisiana

CHRISTMAS APPLE PUDDING

3/4 c. margarine
3 c. sugar
2 eggs, well beaten
Flour
2 tsp. soda
3 tsp. cinnamon
1/2 tsp. salt
4 c. peeled grated apples
1 c. nuts
2/3 c. chopped dates (opt.)
1 1/2 tsp. lemon juice
1 1/2 tsp. grated lemon rind
1 egg yolk

Combine 1/2 cup margarine, 2 cups sugar and 2 eggs in large bowl; blend thoroughly. Sift 2 cups flour, soda, cinnamon and salt together. Add to creamed mixture; mix well. Add apples, nuts and dates; mix well. Pour into greased pan. Bake at 350 degrees for 45 minutes or until cake tests done. Combine 1 cup sugar, 1 tablespoon flour and 1 cup boiling water in saucepan. Cook over medium heat until thickened, stirring constantly. Add lemon juice and lemon rind. Beat egg yolk in small bowl. Add a small amount of hot mixture to egg yolk; add egg yolk to hot mixture. Cook, stirring constantly, until smooth. Remove from heat; stir in 1/4 cup margarine until melted. Serve sauce hot over cake.

Jaralee Wettstein, Unitah H.S.
Vernal, Utah

SPECIAL OCCASION BAKED ALASKA

4 egg whites
Pinch of salt
1/2 c. sugar
4 slices pound cake
4 scoops ice cream
Strawberries

Beat egg whites and salt in medium bowl until soft peaks form. Add sugar gradually, beating until stiff. Place cake slices on cookie sheet. Place 1 scoop ice cream on each slice. Spread meringue over ice cream and cake, covering each completely. Bake at 450 degrees for 4 minutes or until lightly browned. Remove from cookie sheet with spatula. Top with strawberries. Serve immediately.

Sherry Pattison, Epping H.S.
Epping, New Hampshire

BETTY CRACKER CAKE

6 egg whites
3/4 tsp. cream of tartar
2 c. sugar
1 c. chopped nuts
2 c. crushed saltine crackers
1 1-lb. can pie filling
Whipped topping

Beat egg whites and cream of tartar in bowl until soft peaks form. Add sugar gradually, beating until stiff. Fold in nuts and crackers. Place in greased cake pan. Bake at 350 degrees for 30 minutes. Cool. Top with pie filling. Spread whipped topping on top. Refrigerate until serving time.

Bonnie C. Rink, St. Stephens H.S.
Hickory, North Carolina

BLUEBERRY PIZZA

1 pkg. white cake mix
1 1/4 c. quick-cooking rolled oats
1/2 c. butter, softened
1 egg
1/2 c. chopped nuts
1/4 c. (firmly packed) brown sugar
1/2 tsp. cinnamon
1 21-oz. can blueberry pie filling

Combine cake mix, 1 cup oats and 6 tablespoons butter in large bowl. Beat at low speed of electric mixer until crumbly. Reserve 1 cup crumbs for topping. Blend remaining crumb mixture with egg. Press into greased 12-inch pizza pan. Bake at 350 degrees for 12 minutes. Combine reserved crumb mixture, 1/4 cup oats, 2 tablespoons butter, nuts, brown sugar and cinnamon; mix well. Spread crust with pie filling. Sprinkle with crumb mixture. Bake at 350 degrees for 15 to 20 minutes or until crumbs are golden. Cool completely. Cut in wedges.

Cynthia Kolberg, Fairfield Jr.-Sr. H.S.
Goshen, Indiana

BLUEBERRY DELIGHT

2 sticks margarine, melted
2 c. flour
1 c. chopped pecans
1 8-oz. package cream cheese, softened
1 lg. carton Cool Whip
1/2 box confectioners' sugar
1 c. sugar
3 tbsp. cornstarch
1 tbsp. lemon juice
2 c. blueberries

Place first 3 ingredients in bowl; mix well. Pat into 13 x 9-inch baking pan. Bake at 350 degrees for 30 minutes. Cool. Blend cream cheese, Cool Whip and confectioners' sugar in bowl. Spread over baked crust. Combine sugar, cornstarch and lemon juice with 1 cup water in saucepan. Bring to a boil. Cook until clear. Add blueberries. Spread over top of cream cheese mixture.

Terry J. Rakes, Elmwood Jr. H.S.
Rogers, Arkansas

BROKEN GLASS CAKE

1 3-oz. package each orange, cherry,
* lemon and lime gelatins*
1 c. pineapple juice
1/4 c. sugar
1 1/2 c. graham cracker crumbs
1/3 c. butter, melted
2 c. whipping cream, whipped

Place orange, cherry and lime gelatins in separate bowls. Dissolve each in 1 cup boiling water. Add 1/2 cup cold water; mix well. Pour each flavor into separate 8-inch square pans. Chill until firm. Heat pineapple juice and sugar in saucepan until sugar is dissolved. Remove from heat. Dissolve lemon gelatin in hot pineapple juice. Add 1/2 cup cold water. Chill until partially congealed; set aside. Mix graham cracker crumbs and butter until crumbly. Press into 9-inch springform pan. Cut gelatins into 1/2-inch cubes. Fold lemon gelatin into whipped cream. Fold in gelatin cubes. Pour into crumb-lined pan. Chill for 6 hours. Remove from pan before serving. Yield: 12 servings.

Sister Anne Kavanagh, Pius X H.S.
Downey, California

SUPER CHEESECAKE

1 c. graham cracker crumbs
Sugar
2 tbsp. melted butter
32 oz. cream cheese

4 eggs
1 tsp. vanilla extract
1 pt. sour cream
1 can pie filling

Combine crumbs, 2 tablespoons sugar and butter in small bowl; mix well. Press into 10-inch tube pan. Combine cream cheese, 1 cup sugar, eggs and vanilla in bowl; beat well. Pour over graham cracker crumbs. Bake at 350 degrees for 50 minutes. Remove from oven. Mix sour cream and 1/2 cup sugar. Spread over cheesecake. Return to oven. Bake for 5 minutes longer. Cool. Remove from pan. Cover with pie filling. Refrigerate overnight. May substitute fresh fruit for pie filling. Yield: 16 servings.

Martha R. Phillips, Kennett H.S.
Conway, New Hampshire

CHERRY TORTE

2 c. flour
Salt
3 eggs, separated
1 21-oz. can cherry pie filling
1 tsp. vanilla extract
1/4 tsp. cream of tartar
3/4 c. sugar

Sift flour and 1 teaspoon salt together in bowl. Add egg yolks; mix well. Press into bottom of 9 x 13-inch pan. Bake at 425 degrees for 20 minutes. Spread pie filling over crust. Beat egg whites, vanilla, cream of tartar and pinch of salt in bowl until soft peaks form. Add sugar gradually, beating until stiff. Spread over pie filling. Bake at 350 degrees for 20 minutes.

Lois Paguette, Chippewa Falls H.S.
Chippewa Falls, Wisconsin

OREO-ICE CREAM DESSERT

1 lg. package Oreos, crushed
1 stick margarine, melted
1/2 gal. vanilla ice cream, softened
1 can chocolate syrup
1 lg. container Cool Whip
1 2-oz. package slivered almonds

Combine Oreo crumbs and margarine; mix well. Reserve 1/2 cup mixture. Press in greased 13 x 9-inch pan. Spread ice cream over crust. Drizzle with chocolate syrup. Spread Cool Whip over top. Sprinkle with reserved crumbs. Garnish with almonds. Freeze for at least 12 hours before serving.

Jo Frances Bice, William Pitcher Jr. H.S.
Covington, Louisiana

CHERRIES IN THE SNOW

1 c. flour
1/2 c. butter, softened
1/4 c. (firmly packed) brown sugar
1/2 c. chopped nuts
1   8-oz. package cream cheese, softened
2 c. confectioners' sugar
2 tsp. vanilla extract
1/2 pt. whipping cream, whipped
1 can cherry pie filling

Combine flour, butter, brown sugar and nuts in bowl; mix well. Spread in 8-inch square pan. Bake at 375 degrees for 15 minutes. Cool. Crumble into 9 x 13-inch serving dish. Blend cream cheese, confectioners' sugar and vanilla together in large bowl. Fold whipped cream into cheese mixture. Spoon over crust. Top with pie filling. Freeze overnight. Yield: 12 servings.

Judy Cammelot, Johnsburg H.S.
McHenry, Illinois

GRASSHOPPER CHEESECAKE

1 1/2 c. chocolate cookie crumbs
Sugar
2 tbsp. butter, melted
2   8-oz. packages cream cheese
3 eggs
1/4 c. green Creme de Menthe
2 tbsp. white Creme de Cacao
4 oz. sweet cooking chocolate
1/2 c. sour cream

Mix cookie crumbs, 1 tablespoon sugar and butter in bowl. Press into bottom and 1 1/2 inches up sides of 8-inch springform pan. Blend the cream cheese in bowl with 1 cup sugar. Add eggs; beat until smooth. Stir in liqueurs. Pour into prepared crust. Bake in preheated 350-degree oven for 40 to 45 minutes. Cool in pan. Melt chocolate in saucepan; cool 5 minutes. Stir in sour cream. Spread over slightly cooled cheesecake. Refrigerate until set. Remove from springform pan; slice and serve.

Sheila D. Walker, Ygnacio Valley H.S.
Concord, California

CHOCOLATE-MINT DESSERT

10 oz. Oreo cookies, crushed
3/4 c. margarine, melted
4 oz. German's sweet chocolate
2/3 c. sugar
1/8 tsp. salt
2/3 c. evaporated milk
1 tsp. vanilla extract
1/2 gal. chocolate chip-mint ice cream,
softened

Reserve 2/3 cup crushed Oreos. Mix remaining crushed Oreos with 1/4 cup melted margarine in bowl. Press in 9 x 13-inch baking pan. Chill. Melt chocolate in heavy saucepan. Add 1/2 cup margarine, sugar, salt and evaporated milk. Boil for 4 minutes, stirring constantly. Add vanilla; cool. Spread over crust. Chill in freezer until set. Spread ice cream over chocolate layer. Sprinkle reserved Oreos over top. Freeze in covered container until firm.

Mrs. Nicolette Gabrysiak, Warren Township H.S.
Gurnee, Illinois

CHOCOLATE-PEPPERMINT FREEZER DESSERT

3/4 c. butter
2 c. vanilla wafer crumbs
1 1/2 c. confectioners' sugar
3 eggs, slightly beaten
3 sq. sweetened chocolate, melted
1 1/2 c. whipping cream
3 tbsp. sugar
8 oz. miniature marshmallows
1/2 c. crushed hard peppermint candy

Melt 1/4 cup butter in saucepan. Add vanilla wafer crumbs; mix well. Press into 7 x 11-inch cake pan. Cream 1/2 cup butter and confectioners' sugar in bowl. Add eggs and chocolate. Beat until light and fluffy. Pour over crust. Chill in refrigerator until set. Beat whipping cream until soft peaks form, adding sugar gradually. Combine marshmallows and sweetened whipped cream in bowl; pour over chocolate mixture. Sprinkle crushed peppermint candy over top. Freeze until serving time. Yield: 12-15 servings.

Virginia E. Grafe, Bertrand Community School
Bertrand, Nebraska
Avis Crawford, Liberty Jr. H.S.
Hutchinson, Kansas

FUDGE MELTAWAYS

1 1/2 c. butter
5 oz. unsweetened chocolate
1/2 c. sugar
4 tsp. vanilla extract
2 eggs, beaten
4 c. graham cracker crumbs
2 c. coconut
1 c. chopped walnuts

2 tbsp. milk
4 c. confectioners' sugar

Melt 1 cup butter and 2 ounces chocolate in saucepan. Blend sugar, 2 teaspoons vanilla, eggs, graham cracker crumbs, coconut and walnuts into butter-chocolate mixture; mix thoroughly. Press into 11 x 7 x 2-inch serving dish. Refrigerate. Cream 1/2 cup butter, milk, confectioners' sugar and 2 teaspoons vanilla. Spread mixture over butter-chocolate layer. Chill in refrigerator. Melt 3 ounces chocolate. Pour over chilled mixture; spread evenly to edges. Cut into squares before completely firm. Keep refrigerated. Yield: 6-8 dozen.

Joanne L. Wulff, Washburn H.S.
Washburn, Wisconsin

MARBLED ICE CREAM DESSERT

    1 14-oz. can evaporated milk
    1 10-oz. package miniature marshmallows
    1 6-oz. package chocolate chips
    1 can coconut
    1/2 c. margarine
    2 c. graham cracker crumbs
    1/2 gal. square vanilla ice cream
    1 c. chopped nuts

Combine evaporated milk, marshmallows and chocolate chips in top of double boiler. Heat over boiling water until melted. Set aside to cool thoroughly. Brown coconut in margarine in heavy skillet. Remove from heat. Stir in graham cracker crumbs. Press 3/4 of the crumb mixture into 9 x 13-inch pan. Cut ice cream into slices approximately 1/2 inch thick. Place on crust. Pour 1/2 of the cooled sauce over ice cream. Add second layer ice cream. Pour on remaining sauce. Mix remaining 1/4 of the crumb mixture with nuts. Sprinkle over top of dessert. Freeze. Cut into squares.

Carol Tevebaugh, Hallsville H.S.
Hallsville, Texas

CHRISTMAS PEPPERMINT DESSERT

    1 10 1/2-oz. package miniature
       marshmallows
    1/4 c. chopped pecans
    1 c. crushed red and white-striped
       peppermint candy
    1 1/4 c. whipping cream, whipped
    1 1/2 c. Nabisco chocolate wafer crumbs
    1 sm. jar maraschino cherries

Fold marshmallows, pecans and candy into whipped cream. Refrigerate for 2 hours or longer. Form into 12 balls. Roll in cookie crumbs. Top with cherries. Yield: 12 servings.

Carolyn Freeman, Alta H.S.
Sandy, Utah

CRANBERRY-APPLE CRUNCH

    2 c. cranberries
    3 c. peeled sliced apples
    3/4 c. sugar
    1/2 c. butter
    1 c. quick-cooking oats
    1/2 c. flour
    1/2 c. (firmly packed) brown sugar
    1/2 c. chopped nuts

Combine cranberries, apples and sugar in 2-quart casserole. Melt butter in saucepan. Stir in remaining ingredients; blend well. Spread over fruit mixture. Bake at 350 degrees for 1 hour. Serve hot or cold with ice cream.

Marsha McMahon, Newburyport H.S.
Newburyport, Massachusetts

CRANBERRY CASSEROLE

    3 c. unpeeled chopped apples
    1 can whole cranberry sauce
    1 1/2 c. quick-cooking oatmeal
    1/2 c. (firmly packed) brown sugar
    1/3 c. flour
    1/3 c. chopped pecans (opt.)
    1/2 c. margarine, melted

Place apples and cranberries in 2-quart casserole. Combine remaining ingredients in bowl; mix well. Spread over fruit. Bake at 350 degrees for 1 hour.

Frances H. Campbell, Alexander Central H.S.
Taylorsville, North Carolina

CRANBERRY FLUFF

    2 c. fresh cranberries, ground
    3 c. miniature marshmallows
    3/4 c. sugar
    2 c. unpared diced, tart apples
    1/2 c. seedless green grapes
    1/2 c. walnuts
    1/4 tsp. salt
    1 c. whipping cream, whipped

Combine cranberries, marshmallows and sugar; cover. Chill overnight. Add apples, grapes, walnuts and salt. Fold in whipped cream. Chill. Turn into serving bowl. Garnish with cluster of green grapes, if desired. Yield: 8-10 servings.

Carolyn Cotton, Bristow H.S.
Bristow, Oklahoma

CURRIED FRUIT

1 can pineapple chunks, drained
1 can peaches, drained
1 can pears, drained
1 can cherries, drained
2 to 4 tsp. curry powder
1 c. (firmly packed) brown sugar
3/4 stick margarine

Drain fruits overnight. Place in casserole. Combine curry powder with brown sugar. Sprinkle over fruit. Dot with margarine. Bake at 350 degrees for 35 minutes. May add mandarin oranges or fresh fruits in season. Yield: 12 servings.

Mrs. Eloise Scott, Mooreville H.S.
Mooreville, Mississippi

FROZEN FRUIT COCKTAIL

1 c. sugar
1 med. can crushed pineapple
1 can grapefruit sections
Juice of 1 lemon
1 drop of green food coloring
Essence of peppermint to taste
7-Up

Boil sugar and 2 cups water for 5 minutes in saucepan. Cool. Add pineapple, grapefruit and lemon juice; mix well. Add food coloring and essence of peppermint; mix well. Freeze until mushy. Spoon into glasses. Fill glasses with 7-Up. Yield: 12 to 14 servings.

Eunice Pixton, Hillcrest H.S.
Midvale, Utah

FRUIT PIZZA

1 box Nestle's sugar cookie mix
16 oz. cream cheese, softened
3/4 c. sugar
1 tsp. lemon juice
Peaches, strawberries, bananas, drained
3 oz. apricot preserves
2 tbsp. fruit juice

Prepare cookie dough according to package directions. Pat into 12-inch pizza pan, forming rim. Bake according to package directions. Cool. Combine cream cheese, sugar and lemon juice in bowl; mix well. Spread on crust. Arrange fruit over top. Mix apricot preserves with fruit juice. Drizzle over fruit. Refrigerate until serving time. Yield: 8-10 servings.

Jane Tadelski, Apollo Middle School
Burlington, Iowa

GELATIN DELIGHT

2 pkg. red gelatin
3 eggs, beaten
2 sticks margarine, melted
2 c. sugar
1 c. chopped pecans
1 lg. can crushed pineapple, drained
1 box graham crackers
20 pecan halves

Prepare gelatin according to package directions. Chill until partially set. Beat eggs well in bowl; add margarine gradually. Add sugar, pecans and pineapple; mix well. Line broiler pan with whole graham crackers. Add 1/2 of the egg mixture. Top with graham crackers. Add remaining egg mixture. Pour gelatin mixture over top. Garnish with pecan halves. Chill for several hours. Cut into squares. Yield: 20 servings.

Mrs. Frances Tharpe, North Wilkes H.S.
Hays, North Carolina

GRASSHOPPER DESSERT

2 c. finely crushed chocolate cookies
1/2 c. margarine, melted
1 env. unflavored gelatin
1/2 c. sugar
1/2 c. frozen limeade, thawed
4 eggs, separated
1 8-oz. package butter mints, finely crushed
1/4 c. green Creme de Menthe (opt.)
Green food coloring (opt.)
1/2 c. whipping cream, whipped

Combine cookie crumbs and margarine. Press firmly into 11 3/4 x 7 1/4-inch baking dish, reserving 1/4 cup crumbs for top. Chill until set. Combine gelatin and 1/4 cup sugar in saucepan. Stir in limeade and 1/4 cup water. Cook over low heat until hot and gelatin is dissolved, stirring constantly. Beat egg yolks. Stir a small amount hot mixture into egg yolks. Stir egg yolks into hot mixture. Add crushed mints; mix well. Cook until slightly thickened, stirring constantly. Remove from heat. Stir in Creme de Menthe and food coloring. Cover. Cool until thickened. Beat egg whites until soft peaks form. Add 1/4 cup sugar gradually, beating until stiff. Fold egg whites and whipped cream into gelatin mixture. Spoon into crust. Sprinkle with reserved curmbs. Refrigerate for 4 hours or overnight. Cut into squares. Yield: 8-10 servings.

Beth Hilty, Jonathan Adler H.S.
Plain City, Ohio

EASY HOLIDAY TRIFLE

1 angel food cake
1/4 c. rum (opt.)
2   10-oz. packages sweetened, frozen
    strawberries, thawed
2   4-oz. packages French vanilla
    instant pudding mix
2   9-oz. cartons Cool Whip
1   10-oz. package sweetened frozen
    raspberries, thawed

Slice angel food cake into 3 layers. Sprinkle each layer with rum. Pour a small amount of strawberry juice in bottom of bowl large enough for cake layer and at least 10 inches deep. Place layer of cake in bowl; cover with 1 package thawed strawberries and juice. Prepare pudding using package directions. Let set for 5 minutes. Spoon 1/3 of the pudding over strawberry layer. Spread 1/3 of Cool Whip over pudding. Add cake layer. Continue layering until all ingredients are used placing raspberries in middle layer and strawberries in top layer. Garnish with fresh mint leaves. Yield: 12 servings.

Mary Ellen Kile, Ocean View H.S.
Huntington Beach, California

JIFFY HOLIDAY TORTE

Graham crackers
2 pkg. instant vanilla pudding mix
French vanilla extract to taste
1 pt. whipping cream, whipped
2 cans cherry pie filling

Place graham crackers in 9 x 13-inch serving dish. Prepare vanilla pudding according to package directions. Add vanilla to taste. Fold whipped cream into vanilla pudding. Spread half the pudding mixture over graham crackers. Place layer of graham crackers over pudding layer. Cover with remaining pudding mixture. Spread pie filling over top. Refrigerate for 24 hours.

Sharon J. Nelsen, Cameron H.S.
Cameron, Wisconsin

HOLIDAY DELIGHT

2 pkg. lime Jell-O
1/2 pt. whipping cream, whipped
1 sm. can crushed pineapple, drained
1 sm. jar maraschino cherries, sliced
1 c. miniature marshmallows

Prepare Jell-O in large bowl according to package directions. Place in large bowl of ice. Beat with hand mixer until fluffy and firm. Fold in whipped cream. Combine pineapple, cherries and marshmallows with Jell-O. Pour into lightly greased dish or mold. Refrigerate overnight. Yield: 10-12 servings.

Mrs. Dorothy W. Reese, C.L. Harper H.S.
Atlanta, Georgia

HOLIDAY DESSERT PUDDING

6 eggs, separated
1 c. milk
1 c. sugar
2 1/2 env. unflavored gelatin
3 c. crushed coconut macaroon cookies
1 c. Sherry
1 c. whipping cream, whipped
Maraschino cherries

Beat egg yolks in top of double boiler. Add milk and 1/2 cup sugar; mix well. Cook over boiling water, stirring constantly, until thickened. Soften gelatin in 1/2 cup cold water. Add to custard; mix well. Cool. Combine cookie crumbs with Sherry. Stir cookie mixture into cooled custard. Beat egg whites until soft peaks form. Add remaining 1/2 cup sugar gradually, beating until stiff. Fold egg whites into custard mixture. Fold in whipped cream. Pour into 12 individual molds. Chill until firm. Unmold onto serving dishes. Garnish with whipped cream and cherries.

Eloise Scott, Mooreville H.S.
Mooreville, Mississippi

CINNAMON-NOODLE PUDDING

3/4 lb. wide noodles
1 stick margarine
1 lb. cottage cheese
2 tbsp. (heaping) sour cream
1 1/4 c. milk
3/4 c. sugar
2 sm. packages Jell-O egg custard mix
3 eggs
1 tsp. vanilla extract
1 c. white raisins

Boil noodles using package directions; drain. Combine noodles and margarine in bowl; mix well. Combine remaining ingredients except cinnamon in large bowl; mix well. Stir noodles into mixture. Pour into greased baking dish. Sprinkle with cinnamon. Bake at 350 degrees for 1 hour and 30 minutes. May serve hot or cold.

Miriam Graff, McCleary Jr. H.S.
East Meadow, New York

STEAMED APPLE PUDDING

1/2 c. butter, softened
1 c. sugar
2 eggs
2 3/4 c. flour
1 tsp. each cinnamon, nutmeg
1 tbsp. baking powder
1/4 tsp. each ground cloves, salt
1/2 c. milk
1 1/2 c. peeled chopped apples
1/2 c. chopped pecans
1 recipe Hot Buttered Rum Sauce

Cream butter in large mixing bowl. Add sugar gradually, beating until light and fluffy. Add eggs, one at a time, beating well after each addition. Sift dry ingredients together. Add to creamed mixture alternately with milk. Stir in apples and pecans; mix well. Pour into buttered 10-cup mold. Cover tightly with aluminum foil. Place on rack in heavy deep kettle. Add water to 1/2 depth of mold. Bring to a boil; cover. Reduce heat; simmer for 3 hours. Let stand for 10 minutes before unmolding. Serve with Hot Buttered Rum Sauce. May be frozen and reheated in foil at 325 degrees for 45 minutes. Yield: 12-16 servings.

Photograph for this recipe on page 4.

ORANGE CUSTARD FONDUE

1 3-oz. package no-bake custard mix
1 4 1/2-oz. carton frozen whipped
   topping, thawed
2 tbsp. orange liqueur
1 tsp. grated orange rind

Prepare custard according to package directions, omitting egg yolk. Cover surface with clear plastic wrap; cool. Chill for 2 hours or until thickened. Beat custard until smooth. Fold in dessert topping and liqueur. Top with orange rind; chill. Serve as dip for fresh fruit and cake cubes. Yield: 3 1/2 cups.

Mrs. Pamela M. Renaker, Grant Community H.S.
Fox Lake, Illinois

PEACH CREAM FREEZE

1 lg. can peach pie filling
1 15-oz. can sweetened condensed milk
1 8 3/4-oz. can crushed pineapple,
   drained
1/4 c. lemon juice

1/4 tsp. almond extract
1/2 c. whipping cream, whipped

Combine first 5 ingredients in large bowl; mix well. Fold whipped cream into peach mixture. Pour into 9 x 5 x 3-inch loaf pan. Freeze. Unmold. Slice. Top each serving with additional whipped cream and chopped nuts or cherry.

Cindy Gedling, Sidney Phillips Middle School
Mobile, Alabama

PECAN PUDDING

3 eggs, beaten
1 1/2 c. milk
1 c. sugar
1 pkg. unflavored gelatin
1 c. chopped pecans
1 c. whipping cream, whipped
1 tsp. vanilla extract

Combine eggs, milk and sugar in saucepan. Bring to boil over medium heat, stirring constantly. Cook until mixture begins to thicken. Remove from heat. Soften gelatin in 1/4 cup cold water. Add to egg mixture; mix until dissolved. Stir in pecans. Cool. Fold in whipped cream and vanilla. Refrigerate until serving time.

Connie Schlimgen, Washington Sr. H.S.
Sioux Falls, South Dakota

ORANGE-PUMPKIN POTS DE CREME

4 eggs
3/4 c. skim milk
3/4 c. Florida orange juice
1 c. canned pumpkin
1/3 c. sugar
1/2 tsp. each salt, cinnamon
Pinch of ginger

Combine all ingredients in large bowl; mix well. Spoon into eight 6-ounce custard cups. Place in pan filled with 1 inch hot water. Bake at 350 degrees for 25 to 30 minutes or until knife inserted in center comes out clean. Cool. Sprinkle with nutmeg. Yield: 8 servings/100 calories per serving.

Photograph for this recipe on page 8.

ORANGE-PUMPKIN CHIFFON

8 whole oranges
1 env. unflavored gelatin
1/2 c. (firmly packed) dark brown sugar

1/2 tsp. each salt, nutmeg and cinnamon
1/4 tsp. ginger
2 eggs, separated
2/3 c. Florida orange juice
1 c. canned pumpkin
1 tsp. grated orange rind

Cut top from each orange. Scoop out pulp with spoon. Cut picot edge with zig-zag cut with scissors. Set aside. Mix gelatin, 1/4 cup brown sugar, salt, nutmeg, cinnamon and ginger in medium saucepan. Beat egg yolks and 1 cup water; stir into gelatin mixture. Cook over low heat for 5 minutes, stirring constantly, until gelatin dissolves and mixture thickens slightly. Remove from heat. Stir in orange juice, pumpkin and orange rind. Chill, stirring occasionally, until partially set. Beat egg whites until soft peaks form. Add remaining 1/4 cup brown sugar gradually, beating until stiff peaks form. Fold into pumpkin mixture. Turn into prepared orange shells. Chill until set. Garnish with a small amount of whipped topping if desired. Yield: 8 servings/100 calories per serving.

Photograph for this recipe on page 8.

RAINBOW CAKE

1 lg. angel food cake
1 pkg. each strawberry, lime and orange
    Jell-O
1 pkg. frozen strawberries, slightly
    thawed
1/2 gal. vanilla ice cream, softened
1 can blueberries, washed and drained
1 can mandarin oranges, drained

Break cake into 1-inch pieces. Divide equally into 3 large bowls. Add 1 package dry Jell-O to each bowl. Mix well to coat cubes. Arrange layers in angel food cake pan as follows: strawberry-flavored cake cubes, strawberries, 1/3 of the ice cream; lime-flavored cake cubes, blueberries, 1/3 of the ice cream; orange-flavored cake cubes, remaining ice cream, mandarin oranges. Cover with foil. Freeze. Unmold; slice. Serve frozen. Yield: 20 servings.

Nancy A. Marrow, Salisbury H.S.
Salisbury, North Carolina

SOUR CREAM-RAISIN TARTS

1 recipe 2-crust pie pastry
1 c. sugar
2 eggs

1 c. sour cream
1 1/2 c. raisins
3/4 tsp. cinnamon
1/4 tsp. salt

Line tart pans with pie pastry. Mix together sugar and eggs in bowl. Add sour cream, raisins, cinnamon and salt; mix well. Fill each tart shell within 1/8 inch of top with raisin mixture. Bake at 400 degrees for 5 minutes. Reduce temperature to 325 degrees. Bake for 15 to 20 minutes longer.

Vi Raddatz, Port Townsend H.S.
Port Townsend, Washington

ANGEL RHUBARB DESSERT

1 c. margarine
Flour
3 tbsp. confectioners' sugar
3 c. chopped rhubarb
3 eggs, separated
1 3/4 c. sugar
1/2 c. evaporated milk
Dash of salt
1/2 tsp. vanilla extract
3/4 c. coconut (opt.)

Combine margarine, 2 cups flour and confectioners' sugar in bowl; mix well. Pat into 9 x 13-inch baking pan. Bake at 350 degrees for 10 minutes. Mix rhubarb, egg yolks, 1 1/4 cups sugar, 6 tablespoons flour, evaporated milk and salt in bowl; spread over crust. Bake at 350 degrees for 45 to 60 minutes. Beat egg whites in bowl until soft peaks form. Add vanilla and 1/2 cup sugar gradually, beating until stiff. Spread over baked mixture; sprinkle with coconut. Bake at 375 degrees for 10 minutes.

Diane L. Stelten-Dane, Blair Public Schools
Blair, Wisconsin

STRAWBERRY-ANGEL FOOD DESSERT

2 lg. packages strawberry Jell-O
2 10-oz. packages frozen strawberries,
    thawed
1 angel food cake, broken into small
    pieces

Mix Jell-O with 5 cups hot water; stir until dissolved. Add strawberries; mix well. Chill until partially congealed. Fold cake pieces into Jell-O mixture. Pour into angel food cake pan. Refrigerate overnight. Unmold before serving.

Rosa Sparling, Southwood H.S.
Wabash, Indiana

STRAWBERRY CLOUD TORTE

20 to 24 chocolate chip cookies
1 pt. whipping cream
1/4 c. confectioners' sugar
2 tsp. strawberry extract
2 drops of red food coloring
1/2 c. strawberry preserves

Place 8 cookies in 9-inch springform pan. Crumble 2 cookies; fill empty spaces. Beat whipping cream, sugar, strawberry extract and food coloring in bowl. Whip until stiff. Spread half the cream mixture evenly over cookies. Repeat layers, alternating cookies and cream mixture until all ingredients are used. Refrigerate overnight. Remove from pan; cut into serving pieces. Melt preserves in saucepan over low temperature. Drizzle 2 teaspoonfuls over each serving. Yield: 20 servings.

M. V. "Lynne" Fielding, Jordan H.S.
Long Beach, California

STRAWBERRY STRATA SURPRISE

1 box strawberry cake mix
2 8-oz. packages cream cheese, softened
2 c. confectioners' sugar
2 pkg. Dream Whip
2 10-oz. packages frozen strawberries, thawed
2 pkg. strawberry junket

Prepare cake mix according to package directions, using 13 1/2 x 8 1/2-inch baking pans. Cool cake layers. Blend cream cheese and confectioners' sugar in bowl until smooth; mix well. Prepare Dream Whip according to package directions. Add to cream cheese mixture. Spread mixture over each cake layer. Thaw and drain frozen strawberries, reserving liquid. Prepare junket according to package directions, using strawberry juice as part of liquid. Mix strawberries into junket. Spread on top of Dream Whip layer. Refrigerate until serving time. Cut into squares. Yield: 40 to 48 servings.

Shirley Hendricks, Clarks H.S.
Clarks, Nebraska

TUNNEL OF STRAWBERRY CAKE

1 pkg. Butter Cake Mix
1/4 c. sugar
1 qt. fresh sliced strawberries
1 carton sour cream
2 9-oz. cartons Cool Whip
Red food coloring

Prepare cake mix according to package directions. Bake in tube pan. Cool. Sprinkle sugar over strawberries. Allow to stand 10 minutes. Cut cake into 2 layers. Scoop out center of each layer leaving 1/2-inch thick shells. Place cake pieces in large bowl. Add strawberries to cake pieces. Stir in sour cream, 1 carton Cool Whip and a few drops of food coloring; mix well. Fill tunnels in cake layers with strawberry mixture. Reassemble cake on serving dish. Cover with plastic wrap. Refrigerate several hours or overnight. Frost cake with Cool Whip. Garnish with whole strawberries. May substitute one 10-ounce package frozen strawberries for 1 quart of fresh berries.

Dana Horn, Kirby H.S.
Kirby, Arizona

APPLE FRUITCAKE

1/2 c. butter, softened
1 c. (firmly packed) light brown sugar
1 egg
1 tsp. vanilla extract
1 3/4 c. flour
1 tsp. baking powder
1/2 tsp. each soda, cinnamon, nutmeg and salt
1/4 c. milk
1 1/2 c. peeled chopped apples
1 c. raisins
1 c. mixed candied fruit
1 c. chopped nuts

Cream butter in large bowl. Add brown sugar gradually, beating until light and fluffy. Add egg and vanilla; mix well. Sift dry ingredients together. Add to creamed mixture alternately with milk, beginning and ending with dry ingredients. Fold in apples, raisins, candied fruit and nuts. Spread evenly in waxed paper-lined 9 x 5 x 3-inch loaf pan. Bake at 275 degrees for 2 hours and 30 minutes to 3 hours or until cake tests done. Cool in pan. Remove paper. Wrap well before storing in cool place.

Photograph for this recipe on page 4.

GERMAN APPLE CAKE

5 apples, peeled, thinly sliced
Sugar
2 tsp. cinnamon
3 c. flour
1/2 tsp. salt
4 eggs
1 c. oil
1/3 c. orange juice
1 1/2 tsp. soda

1 1/2 tsp. baking powder
3 1/2 tsp. vanilla extract
1 1/2 c. confectioners' sugar
2 tbsp. butter, softened

Combine apples, 5 tablespoons sugar and cinnamon in bowl. Set aside. Combine next 7 ingredients with 2 teaspoons vanilla and 2 1/2 cups sugar in large mixer bowl. Beat at low spead of electric mixer for 1 minute or until blended, scraping side of bowl. Beat at medium speed for 3 minutes. Pour 1/3 of the batter into greased and floured tube pan. Spread with 1/2 of the apple mixture. Repeat layers ending with batter. Bake at 350 degrees for 1 hour and 15 minutes to 1 hour and 30 minutes. Cool on rack for 10 minutes. Remove from pan. Cool thoroughly. Combine confectioners' sugar with butter and 1 1/2 teaspoons vanilla in bowl. Beat until smooth, adding 1 to 2 tablespoons water until of glaze consistency. Drizzle glaze over cooled cake.

Joyce Mann, Harmony Grove School
Camden, Arkansas

FRESH APPLE CAKE

1/2 c. butter, softened
2 c. sugar
2 eggs
2 c. sifted flour
1 tsp. baking powder
3/4 tsp. soda
1/2 tsp. each salt, nutmeg and cinnamon
3 c. peeled chopped apples
1 1/2 c. chopped nuts
Hot Buttered Rum Sauce

Cream butter in mixing bowl. Add sugar gradually, beating until light and fluffy. Add eggs, one at a time, beating well after each addition. Sift dry ingredients together. Add gradually to creamed mixture. Stir in apples and nuts; mix well. Spoon into greased 13 x 9 x 2-inch pan. Bake at 325 degrees for 45 to 50 minutes. Serve with Hot Buttered Rum Sauce. Yield: 12 servings.

Hot Buttered Rum Sauce

1 c. sugar
1/2 c. butter
1/2 c. light cream
1 tsp. rum extract

Combine sugar, butter and cream in saucepan; mix well. Heat over low heat, stirring occasionally, until hot. Stir in rum flavoring. Yield: 1 3/4 cups.

Photograph for this recipe on page 4.

CHANUKAH ORANGE-CARROT CAKE

Margarine
2 c. sugar
Orange rind, grated
1 tsp. cinnamon
1/2 tsp. nutmeg
1 c. cholesterol-free egg substitute
1 1/2 c. grated carrots
2/3 c. finely chopped walnuts
3 c. sifted all-purpose flour
3 tsp. baking powder
1/2 tsp. salt
1/2 c. Florida orange juice
1 1/2 c. sifted confectioners' sugar
Chopped walnuts

Cream 1 cup margarine and sugar in large bowl. Stir in 1 tablespoon orange rind, cinnamon and nutmeg; mixing well. Beat in egg substitute gradually. Stir in carrots and walnuts. Sift together dry ingredients. Add to creamed mixture alternately with 1/3 cup orange juice. Pour into greased 10-inch tube pan. Bake at 350 degrees for 50 to 60 minutes or until cake tests done. Cool in pan for 15 minutes. Remove from pan; cool completely. Beat confectioners' sugar with 1 tablespoon margarine, 1/2 teaspoon orange rind and 2 to 3 tablespoons remaining juice in small bowl to make thin glaze. Pour over cake. Sprinkle with walnuts. Yield: 12 servings.

Photograph for this recipe above.

AMARETTO-RAISIN BUNDT CAKE

1 pkg. pound cake supreme bundt cake mix
Margarine, softened
Amaretto
3 eggs
1 1/2 c. sour cream
2 c. candied fruit
1 1/2 c. raisins
1 c. chopped nuts
Confectioners' sugar
1 1/2 c. sugar
4 tbsp. cornstarch
2 tbsp. lemon juice

Combine cake mix, 1/4 cup margarine, 1/3 cup Amaretto, 1/2 cup water, eggs and sour cream in large bowl. Blend until moistened. Beat for 2 minutes at medium speed of electric mixer. Fold in candied fruit, 1 cup raisins and nuts. Pour into greased 12-cup bundt pan. Bake at 325 degrees for 1 hour and 10 minutes or until cake tests done. Cool on rack for 25 minutes. Invert on plate; cool completely. Sprinkle with confectioners' sugar. Mix sugar and cornstarch in saucepan. Stir in 1 1/2 cups water gradually. Heat to boiling point; boil for 1 minute, stirring constantly. Remove from heat. Stir in 1/4 cup margarine, 2 tablespoons Amaretto, lemon juice and 1/2 cup raisins. Serve warm over cooled cake.

Rosemary Gasper, Shawnee Mission East H.S.
Shawnee Mission, Kansas

SOUR CREAM-COCONUT CAKE

1 pkg. deluxe yellow cake mix
2 c. sour cream
2 c. sugar
16 oz. fresh coconut
1 lg. carton Cool Whip

Bake cake using package directions. Cool. Split layers in half, with thread, to make 4 layers. Combine sour cream, sugar and coconut in bowl; mix well. Reserve 1 cup. Spread remaining mixture between cake layers. Mix Cool Whip with reserved mixture. Frost sides and top of cake. May garnish with crushed nuts and cherries if desired. Store in refrigerator.

Anne Holder, Glasgow H.S.
Glasgow, Kentucky

THEOLA'S OLD-FASHIONED FRUITCAKE

1 qt. pecan halves
1 lg. box seedless raisins
1 lb. candied fruitcake mix
1/2 c. cherries (opt.)
1 14-oz. package coconut
1 c. flour
2 c. self-rising flour
1 tsp. each cinnamon, nutmeg and allspice
1/2 lb. butter, softened
1 c. sugar
1 c. light corn syrup
5 eggs
1 c. orange juice

Combine first 5 ingredients in large bowl. Sift flour over top. Stir to coat; set aside. Sift self-rising flour with spices. Cream butter, sugar and corn syrup in separate bowl. Add dry ingredients gradually to creamed mixture, mixing well. Add eggs one at a time, beating well after each addition. Beat in orange juice. Add batter to fruit mixture; mix well. Pour into well-greased tube pan. Bake at 250 degrees for 3 to 4 hours.

Louise Preyer Richardson, Monroe County H.S.
Monroeville, Alabama

CHOCOLATE POUND CAKE

1/2 lb. butter, softened
1/2 c. shortening
3 c. sugar
5 eggs
3 c. flour
1/2 tsp. baking powder
1/2 tsp. salt
4 tbsp. cocoa
1 c. milk
1 tsp. vanilla extract

Cream butter and shortening in large bowl. Add sugar; blend until smooth. Add eggs one at a time, beating well after each addition. Sift dry ingredients together. Add to egg mixture alternately with milk, mixing well after each addition. Add vanilla. Pour into greased and floured tube pan. Bake at 350 degrees for 1 hour and 20 minutes. Cool. Remove from pan. Frost with Chocolate-Mocha Icing.

Chocolate-Mocha Icing

6 tbsp. cocoa
6 tbsp. cold coffee
6 tbsp. butter, softened
1 tsp. vanilla extract
3 c. (or more) confectioners' sugar

Combine cocoa and coffee; mix well. Blend in butter and vanilla. Beat until smooth. Add enough confectioners' sugar until creamy and of spreading consistency.

Mrs. Peggy White, Califf Middle Grades
Gray, Georgia

GRANNY'S SOUR CREAM POUND CAKE

    1 c. butter, softened
    2 3/4 c. sugar
    6 eggs
    3 c. sifted all-purpose flour
    1/2 tsp. salt
    1/2 tsp. each vanilla extract, almond
        extract
    1/4 tsp. soda
    1 c. sour cream

Cream butter in large bowl until fluffy. Add sugar; beat until light and fluffy. Add eggs one at a time, beating well after each addition. Sift flour and salt together 3 times. Add vanilla and almond extracts. Add soda to sour cream. Add dry ingredients alternately with sour cream, mixing well after each addition. Pour into greased and floured tube pan. Bake at 350 degrees for 1 hour and 20 minutes. Cool. Remove from pan.

Camille M. Yates, Lee Academy
Clarksdale, Mississippi

ITALIAN CREAM CAKE

    1/2 c. Crisco
    1 stick butter
    2 c. sugar
    5 eggs, separated
    2 c. flour
    1/2 tsp. salt
    1 tsp. soda
    1 c. buttermilk
    1 tsp. vanilla extract
    2 c. coconut
    1 c. chopped pecans

Cream Crisco, butter and sugar. Add egg yolks one at a time, beating well after each addition. Sift dry ingredients together. Add to creamed mixture alternately with buttermilk, beating well after each addition. Add vanilla. Stir in coconut and pecans. Fold in stiffly beaten egg whites. Pour into 3 greased and floured 9-inch cake pans. Bake at 350 degrees for 30 to 35 minutes or until cake tests done. Cool on racks.

Icing

    1 stick butter
    1 8-oz. package cream cheese
    1 lb. confectioners' sugar, sifted
    1 tsp. vanilla extract
    1 c. chopped pecans

Combine first 4 ingredients until smooth. Stir in pecans. Frost tops and sides of cake.

Barbara E. Smoot, Wapahani H.S.
Selma, Indiana

GERMAN RAISIN CAKE

    2 c. raisins, coarsely chopped
    1 c. finely cut citron
    1 1/2 c. currants
    2 1/2 c. sifted cake flour
    1 1/2 c. butter, softened
    1 1/4 c. sugar
    5 eggs
    1 tsp. grated lemon rind
    Vanilla extract
    3/4 tsp. baking powder
    Salt
    2 oz. unsweetened chocolate
    3 c. sifted confectioners' sugar

Combine raisins, citron and currants with 1/2 cup flour in bowl; mix until coated. Cream 1 1/4 cups butter until soft in bowl. Add sugar gradually, beating until mixture is fluffy. Add eggs one at a time, beating well after each addition. Blend in lemon rind and 1 tablespoon vanilla. Sift remaining 2 cups flour with baking powder and 1/4 teaspoon salt. Add to batter; beat for 1 minute. Fold in floured fruit. Turn into greased and floured 2-quart baking mold. Bake at 325 degrees for 1 hour and 30 minutes. Cool cake in pan for 10 minutes. Turn onto cake rack. Cool. Melt chocolate and 1/4 cup butter in saucepan; mix well. Add 1/4 cup boiling water, confectioners' sugar, 1/8 teaspoon salt and 1/2 teaspoon vanilla. Beat until smooth and thick. Frost cake. Yield: 12 servings.

Photograph for this recipe below.

CRANBERRY CAKE WITH BUTTER SAUCE

Butter
Sugar
Evaporated milk
2 eggs, beaten
Flour
2 tsp. soda
2 c. fresh cranberries
2 tsp. vanilla extract

Cream 3 tablespoons butter and 1 cup sugar together in bowl. Stir in 1/4 cup water, 1/2 cup evaporated milk and eggs; mix well. Combine 2 cups flour and soda. Add to egg mixture; beat well. Stir in cranberries. Place in greased 9 x 13-inch pan. Bake at 350 degrees for 25 minutes or until cake tests done. Combine 1 cup butter, 2 cups sugar, 2 tablespoons flour, 1 cup evaporated milk and vanilla in 1-quart saucepan; mix well. Bring to a boil. Boil for 2 minutes or until thick. Serve warm over cranberry cake.

Barbara Sanders, Oelwein H.S.
Oelwein, Iowa

GREEN VELVET CAKE

2 eggs, beaten
1 1/2 c. sugar
1 1/4 c. oil
1 tsp. vinegar
2 1/2 c. self-rising flour
1 tsp. soda
1 c. buttermilk
1 tsp. vanilla extract
Green food coloring

Combine eggs, sugar, oil and vinegar in bowl; mix well. Sift flour and soda together. Add to egg mixture alternately with buttermilk, beating well after each addition. Add vanilla and food coloring; mix well. Pour batter into 3 greased and floured 8-inch cake pans. Bake at 350 degrees for 25 minutes. Cool. Frost with white icing.

Karen Overstreet, Groves H.S.
Savannah, Georgia

LAURA'S GINGERBREAD

1 c. (firmly packed) brown sugar
1/2 c. oil
1 c. dark molasses
2 tsp. soda
3 c. flour
1 tsp. each ginger, cloves, allspice,
*   nutmeg and cinnamon*

1/2 tsp. salt
2 eggs, beaten

Combine brown sugar and oil in large bowl; blend well. Combine molasses, soda and 1 cup boiling water; mix well. Add brown sugar mixture; mix well. Sift dry ingredients together. Add to brown sugar mixture; mix well. Add eggs; mix well. Batter will be quite thin. Pour into greased baking pan. Bake at 375 degrees for 20 minutes. May add raisins, candied fruit, or dates if desired.

Cheryl Yates, Mountain View H.S.
Mesa, Arizona

POPPY SEED CAKE

1 pkg. white cake mix
1 sm. package instant vanilla pudding mix
1/4 c. poppy seed
5 eggs
1/2 c. oil
1 tsp. almond extract

Combine all ingredients with 1 cup water in large bowl. Beat with electric mixer for 5 minutes. Pour into 2 greased and floured loaf pans. Bake at 350 degrees for 40 to 50 minutes. Cool for 15 minutes. Remove from pan. May dust with confectioners' sugar if desired.

Leslie A. Nuttman, North Mason H.S.
Belfair, Washington

PRUNE CAKE

2 c. sugar
Butter
5 eggs
1 tsp. each baking powder, soda
2 tsp. cinnamon
1 tsp. allspice
Pinch of salt
2 c. sifted flour
1/2 c. prune juice
2 c. cooked, mashed prunes
1/2 c. sour milk

Cream 1 cup sugar and 3/4 cup butter in large bowl until smooth. Add 3 eggs one at a time, beating well after each addition. Set aside. Sift dry ingredients together 3 times. Add sifted ingredients to creamed mixture alternately with prune juice, beating well after each addition. Stir in 1 cup prunes. Pour into 2 greased and floured cake pans. Bake at 350 degrees for 25 to 30 minutes. Cool. Remove from pans. Beat 2 eggs in saucepan. Add 1 cup sugar and sour milk. Cook over low heat, stirring constantly until thickened. Stir in 1 cup prunes and 2 tablespoons butter. Cool until thickened. Spread between layers.

Carla Voelkel, Texas City H.S.
Texas City, Texas

PUMPKIN ROLL

3 eggs
1 c. sugar
2/3 c. canned pumpkin
1 tsp. lemon juice
3/4 c. flour
1 tsp. baking powder
2 tsp. cinnamon
1 tsp. ginger
1/2 tsp. each salt, nutmeg
Confectioners' sugar
1 6-oz. package cream cheese, softened
5 tbsp. butter, softened
1/2 tsp. vanilla extract
1/2 c. chopped pecans

Beat eggs in bowl at medium speed of electric mixer for 5 minutes. Add sugar, pumpkin and lemon juice gradually. Mix next 5 ingredients; fold into pumpkin mixture. Line jelly roll pan with waxed paper. Pour batter into pan. Bake at 350 degrees for 15 minutes. Invert on towel sprinkled with confectioners' sugar. Roll cake and towel together as for jelly roll. Cool completely. Combine cream cheese, 1 cup confectioners' sugar, butter and vanilla in bowl; mix well. Stir in pecans. Spread on cake. Reroll. Refrigerate until serving time.

Winn Williams, Lake Hamilton H.S.
Pearcy, Arkansas

VENETIAN CREME TORTE

1 1/2 c. butter
Sugar
3 eggs
2 tsp. vanilla extract
2 c. sifted cake flour
1/2 c. cocoa
1/2 tsp. soda
3/4 tsp. salt
1 c. buttermilk
1/2 c. all-purpose flour
2 2/3 c. milk
1 1/2 c. confectioners' sugar

Cream 1/2 cup butter in bowl; add 1 2/3 cups sugar gradually, beating until light and fluffy.

Beat in eggs one at a time, beating well after each addition. Add 1 teaspoon vanilla. Sift together cake flour, cocoa, soda and 1/4 teaspoon salt. Add to creamed mixture alternately with buttermilk. Spoon into 3 greased and floured 9-inch cake pans. Bake at 350 degrees for 20 to 22 minutes. Cool for 10 minutes on wire racks. Turn onto racks; cool completely. Slice each layer in half with long thin knife. Combine 1/2 cup sugar, all-purpose flour and 1/2 teaspoon salt in 1 1/2-quart saucepan. Add milk gradually. Cook over medium heat until thickened, stirring constantly. Cook for 2 additional minutes. Cover; cool. Chill until set. Cream 1 cup butter and 3/4 cup confectioners' sugar together in large mixing bowl until light and fluffy. Add chilled mixture to creamed ingredients alternately with remaining 3/4 cup confectioners' sugar; mix well after each addition. Add 1 teaspoon vanilla; beat until smooth. Spread between layers and on top of torte. Stabilize with wooden picks; refrigerate until firm. May be frozen.

Photograph for this recipe on page 15.

YULE LOG CAKE

1/2 c. flour
1/3 c. cocoa
1/4 tsp. soda
1/4 tsp. salt
4 eggs, separated
3/4 c. sugar
1 tsp. vanilla extract
2 to 3 drops of red food coloring
Confectioners' sugar
1 qt. vanilla ice cream, softened
1 recipe chocolate frosting

Sift together first 4 ingredients; set aside. Beat egg whites in bowl until soft peaks form. Add sugar gradually, beating well after each addition. Beat until stiff peaks form. Beat egg yolks, vanilla and food coloring in separate bowl. Fold egg yolks into egg whites. Fold in dry ingredients. Line jelly roll pan with greased waxed paper. Pour batter into pan. Bake at 400 degrees for 12 to 15 minutes. Turn onto towel dusted with confectioners' sugar. Roll up in towel. Cool. Unroll cake. Spread with ice cream. Reroll. Wrap in plastic wrap. Freeze overnight. Frost with chocolate frosting to resemble log before serving.

Viola B. Farner, Central H.S.
Louisville, Kentucky

CHEESECAKE CUPCAKES

24 vanilla wafers
3/4 c. sugar
2 8-oz. packages cream cheese, softened
2 tsp. lemon juice
2 eggs
1 tsp. vanilla extract
1 can cherry pie filling

Line 24 muffin tins with paper liners. Place 1 vanilla wafer in bottom of each muffin tin. Blend sugar, cream cheese, lemon juice, eggs and vanilla in bowl. Spoon enough mixture in tins to fill half full. Bake at 350 degrees for 20 minutes. Cool. Top with pie filling. Yield: 24 servings.

Marcy Poulton, Millcreek Jr. H.S.
Bountiful, Utah

SUSAN'S CHEESE CUPCAKES

3 8-oz. packages cream cheese, softened
5 eggs, beaten
1 1/4 c. sugar
1 3/4 tsp. vanilla extract
1 c. sour cream

Blend cream cheese, eggs, 1 cup sugar and 1 1/2 teaspoons vanilla in bowl; mix well. Fill 24 paper-lined cupcake tins 3/4 full. Bake at 325 degrees for 40 minutes or until lightly browned. Combine sour cream, 1/4 cup sugar and 1/4 teaspoon vanilla in bowl; mix well. Remove cupcakes from oven. Allow cupcakes to stand for several seconds until centers fall. Fill depressions with a small amount of filling. Bake for 5 minutes longer. Keep refrigerated.

Susan Vannoy, North Wilkes School
Hays, North Carolina

CARAMEL-COATED YULE LOGS

1/3 c. margarine, softened
1/3 c. light corn syrup
1/2 tsp. salt
1 tsp. vanilla extract
1 lb. confectioners' sugar
Green and red food coloring
1/4 tsp. mint extract
1 lb. caramels
2 tbsp. cream
Pecan halves

Blend margarine, corn syrup, salt and vanilla in large mixing bowl. Add confectioners' sugar. Mix with spoon; knead with hands. Turn onto board; knead until mixture is well-blended and smooth. Divide into halves. Blend green food coloring and mint extract into half; blend red food coloring into remaining half. Roll into two 10-inch logs. Cover with dampened cloth; refrigerate for several hours or overnight. Melt caramels with cream in top of double boiler. Place logs on waxed paper. Spoon caramel mixture over fondant logs; roll in pecan halves. Chill until set. Slice to serve.

Barbara Johnson, Ord Jr.-Sr. H.S.
Ord, Nebraska

OVEN CARAMEL CORN

2 c. (firmly packed) brown sugar
1 c. butter
1/2 c. dark corn syrup
1 tsp. salt
1 tsp. soda
6 qt. popped popcorn

Combine first 4 ingredients in saucepan. Cook for 5 minutes. Add soda; stir well. Pour over popcorn. Stir to coat well. Spread onto greased cookie sheets. Bake for 1 hour at 200 degrees, stirring every 15 minutes. Spread onto waxed paper to dry.

Mary Alsteens, Tomahawk H.S.
Tomahawk, Wisconsin

BUCKEYES

2 c. chunky peanut butter
1 stick margarine, softened
2 c. confectioners' sugar
3 c. Rice Krispies
1 6-oz. package chocolate chips
1/3 bar paraffin wax

Combine first 4 ingredients in large bowl; mix well. Chill. Form into walnut-sized balls. Melt chocolate chips and paraffin in saucepan. Dip balls into chocolate mixture to partially coat, leaving an eye uncoated. Place on waxed paper until firm. Store in freezer.

Cindy Fischer, Roncalli H.S.
Aberdeen, South Dakota

CHOCOLATE MILLIONAIRES

1 pkg. Kraft caramels
2 tbsp. evaporated milk
2 c. chopped pecans
1 lg. Hershey bar
2 tbsp. shortening

Melt caramels in milk in double boiler. Add pecans; mix well. Drop by spoonfuls onto greased cookie sheet. Cool. Mix Hershey bar with shortening in saucepan until melted. Dip cooled balls in chocolate mixture to coat. Drop onto waxed paper to harden. May use 1/4 block paraffin instead of shortening.

Mrs. Una Kernodle, Chugiak H.S.
Eagle River, Alaska

KAY'S FUDGE

2 c. sugar
2 tbsp. cocoa
1 tbsp. corn syrup
1 c. cream
Dash of salt
Nuts
1 tsp. vanilla extract

Combine first 5 ingredients in heavy saucepan. Cook to soft-ball stage or 234 to 240 degrees on candy thermometer. Pour onto buttered platter. Cool. Return to bowl; add nuts and vanilla. Beat until loses its gloss. Place on waxed paper; roll into a roll. Wrap in waxed paper. Slice to serve. Store in cool place.

Kay Caskey, Manogue H.S.
Reno, Nevada

QUICK AND EASY CANDY

2 c. sugar
2/3 c. milk
24 saltine crackers, crumbled
6 tbsp. peanut butter

Combine sugar and milk in saucepan. Boil for 4 minutes. Stir in cracker crumbs and peanut butter. Drop by spoonfuls onto waxed paper. Cool until firm.

Ruth Cross, Sullivan Central H.S.
Blountville, Tennessee

BUTTERMILK PRALINES

2 c. sugar
1 c. buttermilk
1 tsp. soda
2 tbsp. light corn syrup
1/2 stick butter, softened
1 tsp. vanilla extract
2 c. pecans

Combine first 5 ingredients in 3-quart saucepan. Cook to soft-ball stage, 240 degrees on candy thermometer, stirring constantly. Cool slightly.

Add vanilla and pecans. Beat until mixture loses its gloss. Drop by teaspoonfuls onto waxed paper. Yield: 3 dozen.

Caroline L. Bode, Robert E. Lee H.S.
San Antonio, Texas

HOLIDAY LOGS

1/3 c. butter, softened
1/4 c. light corn syrup
Vanilla extract
1/2 tsp. salt
1 1-lb. box confectioners' sugar
Green and red food coloring
Cinnamon or peppermint oil to taste
1 lb. caramels
3 tbsp. evaporated milk
1 1/2 c. chopped pecans, toasted

Combine butter, corn syrup, 1 teaspoon vanilla and salt in large mixing bowl; mix well. Add confectioners' sugar, mixing well with fork. Knead with hands until softened. Sivide into thirds. Knead each part on board. Blend green food coloring and peppermint oil into one third. Blend red food coloring and cinnamon oil into one third. Flavor remaining third with vanilla to taste, if desired. Form into 1-inch rolls. Wrap individual rolls well. Refrigerate or freeze overnight. Melt caramels with evaporated milk in top of double boiler, stirring constantly. Dip rolls to coat with melted caramel. Roll in pecans.

Marie R. Duggan, Johnson County H.S.
Wrightsville, Georgia

PEANUT BRITTLE

2 c. sugar
1 c. light corn syrup
2 c. raw peanuts
2 tbsp. butter
2 tsp. vanilla extract
2 tsp. soda

Bring 1/2 cup water to a boil in heavy saucepan. Add sugar and syrup. Boil until 300 degrees on candy thermometer, or mixture spins a thread. Stir in peanuts. Cook until golden brown and peanuts begin to pop. Add butter, vanilla and soda. Stir down quickly. Pour onto greased cookie sheet, spreading thin. Cool. Break into small pieces.

Baubie Fay Dillard, Spring Hill School
Hope, Arkansas

MOLASSES-WHEAT GERM CANDY

2 1/2 c. toasted wheat germ
1 c. instant nonfat milk
1 c. crunchy peanut butter
1 c. raisins
1/2 c. blackstrap molasses
1/2 c. honey

Combine all ingredients in large bowl. Knead with hands to mix well. Press into oiled pan. Cut into squares. Refrigerate until firm.

Paul F. Kallona, Gordon Center School
Washington, D.C.

CHRISTMAS WREATH CANDIES

32 lg. marshmallows
7 tbsp. butter
1/2 tsp. vanilla extract
1/2 tsp. almond extract
1 tsp. green food coloring
6 c. corn flakes
Red cinnamon candies

Melt marshmallows and butter in large saucepan over low heat. Stir in flavorings and food coloring. Add corn flakes; stir well to coat. Shape by spoonfuls into wreaths on waxed paper with buttered hands. Decorate with cinnamon candies.

Debra Nelson, Donnybrook H.S.
Donnybrook, North Dakota

PANOCHA WALNUTS

1 c. (firmly packed) brown sugar
1/2 c. sugar
1/4 tsp. salt
1 tsp. vanilla extract
2 1/2 c. walnut halves

Combine brown sugar, sugar, 1/2 cup water and salt in 3-quart saucepan. Bring slowly to a boil, stirring constantly until sugar dissolves. Cook to firm-ball stage, 246 degrees on candy thermometer. Remove from heat. Add vanilla and walnuts. Stir until walnuts are well coated. Spread onto waxed paper. Separate walnuts with 2 forks. Cool.

Photograph for this recipe on page 110.

APRICOT BROWNIES

2/3 c. dried apricots
1/4 c. sugar
1 1/3 c. flour
1/2 c. butter, softened
2 eggs, well beaten
1 c. (firmly packed) brown sugar
1/2 tsp. baking powder
1/4 tsp. salt
1 tsp. vanilla extract
1/2 c. chopped nuts
Confectioners' sugar

Rinse apricots. Place in saucepan with water to cover. Boil for 10 minutes; drain. Cool; chop. Combine sugar with 1 cup flour in bowl. Cut in butter until crumbly. Press into greased 9 x 9-inch pan. Bake at 350 degrees for 25 minutes or until light brown. Combine eggs and brown sugar in bowl; beat well. Sift 1/3 cup flour with baking powder and salt. Add flour mixture to egg mixture gradually; mix well. Stir in vanilla, nuts and apricots. Spread over baked layer. Bake at 350 degrees for 30 minutes. Cool. Cut into squares. Sprinkle with confectioners' sugar.

Esther Moorhead, Berryhill H.S.
Tulsa, Oklahoma

CHERRY BARS

1 1/4 c. flour
1 1/4 c. confectioners' sugar
1/2 c. margarine, softened
3/4 c. sugar
1/2 tsp. baking powder
Pinch of salt
2 eggs, beaten
1/2 c. chopped nuts
1/2 c. chopped maraschino cherries
1/2 c. coconut
Maraschino cherry juice

Mix 1 cup flour and 1/4 cup confectioners' sugar in bowl. Cut in margarine until crumbly. Press firmly into 8 x 8-inch baking pan. Bake at 350 degrees for 10 minutes. Combine 1/4 cup flour with next 3 ingredients in large bowl. Blend in eggs. Stir in next 3 ingredients; mix well. Spread over crust. Bake for 30 minutes longer. Combine 1 cup confectioners' sugar with small amount of cherry juice. Glaze hot cookies. Cool. Cut into bars.

Pat Duncan, Haltom Jr. H.S.
Fort Worth, Texas

CHERRY SURPRISE

2 cans cherry pie filling
1 box white cake mix
1 lb. walnuts, chopped
1/2 lb. butter, melted

Spread cherry pie filling in greased 13 x 9-inch cake pan. Sprinkle cake mix over pie filling.

Sprinkle walnuts over cake mix. Drizzle with melted butter. Bake at 350 degrees for 50 to 60 minutes. Cut into squares. Serve plain or with whipped topping.

Elaine Buerkel, West H.S.
Columbus, Ohio

CHOCOLATE MACAROONS

1/2 c. shortening
4 sq. chocolate
2 c. sugar
4 eggs
1 tsp. vanilla extract
2 c. flour
2 tsp. baking powder
1/2 tsp. salt
Confectioners' sugar

Melt shortening and chocolate in small saucepan. Combine with sugar in large bowl; mix well. Add eggs one at a time, beating well after each egg. Add vanilla and next 3 ingredients; mix well. Chill thoroughly, about 1 hour. Shape into walnut-sized balls. Roll in confectioners' sugar; place on cookie sheet. Bake at 350 degrees for 10 to 12 minutes.

Peggy Sumner, Bishop Ward H.S.
Kansas City, Kansas

ORANGE-CHOCOLATE BALLS

2 8 1/2-oz. boxes chocolate wafers,
crushed

1 c. confectioners' sugar
1/3 c. Florida frozen orange juice,
thawed
1/4 c. light corn syrup
1/4 c. butter, melted
1 c. finely chopped walnuts

Mix all ingredients together in large bowl. Shape into 1-inch balls. Chill until firm. Roll in confectioners' sugar just before packing in gift containers. Yield: 4 dozen.

Photograph for this recipe on this page.

CANDIED ORANGE SLICES

6 Florida oranges
1 1/2 c. (firmly packed) dark brown sugar
Sugar

Place oranges in large saucepan. Fill with water to cover. Cover. Bring to a boil over medium heat. Reduce heat. Simmer for 40 minutes or until peel is tender. Drain. Cool. Cut oranges into 3/8-inch crosswise slices. Cut slices into halves. Place in bowl; set aside. Mix together brown sugar and 2 cups water in medium saucepan. Bring to a boil over low heat, stirring until sugar dissolves. Boil for 20 minutes or until mixture becomes thick and syrupy, stirring frequently. Pour over orange slices. Cover. Refrigerate overnight. Remove orange slices from syrup. Roll in sugar. Dry overnight on rack. Roll in sugar again just before packing into gift boxes. Yield: About 6 cups.

Photograph for this recipe on this page.

ORANGE MACAROON BARS

1/4 c. butter, softened
1 c. sugar
1 egg
1 tsp. grated orange rind
2 tbsp. Florida frozen orange juice,
thawed
1 c. sifted all-purpose flour
1 tsp. baking powder
1/2 tsp. salt
1 c. flaked coconut

Cream butter and sugar in medium bowl. Beat in egg, orange rind and orange juice. Stir in remaining ingredients; mix well. Spread in greased 8 x 8 x 2-inch baking pan. Bake at 350 degrees for 40 to 50 minutes or until cake tests done. Cool. Cut into 1 1/4-inch squares. Yield: 36 bars.

Photograph for this recipe on this page.

ORANGE-FRUITCAKE BARS

1 6-oz. can Florida frozen orange
     juice, thawed
Light brown sugar
1 c. raisins
1 8-oz. package pitted dates, chopped
1 1-lb. jar mixed candied fruit,
     finely chopped
Butter, softened
4 eggs
1 c. unsifted all-purpose flour
Pinch of soda
1/2 tsp. each cinnamon, nutmeg
1/4 tsp. each allspice, cloves
1 1/2 c. sifted confectioners' sugar
1 c. chopped nuts
1/4 c. orange juice

Combine orange juice and 1/2 cup firmly packed brown sugar in medium saucepan. Bring to a boil over low heat, stirring constantly. Add raisins and dates. Bring to a boil again. Remove from heat. Stir in candied fruit. Set aside. Cream 1/2 cup butter and 2/3 cup firmly packed brown sugar in large bowl. Add eggs one at a time, mixing well after each addition. Blend in dry ingredients except confectioners' sugar; mix well. Stir in nuts and fruit mixture. Turn into 2 waxed paper-lined 15 x 10 x 1-inch baking pans. Bake at 300 degrees for 35 to 40 minutes or until cake tests done. Cool. Mix confectioners' sugar, 1 tablespoon butter and orange juice in small bowl until smooth. Frost cakes. Cut into 3 x 1-inch bars. Garnish with halved candied cherries. Yield: 100 bars.

Photograph for this recipe on page 129.

EASY-DO DONUTS

Sugar
1/2 c. milk
1 egg
2 tbsp. oil
1 1/2 c. sifted all-purpose flour
2 tsp. baking powder
1/2 tsp. salt
1/2 c. seedless raisins
Oil for deep frying
1/2 tsp. nutmeg

Blend together 1/3 cup sugar, milk, egg and oil. Sift together flour, baking powder and salt. Add to liquid mixture; stir lightly. Add raisins; mix well. Drop by heaping teaspoonfuls into hot oil. Fry at 365 degrees for 2 to 3 minutes or until golden brown. Drain on absorbent paper. Mix 1/4 cup sugar and nutmeg in bag. Add warm donuts. Shake to coat. Yield: 2 1/2 dozen.

Photograph for this recipe on page 45.

CHOCOLATE NO-BAKE COOKIES

2 c. sugar
1/2 tsp. salt
1/4 c. cocoa
1/2 stick margarine
1/2 c. milk
2 c. quick-cooking oats
1/2 c. peanut butter
1 tsp. vanilla extract

Mix sugar, salt and cocoa in saucepan. Add margarine and milk. Bring to a boil. Cook for 1 minute and 30 seconds. Add remaining ingredients; mix well. Drop by teaspoonfuls onto waxed paper; cool.

Marilake Farmer, Foreman H.S.
Foreman, Arkansas

CHOCOLATE-RUM BALLS

1 6-oz. package semisweet chocolate
     bits
1 7-oz. jar marshmallow creme
1 tbsp. rum flavoring
3 c. crisp rice cereal
Shredded coconut
Chopped pecans

Melt chocolate in double boiler over hot water. Combine marshmallow creme and rum flavoring in small bowl. Stir into chocolate, mixing well. Add cereal, 1/2 cup coconut and 1/2 cup pecans; mix well. Form into small balls. Roll in additional coconut or chopped pecans. Chill until firm. Yield: 4 dozen.

Pauline Emerson, Greenville Jr. H.S.
Greenville, Texas

CREAM CHEESE BROWNIES

1 8-oz. package cream cheese, softened
2 1/2 c. sugar
3 eggs
1/2 c. margarine
1 1/2 sq. unsweetened chocolate
2 c. flour
1/2 c. sour cream
1 tsp. soda
1/2 tsp. salt
1 c. chocolate bits

Combine cream cheese, 1/2 cup sugar and 1 egg in bowl; mix well. Set aside. Combine margarine, 3/4 cup water and chocolate in saucepan. Bring to a boil. Remove from heat. Stir in flour, 2 cups sugar, 2 eggs, sour cream, soda and salt; mix well. Pour into well-greased 15 1/2 x 10 1/2-inch pan. Spoon cream cheese mixture over chocolate mixture. Swirl into batter with knife. Sprinkle chocolate bits on top. Bake at 375 degrees for 25 to 30 minutes. Cool. Cut into squares.

Patricia A. Marcotte, Newburyport H.S.
Newburyport, Massachusetts

UNUSUAL BROWNIES

1 pkg. German's chocolate cake mix
3/4 c. margarine, melted
2/3 c. evaporated milk
1 c. chopped pecans
1 6-oz. package semisweet chocolate chips
1 14-oz. bag caramels

Combine cake mix, margarine and 1/3 cup evaporated milk in bowl; mix well. Press half the mixture into bottom of 13 x 9-inch baking pan. Bake at 350 degrees for 5 minutes. Sprinkle pecans and chocolate chips over crust. Melt caramels with remaining 1/3 cup evaporated milk in saucepan over low heat, stirring frequently until smooth. Spread caramel mixture evenly over pecans and chocolate pieces. Top with remaining cake mix mixture, spreading gently to cover. Bake at 350 degrees for 20 minutes. Cool slightly before cutting into 2-inch squares. Yield: 24 servings.

Patricia Donahoo, Webster County H.S.
Dixon, Kentucky

BROWNIES

1/4 c. butter
1 c. (firmly packed) brown sugar
2 eggs
2 sq. unsweetened chocolate, melted
3 1/2 tbsp. all-purpose flour
1 tsp. vanilla extract
1 c. coarsely chopped nuts
Confectioners' sugar

Cream butter and sugar in bowl until fluffy. Add eggs one at a time, beating well after each addition. Stir in melted chocolate; add flour, vanilla and nuts. Pour into greased 8 x 8-inch pan. Bake at 325 degrees for 30 minutes. Cool in pan; cut into bars. Dust with confectioners' sugar.

Photograph for this recipe on page 110.

HOLIDAY MINT BARS

Butter
1 c. sugar
2 eggs
1 tsp. vanilla extract
3 1-oz. squares unsweetened chocolate
1/2 c. sifted flour
1/2 c. chopped nuts
1 c. confectioners' sugar
1 tbsp. cream
1/2 tsp. peppermint extract

Cream 1/2 cup butter and sugar in bowl. Beat in eggs and vanilla. Blend in 2 squares melted chocolate. Stir in flour and nuts. Spoon batter into greased 8-inch square pan. Bake at 350 degrees for 25 minutes. Cool. Combine next 3 ingredients with 2 tablespoons butter in small bowl; beat until creamy. Spread mint frosting over brownies. Let stand until set. Combine remaining square melted chocolate with 1 tablespoon melted butter. Spread chocolate glaze over frosting. Chill until firm. Cut into 2 x 3/4-inch bars. Yield: 40 servings.

Dolores Weber, Sacred Heart H.S.
Miles City, Montana

RAISIN-NUT COOKIES

2 c. seedless raisins
1 tsp. soda
1 c. shortening
2 c. sugar
1 1/2 tsp. cinnamon
1/4 tsp. each nutmeg, allspice
3 eggs
1 tsp. vanilla extract
4 c. sifted all-purpose flour
2 tsp. salt
1 tsp. baking powder
1 c. chopped walnuts

Boil raisins with 1 cup water in saucepan for 5 minutes. Drain, reserving 1/2 cup liquid. Cool. Stir in soda. Cream shortening, sugar and spices in bowl. Add eggs, one at a time, beating well after each addition. Add vanilla and raisin liquid; mix well. Sift dry ingredients together. Stir into creamed mixture. Add raisins and walnuts; mix well. Chill until stiff. Drop by spoonfuls onto lightly greased baking sheet 1 inch apart. Bake at 375 degrees for 10 to 15 minutes or until golden brown. Cool on rack. Store in covered jar between sheets of waxed paper. Yield: 6 dozen.

Photograph for this recipe on page 110.

TOFFEE BARS

1 c. margarine, softened
1 c. (firmly packed) brown sugar
1 tsp. vanilla extract
1 egg
2 c. sifted flour
1/4 tsp. salt
Chocolate chips
Nuts

Cream margarine and brown sugar in large bowl. Add vanilla and egg; beat well. Sift flour and salt. Add to creamed mixture gradually, blending thoroughly. Spread mixture evenly in greased 10 x 14-inch baking pan. Bake at 350 degrees for 20 to 25 minutes. Remove from oven. Spread chocolate chips over top; allow to melt. Sprinkle with nuts. Cool. Cut into bars.

Aleene Alder, Dixon Jr. H.S.
Provo, Utah

APPLE-DATE COOKIES

3/4 c. butter, softened
2 c. sugar
2 eggs
3 3/4 c. flour
3/4 tsp. salt
1 tbsp. baking powder
1/3 c. milk
1/2 tsp. vanilla extract
2 1/2 c. peeled chopped apples
1 c. chopped dates

Cream butter in large mixing bowl. Add 1 cup sugar gradually, beating until light and fluffy. Add eggs one at a time, beating well after each addition. Sift 3 1/2 cups flour, 1/2 teaspoon salt and baking powder together. Add to creamed mixture alternately with milk and vanilla, mixing well after each addition. Refrigerate until chilled. Combine 1 cup sugar, 1/4 cup flour and 1/4 teaspoon salt in saucepan. Stir in 1 cup water gradually, mixing well. Stir in apples and dates. Cook over medium heat until thickened, stirring frequently. Chill thoroughly. Roll out dough on lightly floured surface to 1/8-inch thickness. Cut into 2 1/2-inch rounds. Place half the cookies on baking sheet. Top each with 1 rounded teaspoon filling. Cut out center of remaining cookies with round or star-shaped cutter. Place on top of filled cookies. Press edges together with fork. Bake at 400 degrees for 10 to 12 minutes. Cool on wire rack. Store in covered container.

Photograph for this recipe on page 4.

BROWN SUGAR CUT-OUTS

1/2 c. butter, softened
1 c. (firmly packed) brown sugar
1 egg
1 tsp. vanilla extract
2 tsp. grated orange rind
1 3/4 c. sifted all-purpose flour
1/4 tsp. salt
1 tsp. baking powder

Beat together butter, brown sugar, egg, vanilla and orange rind in bowl. Combine flour, salt and baking powder; sift into first mixture, mixing well. Chill until stiff. Shape into 1 1/2-inch roll. Wrap in foil. Store in refrigerator. Unwrap; cut into 1/8-inch slices. Cut slices with floured cookie cutters. Place on greased cookie sheet. Bake at 400 degrees for 6 to 8 minutes. Yield: 4-5 dozen.

Photograph for this recipe on page 110.

CHRISTMAS COOKIES

1 c. Crisco
1 c. sugar
1 c. (firmly packed) brown sugar
2 eggs
1 tsp. vanilla extract
2 c. flour
1 tsp. soda
1 tsp. baking powder
1/2 tsp. salt
2 c. oatmeal
2 c. crushed corn flakes
1 c. chopped pecans
1 c. raisins
1 c. coconut
1 c. chopped red cherries
1 c. chopped green cherries

Cream Crisco and sugars in large bowl. Add eggs and vanilla. Sift in dry ingredients; mix well. Add oatmeal, corn flakes, pecans, raisins, coconut and cherries; mix thoroughly. Form into small balls. Place on cookie sheet; press lightly. Bake at 375 degrees for 8 to 10 minutes. Yield: 100 cookies.

Lecia Simmons, St. Stephens H.S.
Hickory, North Carolina

CHRISTMAS DROPS

1/2 c. butter
1 c. sugar

2 eggs
1/4 c. sour cream
1 1/4 c. flour
1/2 tsp. soda
1/2 tsp. ground cinnamon
1/4 tsp. salt
1/4 tsp. ground cloves
1 c. quick-cooking rolled oats
1 c. chopped pecans
1 c. finely chopped dates
1/2 c. raisins
1/2 c. chopped candied cherries
Candied cherry halves

Cream butter, sugar and eggs in large bowl until fluffy. Stir in sour cream. Sift together next 5 ingredients. Add to creamed mixture. Stir in remaining ingredients except cherry halves. Drop by rounded teaspoonfuls, 2 inches apart onto lightly greased cookie sheet. Top each cookie with cherry half. Bake at 350 degrees for 10 to 12 minutes. Yield: 5 dozen cookies.

Anita Weintraub, Aberdeen Middle School
Aberdeen, Maryland

COCOONS

8 tbsp. confectioners' sugar
2 1/2 c. flour
1 c. margarine
1 tsp. vanilla extract
1 c. chopped pecans

Combine dry ingredients in bowl; mix well. Cut in margarine until crumbly. Add vanilla; mix well. Stir in pecans. Shape dough into 1 1/2-inch long Cocoons. Bake at 325 degrees for 5 to 7 minutes until set but not brown. Cool on rack. Sprinkle with additional confectioners' sugar.

Lela Reed, Lyon Elementary School
Lyon, Mississippi

COTTAGE CHEESE COOKIES

1 c. sugar
1/2 c. shortening
1/2 c. cottage cheese
1 egg
1 3/4 c. flour
1/2 tsp. soda
1/2 tsp. salt
1 tsp. vanilla extract
Shredded coconut
Maraschino cherries, halved

Combine first 4 ingredients in bowl; blend well. Sift dry ingredients together. Add to sugar mixture; mix thoroughly. Add vanilla; mix well. Drop by teaspoonfuls onto waxed paper. Roll in coconut. Place maraschino cherry half on each cookie. Place on greased cookie sheet. Bake at 375 degrees for 10 to 12 minutes. Yield: 3-4 dozen.

Ann Iverson, Skyline H.S.
Salt Lake City, Utah

DREAM COOKIES

1 1/2 c. butter, softened
1 c. sugar
1/4 tsp. soda
1 tbsp. cream
2 eggs, well beaten
1 1/2 tsp. baking powder
3 to 3 1/2 c. flour
1 3-oz. package cream cheese, softened
2 tbsp. milk
Almond extract to taste
Confectioners' sugar

Cream together 1 cup butter and sugar in large bowl. Dissolve soda in cream. Add to creamed mixture; mix well. Add eggs, baking powder and enough flour to make stiff dough. Roll dough 1/4 to 1/8 inch thick. Cut with cookie cutter. Bake at 350 degrees until very lightly browned. Blend 1/2 cup butter, cream cheese, milk and extract in bowl. Beat in enough confectioners' sugar to spreading consistency. Frost half the cookies; top with remaining cookies. Store in airtight container in refrigerator. Frosting may be tinted.

Donnette Vachal, Scobey Public Schools
Scobey, Montana

HEALTH BALLS

1/2 c. peanut butter
1 tbsp. honey (opt.)
3/4 c. nonfat dry milk
6 tbsp. finely chopped apricots
Granola

Cream peanut butter and honey in bowl. Add dry milk gradually, mixing well. Stir in apricots. Shape into 1-inch balls. Roll in Granola. May substitute raisins for apricots and toasted sesame seed for Granola.

Wanda Bain Gary, El Sereno Jr. H.S.
Los Angeles, California

GUMDROPLESS COOKIES

1 c. shortening
1 c. (firmly packed) brown sugar
1 c. sugar
2 eggs
1 tsp. vanilla extract
2 c. flour
1 tsp. each soda, baking powder
2 c. oatmeal
1 c. ground coconut

Cream shortening and sugars in large bowl until light and fluffy. Add eggs and vanilla; beat well. Add dry ingredients gradually to creamed mixture; mix well. Fold in oatmeal and coconut. Drop by teaspoonfuls onto greased cookie sheet. Bake at 325 degrees for 12 to 15 minutes. Yield: 8 dozen.

Christine Lawrence, Miami H.S.
Miami, Arizona

HOLIDAY WREATHS

1 c. butter
3/4 c. confectioners' sugar
2 c. all-purpose flour
1/2 tsp. salt
1/2 tsp. almond extract
1 c. quick-cooking oats
Red or green food coloring (opt.)
Red or green candied cherries, chopped

Beat together butter and sugar in bowl until light and fluffy. Add flour, salt and almond extract; mix well. Stir in oats. Tint with food coloring. Shape rounded teaspoonfuls dough to form 6-inch long ropes. Shape ropes on ungreased cookie sheet to form circle, overlapping ends to form top of wreath. Decorate top of wreath with candied cherry pieces. Bake in 350-degree oven for 10 minutes. Cool for 1 minute on cookie sheet. Cool completely on rack. Yield: 3 dozen cookies.

Mrs. Marjorie West, Northeast H.S.
Meridian, Mississippi

LEMON BARS

1 c. flour
Confectioners' sugar
1/2 c. margarine, softened
2 eggs
1 c. sugar
1/2 tsp. baking powder
1/4 tsp. salt
3 tbsp. lemon juice

Combine flour, 1/4 cup confectioners' sugar and margarine in bowl; mix well. Press into 8 x 8-inch pan to cover bottom and 1/2 inch up sides. Bake at 350 degrees for 20 minutes. Beat remaining ingredients together in bowl. Pour over crust. Bake for 25 minutes longer. Cool. Sprinkle with confectioners' sugar. Cut into squares.

Connie Hansen, Magee Jr. H.S.
Tucson, Arizona
Sharon Johnson, Upper Arllington H.S.
Columbus, Ohio

MOON CAKES

1 lb. butter, softened
1 1/3 c. sugar
1/2 lb. almonds, ground
3 1/2 c. flour
Confectioners' sugar

Cream butter and sugar in large mixing bowl. Add almonds and flour; mix well. Chill until firm. Shape into half-moons. Place on baking sheet. Bake at 375 degrees until golden brown. Cool. Dip in confectioners' sugar. Yield: 10 dozen.

Beate Sachnowitz, R.L. Turner H.S.
Carrollton, Texas

MOIST OATMEAL COOKIES

1 c. shortening
1 c. sugar
2 eggs, beaten
1 c. raisins
2 c. flour
1/2 tsp. each soda, salt
1 tsp. cinnamon
1/4 tsp. nutmeg
2 c. rolled oats
Chopped nuts (opt.)

Cream shortening and sugar in large bowl. Add eggs; mix well. Cook raisins in water to cover. Drain, reserving 6 tablespoons liquid. Stir next 5 ingredients together. Add alternately to creamed mixture with raisin liquid. Stir in oats, nuts and raisins. Drop by teaspoonfuls onto cookie sheet. Bake at 375 degrees about 6 to 7 minutes. Do not overbake. Cool on rack. Store in cookie jar.

Sally G. Mace, Hendersonville H.S.
Hendersonville, Tennessee

PHILLY THINS

1/2 c. Crisco
1 stick margarine
1 sm. package cream cheese, softened
1 c. sugar
2 c. flour
1/2 tsp. salt

Cream Crisco and margarine in medium bowl. Add cream cheese; mix well. Sift together sugar, flour and salt. Add to cream cheese mixture gradually, blending well. Divide dough in half. Shape into rolls. Wrap in waxed paper. Chill or freeze overnight. Slice into 1/4-inch slices. Place on ungreased baking sheet. Bake at 350 degrees for 10 minutes. Cool on rack.

Patricia Taylor, Western Middle School
Louisville, Kentucky

SKILLET COOKIES

1 stick margarine
1 c. chopped dates
1 c. sugar
2 eggs
1 tsp. vanilla extract
2 c. (heaping) Rice Krispies
1 c. nuts
Coconut

Melt margarine in large skillet. Stir in dates, sugar and eggs. Cook until thickened, stirring constantly. Add vanilla. Remove from heat. Stir in Rice Krispies and nuts; mix well. Spread 1/2 of the coconut on 2 sheets of foil. Pour 1/2 of the Rice Krispie mixture over coconut. Form into logs 12 to 15 inches long. Repeat with remaining coconut and Rice Krispie mixture. May store in refrigerator for several weeks. Flavor improves after several days.

Sherry R. Staton, Independence Jr. H.S.
Independence, Kansas

STIR AND DROP SUGAR COOKIES

2 eggs, beaten
3/4 c. sugar
2/3 c. oil
1 tsp. grated lemon rind
2 tsp. vanilla extract
2 c. flour, sifted
2 tsp. baking powder
1/2 tsp. salt
Colored sugar

Combine eggs, sugar, oil, lemon rind and vanilla in large bowl. Sift flour, baking powder and salt together. Stir into oil mixture; mix well. Drop onto ungreased cookie sheet 2 inches apart. Flatten with glass dipped in colored sugar. Bake at 400 degrees for 8 to 10 minutes or until slightly brown around edges. Remove from cookie sheet at once. Cool on rack. Yield: 3 dozen.

Mildred E. Wilson, Shawnee Mission West H.S.
Overland Park, Kansas

RICH PEANUT BUTTER COOKIES

1/2 c. shortening
1/2 c. butter
1 c. sugar
1 c. (firmly packed) brown sugar
1 c. crunchy peanut butter
2 eggs, beaten
3 c. sifted self-rising flour
1 tsp. vanilla extract

Cream shortening, butter and sugars in large bowl. Add peanut butter; mix well. Add eggs; mix well. Add flour; blend thoroughly. Add vanilla; mix well. Shape dough into 1-inch balls. Place 2 inches apart on greased cookie sheet. Press with floured fork to flatten slightly. Bake at 350 degrees for 8 to 10 minutes or until lightly browned.

Renee A. Jenkins, Glenmore Academy
Memphis, Tennessee

PECAN PIE BARS

1 1/2 c. flour
Brown sugar
Butter
2 eggs, beaten slightly
1/2 c. dark corn syrup
1/2 c. chopped pecans
1 tsp. vanilla extract
1/2 tsp. salt

Combine flour and 2 tablespoons brown sugar in mixing bowl. Cut in 1/2 cup butter until crumbly. Pat into ungreased 11 x 7 1/2 x 1 1/2-inch baking pan. Bake at 350 degrees for 15 minutes; set aside. Combine 1/2 cup firmly packed brown sugar with next 5 ingredients. Add 2 tablespoons melted butter; mix well. Pour over baked layer. Bake for 25 minutes longer. Cool until pecan layer is slightly firm. Cut into bars. Yield: 32 bars.

Diane Lindsey, Claymont H.S.
Uhrichsville, Ohio

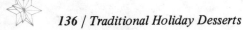

PEANUT STICKS

1 pkg. white cake mix
2 tbsp. melted butter
2 c. confectioners' sugar
Crushed peanuts

Prepare cake mix using package directions. Bake in 9 x 13-inch baking pan. Cool on rack. Wrap; freeze. Cut frozen cake into 1-inch bars. Combine butter and confectioners' sugar with enough hot water to make thin frosting. Coat cake pieces with frosting. Roll in peanuts.

Marcy Holen, Cozad Jr. H.S.
Cozad, Nebraska

QUICK CRESCENT PECAN PIE BARS

1 8-oz. can Crescent Dinner Rolls
1 egg, beaten
1/2 c. chopped pecans
1/2 c. sugar
1/2 c. corn syrup
1 tbsp. margarine, melted
1/2 tsp. vanilla extract

Separate roll dough into 2 large rectangles. Press rectangles over bottom and 1/2 inch up sides of lightly greased 9 x 13-inch pan to form crust. Seal perforations. Bake at 375 degrees for 5 minutes. Combine remaining ingredients in medium bowl; mix well. Pour over crust. Bake at 375 degrees for 18 to 22 minutes. Cool. Cut into squares. Yield: 2 dozen.

Eujana Rasnake, Campbell County H.S.
Jackson, Tennessee

SNOWBALL COOKIES

1 lb. margarine
1/2 c. sugar
4 tsp. vanilla extract
3 1/2 c. flour
1/2 c. chopped nuts
3/4 c. confectioners' sugar

Cream margarine and sugar in bowl. Add vanilla. Stir in flour, blending well. Stir in nuts; mix well. Shape teaspoonfuls dough into balls. Bake at 350 degrees for 10 minutes. Cool. Roll in confectioners' sugar.

Myrna Orr, McFadden Jr. H.S.
Santa Ana, California

SUGAR AND SPICE COOKIES

3/4 c. butter, softened
Sugar

1 egg
1/4 c. molasses
2 c. flour
2 tsp. soda
1/4 tsp. salt
1 tsp. each cinnamon, cloves and ginger

Cream butter, 1 cup sugar, egg and molasses in large bowl until smooth. Sift together dry ingredients. Stir into creamed ingredients; mix well. Roll into 1-inch balls. Dip into additional sugar. Bake at 350 degrees for 10 to 12 minutes.

Jane A. Solinsky, James B. Conant H.S.
Hoffman Estates, Illinois

OLD-FASHIONED TEA CAKES

1/2 c. butter, softened
1 c. sugar
1 egg
2 1/3 c. sifted self-rising flour

Cream butter and sugar in large bowl. Add egg; beat well. Add flour; mix well. Refrigerate overnight. Roll out dough on lightly floured surface to 1/8-inch thickness. Cut into desired shapes with cookie cutter. Place on cookie sheet. Bake at 350 degrees for 10 to 12 minutes.

Cleo Surles, Columbia H.S.
Decatur, Georgia

SWAN CREAM PUFFS

1/2 c. margarine
1/2 tsp. salt
3/4 c. sifted flour
3 eggs
3/4 c. cocoa
2/3 c. sugar
3/4 c. corn syrup
1 tsp. vanilla extract
1 qt. vanilla ice cream, slightly softened

Combine 1/2 cup water, 6 tablespoons margarine and 1/4 teaspoon salt in saucepan. Bring to a boil. Add flour all at once. Cook over low heat, stirring constantly, until mixture forms smooth ball. Remove from heat. Add eggs one at a time, beating well after each addition. Divide mixture into fourths. Press 1/4 of the dough through 1/4-inch pastry tube onto ungreased cookie sheet, forming seven 2 1/2-inch S-shaped strips for necks; shape 1/2 of the mixture into fourteen 2-inch N-shaped curves, one loop higher than the other, for wings; shape remaining mixture to form 7 marble-sized dots for tails. Bake at 400 degrees for 15 minutes or until golden brown. Cool on wire rack. Combine cocoa and sugar in saucepan. Add corn syrup, 1/4 teaspoon salt and 1 cup water, mixing well. Bring to a boil over medium heat, stirring constantly. Boil for 5 minutes. Remove from heat. Stir in 2 tablespoons margarine and vanilla. Cool. Pack ice cream into 1/2 cup measure to form balls. Place on cookie sheet. Press neck, 2 wings, longest strip on top, and tail into each ice cream ball. Freeze until serving time. Place in dessert dishes. Freeze until serving time. Pour chocolate sauce around each swan.

Photograph for this recipe on page 11.

CARAMEL PIE

    4 eggs, separated
    2 c. sugar
    2 tbsp. flour
    2 c. milk
    3 tbsp. butter
    1 unbaked pie shell
    1 recipe meringue

Beat egg yolks in saucepan. Add 1 1/2 cups sugar and flour, mixing well. Add milk; mix well. Melt 1/2 cup sugar in skillet over low heat until golden brown, stirring constantly. Add to milk mixture. Cook over medium heat, stirring constantly until mixture thickens. Add butter; mix well. Pour into pie shell. Bake at 350 degrees until pastry browns. Top with meringue. Bake at 300 degrees until browned.

Mrs. Carrie Ward, Baldwyn H.S.
Baldwyn, Mississippi

CRANBERRY BAVARIAN PIE

    1 env. unflavored gelatin
    1/2 c. sugar
    Pinch of salt
    3 eggs, separated
    1 1/4 c. milk
    1 tsp. almond extract
    1/2 c. whipping cream, whipped
    1 baked 9-inch pie shell
    1 can whole cranberry sauce
    1 tbsp. cornstarch

Soften gelatin in small amount of cold water. Combine with 1/4 cup sugar and salt in bowl. Beat egg yolks in top of double boiler. Stir in milk and gelatin mixture. Cook over hot water, stirring constantly until mixture coats spoon. Stir in almond flavoring. Refrigerate, stirring occasionally, until mixture mounds when dropped from spoon. Beat until smooth. Beat

egg whites in bowl until soft peaks form. Add 1/4 cup sugar gradually, beating until stiff. Fold in custard. Fold in whipped cream. Pour into pie shell. Refrigerate until set. Heat cranberry sauce with cornstarch in saucepan until clear and thick. Cool. Spread over gelatin layer. Chill until serving time.

Ardys Robbins, Bluejacket H.S.
Bluejacket, Oklahoma

CRANBERRY CHIFFON PIE

    1 c. cooked cranberries
    2/3 c. sugar
    4 eggs, separated
    1 tbsp. unflavored gelatin
    1/2 tsp. salt
    1 tbsp. lemon juice
    1 baked pie shell
    1/2 c. whipping cream, whipped

Place cranberries in saucepan; add half as much water. Cook until skins pop. Strain through a sieve; measure 1 cup. Place cranberries, 1/3 cup sugar and egg yolks in top of double boiler. Cook over hot water for 8 minutes or until thickened and smooth, stirring constantly. Soften gelatin in 1/4 cup cold water in large bowl. Pour cranberry mixture over gelatin; mix well. Beat in salt and lemon juice. Beat egg whites until soft peaks form. Add 1/3 cup sugar gradually, beating until stiff. Fold into cranberry mixture. Pour into baked pie shell. Chill until firm. Top each serving with whipped cream.

Barbara Johnson, Boardman H.S.
Youngstown, Ohio

CHOCOLATE-MINT PIE

    Butter
    2/3 pkg. vanilla wafers, crushed
    1 c. confectioners' sugar
    2 sq. chocolate, melted
    3 eggs, well beaten
    5 drops of peppermint oil

Melt 1/3 cup butter in saucepan. Combine with wafer crumbs; mix well. Press into 8-inch pie pan. Bake at 350 degrees for 10 minutes. Cool. Cream 1/2 cup butter and confectioners' sugar in bowl. Add melted chocolate and eggs. Beat for 5 minutes until light and fluffy. Add peppermint oil; mix for 1 minute. Pour into crust. Chill for several hours before serving.

Annette Cook, Somerset Sr. H.S.
Somerset, Wisconsin

CRANBERRY-ICE CREAM PIE

1 c. rolled oats
1/2 c. (firmly packed) brown sugar
1/2 c. grated coconut
1/3 c. butter, melted
1 qt. vanilla ice cream, softened
2 c. fresh cranberries
1 c. sugar

Spread oats in shallow pan; bake at 350 degrees for 10 minutes. Combine with brown sugar, coconut and butter; mix well. Press into bottom and side of 9-inch pie pan. Chill. Spoon ice cream into crust. Cover with aluminum foil; freeze until firm. Cook cranberries in 1/2 cup water in saucepan until cranberries pop. Add sugar. Cool for 10 minutes or until mixture thickens. Cool. Spread over ice cream. Serve immediately or freeze until serving time.

Marilyn J. Ziegler, Bloomington H.S. South
Bloomington, Indiana

FAMOUS BROWNIE PIE

3 egg whites
Pinch of salt
Sugar
3/4 c. chocolate wafer crumbs
1/2 c. chopped pecans
1/2 tsp. vanilla extract
1/2 pt. whipping cream

Beat egg whites and salt until soft peaks form. Add 3/4 cup sugar gradually, beating until stiff peaks form. Fold in crumbs, pecans and vanilla. Spread evenly in lightly buttered 9-inch pie pan. Bake at 325 degrees for 35 minutes. Cool completely. Whip cream with sugar to taste; spread over pie. Chill for 3 to 4 hours. Garnish with curls of unsweetened chocolate.

Sally Johnson, Central H.S.
Springfield, Missouri

PEPPERMINT FUDGE PIE

1 graham cracker crust
2 c. sugar
3 tbsp. cocoa
1 stick butter, softened
1/2 c. milk
1 tsp. vanilla extract
3 c. peppermint ice cream
Whipping cream, whipped

Prepare graham cracker crust according to package directions; press into pie pan. Chill crust for 30 minutes. Combine sugar, cocoa, butter and milk in saucepan. Cook to soft-ball stage, 234 degrees on candy thermometer. Remove from heat; cool to 110 degrees on candy thermometer. Add vanilla. Beat until fudge loses gloss. Pour into graham cracker crust; cool. Spread peppermint ice cream over fudge layer. Top with whipped cream. Serve immediately. May be frozen. Remove from freezer several minutes before serving.

Lana J. Crawford, Tarkington H.S.
Cleveland, Texas

FRENCH WALNUT PIE

1 c. sugar
1/2 c. margarine, softened
1/4 c. sweetened condensed milk
1 tsp. vanilla extract
1 c. chopped walnuts
1 c. raisins
2 eggs, beaten
1 unbaked 9-in. pie shell

Cream sugar and margarine in large bowl. Stir in condensed milk, vanilla, walnuts and raisins. Fold eggs into creamed mixture. Pour into pie shell. Bake at 325 degrees for 1 hour. May serve with whipped cream or vanilla ice cream.

Carol Winter, Millcreek Jr. H.S.
Bountiful, Utah

PINK PARTY PIE

2 eggs
1 c. sugar
1 sm. can crushed pineapple
1 pkg. strawberry gelatin
1 lg. can evaporated milk, chilled
1 vanilla wafer pie crust

Combine eggs, sugar and pineapple in saucepan; mix well. Bring to a boil. Remove from heat. Stir in gelatin until dissolved. Cool. Whip milk in bowl until soft peaks form. Fold milk into gelatin mixture. Pour into pie crust. Refrigerate until chilled. Yield: 6-8 servings.

Mary C. James, Greenville H.S.
Greenville, Alabama

ICE CREAM PIE

1 c. chopped pecans
1 c. crushed graham crackers
1 c. sugar
1 tsp. baking powder
3 egg whites
1 qt. butter brickle ice cream, softened
1 Heath bar, crushed

Mix pecans, graham crackers, sugar and baking powder together in bowl. Set aside. Beat egg whites in mixer bowl until stiff peaks form. Fold pecan mixture into egg whites. Turn into buttered pie pan, spreading over bottom and side. Bake at 325 degrees for 20 minutes. Cool. Fill with ice cream. Top with Heath bar. Freeze until serving time.

Lynda Hofeldt, Grant H.S.
Fox Lake, Illinois

NANCY'S PECAN PIE

> 4 eggs
> 1 1-lb. package light brown sugar
> 1/4 c. margarine, softened
> 1 tsp. vanilla extract
> 1 unbaked pie shell
> 1 c. pecans

Beat eggs in small mixing bowl until frothy. Set aside. Combine brown sugar and 3/4 cup water in 2-quart saucepan. Cook over moderate heat, stirring constantly until sugar dissolves. Bring to full boil. Cook, stirring constantly for 4 minutes. Stir a small amount of hot mixture into eggs. Stir eggs into hot mixture. Blend in marga-rine and vanilla. Pour into pie shell. Arrange pecans over top. Bake at 350 degrees for 1 hour or until set.

Nancy J. Garland, Plymouth Area H.S.
Plymouth, New Hampshire

MOTHER'S PECAN PIE

> 3 eggs, slightly beaten
> 1 c. dark corn syrup
> 1 c. sugar
> 2 tbsp. melted margarine
> 1 tsp. vanilla extract
> Pinch of salt
> 1 c. pecans
> 1 unbaked 9-in. pie shell

Combine first 6 ingredients in bowl; mix well. Stir in pecans. Pour into pie shell. Bake at 400 degrees for 15 minutes. Reduce temperature to 350 degrees; bake for 30 to 35 minutes or until firm around edges.

Margie Petro, Cannon County H.S.
Woodbury, Tennessee

YUMMY PEANUT BUTTER PIE

2 c. graham cracker crumbs
1 1/4 c. peanut butter
Sugar
1 env. unflavored gelatin
1 tsp. vanilla extract
1 c. marshmallow fluff
1 c. whipping cream, whipped

Combine graham cracker crumbs, 1/4 cup peanut butter, 1/4 cup sugar and 2 tablespoons water; mix well. Press into bottom of 9-inch pie plate. Refrigerate until firm. Sprinkle gelatin over 1/3 cup cold water in small saucepan. Stir over medium heat until gelatin dissolves. Remove from heat. Add 2/3 cup water, 3 tablespoons sugar and vanilla; stir well. Blend 1 cup peanut butter and marshmallow fluff in bowl. Pour in gelatin mixture; stir well. Fold in whipped cream. Pour into chilled pie crust. Chill for 3 hours.

Nancy Finck, Brattleboro Union H.S.
Brattleboro, Vermont

FUDGE SUNDAE PIE

Corn syrup
2 tbsp. brown sugar
3 tbsp. margarine
2 1/2 c. Rice Krispies
1/4 c. peanut butter
1/4 c. fudge sauce
1 qt. vanilla ice cream, softened

Combine 1/4 cup corn syrup, brown sugar and margarine in medium saucepan. Cook over low heat, stirring occasionally, until mixture begins to boil. Remove from heat. Add Rice Krispies, stirring until well coated. Press evenly into 9-inch pie pan. Combine peanut butter, fudge sauce and 3 tablespoons corn syrup; mix well. Spread half the peanut butter mixture over crust. Freeze until firm. Spoon ice cream into frozen pie crust, spreading evenly. Freeze until firm. Let stand at room temperature for about 10 minutes before slicing. Warm remaining peanut butter mixture; drizzle over top. Yield: 8 servings.

Annie Fischer, Roncalli H.S.
Aberdeen, South Dakota

PINEAPPLE-SOUR CREAM PIE

1 sm. package instant vanilla pudding mix
1 8-oz. can crushed pineapple
2 c. sour cream
1 tbsp. sugar
1 baked 9-inch pie shell, cooled

Combine pudding mix, undrained pineapple, sour cream and sugar in bowl. Beat slowly with rotary beater until smooth. Pour into pie shell. Chill until firm, about 3 hours.

Patricia Swahn, Oliver Wendel Holmes H.S.
San Antonio, Texas

PINEAPPLE BAVARIAN PIE

1 can sweetened condensed milk
4 tbsp. fresh lemon juice
1 lg. can crushed pineapple, drained
1 c. chopped pecans
1 lg. carton Cool Whip
2 graham cracker pie crusts

Combine condensed milk and lemon juice in large bowl; mix well. Stir in pineapple and pecans. Fold in Cool Whip. Pour into graham cracker crusts. Chill until set. May be tinted with food coloring if desired.

Jane Crussell, Sullivan East H.S.
Bluff City, Tennessee

FROZEN PUMPKIN PIE

1 pt. vanilla ice cream, softened
1 9-inch pie shell
1 c. canned pumpkin
1/2 tsp. each nutmeg, allspice, cinnamon
*   and salt*
1/4 tsp. ginger
1 1/4 c. sugar
1/2 pt. whipping cream, whipped

Mold slightly softened ice cream into bottom and up side of pie shell. Combine remaining ingredients, except whipped cream, in large bowl; mix well. Fold in whipped cream. Pour into ice cream filled crust. Freeze for 24 hours or longer. Remove from freezer 20 minutes before serving.

Barbara E. Smoot, Wapahani H.S.
Selma, Indiana

PUMPKIN CUSTARD PIES

2 c. cooked pumpkin
1 1/2 c. sugar
1 tbsp. cornstarch
1 1/2 tsp. cinnamon
1 tsp. each salt, ginger
1/2 tsp. each cloves, nutmeg
6 eggs
2 13 1/2-oz. cans evaporated milk
2 unbaked 9-inch pie shells

Combine first 8 ingredients in bowl; mix well. Beat eggs until light and lemon colored. Add to pumpkin mixture; mix well. Add evaporated milk gradually, stirring until smooth. Pour into pie shells. Bake at 350 degrees for 15 minutes. Reduce temperature to 325 degrees. Bake for 30 minutes or until set. Cool on racks. Serve with dollop of whipped cream on each slice.

Joyce A. Fletcher, Clear Spring Middle School
Clear Spring, Maryland

SPICY PUMPKIN PIE

    1 c. milk
    1 1/2 c. cooked, mashed pumpkin
    1 c. sugar
    1/4 tsp. salt
    1 tsp. pumpkin pie spice
    1/4 tsp. nutmeg
    1 tsp. vanilla extract
    2 eggs, beaten
    2 tsp. margarine
    1 unbaked 9-inch pie shell

Stir milk into pumpkin in bowl, mixing thoroughly. Add next 7 ingredients; beat well with electric mixer. Pour into pie shell. Bake at 400 degrees for 40 to 45 minutes.

Gloria Whitted, Northwest Sr. H.S.
Greensboro, North Carolina

WHITE CHRISTMAS PIE

    1 tbsp. gelatin
    1 c. sugar
    4 tbsp. flour
    1/2 tsp. salt
    1 1/2 c. milk
    3/4 tsp. vanilla extract
    1/4 tsp. almond extract
    1/2 c. whipping cream, whipped
    3 egg whites
    1/4 tsp. cream of tartar
    1 1/2 c. moist shredded coconut
    2 baked 9-inch pie shells

Soften gelatin in 1/4 cup cold water; set aside. Combine 1/2 cup sugar, flour and salt in saucepan. Stir in milk. Bring to a boil over low heat, stirring constantly. Boil for 1 minute. Remove from heat. Stir in softened gelatin. Cool until partially set. Pour into large bowl. Beat with rotary beater until smooth. Blend in vanilla and almond extracts. Fold whipped cream into custard. Beat egg whites until soft peaks form. Add cream of tartar and 1/2 cup sugar gradually, beating until stiff. Fold into custard mixture carefully. Fold in 1 cup coconut. Spoon

into cooled pie shells. Sprinkle with remaining coconut. Chill for about 2 hours or until set. Remove from refrigerator 20 minutes before serving.

Wana Miller, Trenton H.S.
Trenton, Texas

CHEESECAKE TARTS

    1/3 c. (firmly packed) light brown sugar
    1 c. flour
    1/2 c. chopped nuts
    6 tbsp. melted butter
    1 8-oz. package cream cheese
    1/4 c. sugar
    1 egg
    2 tbsp. milk
    1 tbsp. light rum
    1 tsp. vanilla extract
    Maraschino cherries

Grease 30 mini-tart pans. Mix first 4 ingredients. Press 1 tablespoon mixture into each mini-tart pan. Bake at 350 degrees for 8 to 10 minutes. Combine next 6 ingredients in bowl. Beat until smooth. Spoon cream cheese mixture into baked crusts. Bake at 350 degrees for 15 to 18 minutes or until set. Cool. Top with a maraschino cherry half. Chill until serving time. Yield: 30 servings.

Pauline S. Morian, New Smyrna Beach Sr. H.S.
New Smyrna Beach, Florida

PECAN SASSIES

    1 3-oz. package cream cheese, softened
    Margarine, softened
    1 c. sifted flour
    1 egg
    3/4 c. (firmly packed) light brown sugar
    1 tsp. vanilla extract
    Dash of salt
    2/3 c. chopped pecans

Combine cream cheese and 1/2 cup margarine in bowl; mix well. Stir in flour. Chill for 1 hour. Shape into twenty-four 1-inch balls. Press into ungreased 1 3/4-inch muffin cups to cover bottoms and sides. Beat egg, brown sugar, 1 tablespoon margarine, vanilla and salt together in bowl until smooth. Spoon half the pecans into pastry-lined cups. Add egg mixture; top with remaining pecans. Bake at 325 degrees for 15 minutes or until filling is set. Cool; remove from pans.

Shirley Slemp, Dryden H.S.
Dryden, Virginia

Homemade Holiday Gifts

There's no gift more welcome than a home-baked surprise. It's a gift that's a part of us . . . and says "I care."

Be creative with containers! Wrap your holiday treats with imagination and express your thoughtfulness for years to come.

Tie a loaf of homemade bread with reusable holiday ribbon and set it on a wooden bread board. Store cookies in a ceramic cookie jar or in a pretty piece of pottery. Pack candies in Mason jars or popular cork-topped glass containers. When giving cakes, why not present it on a stylish cake stand?

Sometimes you don't need containers at all. Tuck holiday goodies inside cloth napkins, holiday hand towels, or a wicker basket.

Homemade desserts are such nice hostess gifts as well to take on a holiday visit. A jar of jelly or a tin of peppermint sticks, topped with a copy of the recipe itself, would be appreciated by any hostess.

If you think your family enjoys the homemade treats in this chapter — just imagine the joy of giving them!

SPICED TEA MIX

2 c. instant orange breakfast drink mix
1 1/2 c. instant tea
2 1/2 c. sugar
1 pkg. unsweetened lemonade mix
1 tbsp. cloves
2 tbsp. cinnamon

Combine all ingredients; mix well. Store in airtight container. Place 3 teaspoons mix in cup. Fill cup with boiling water to serve.

Helen Kelley, Lockhart Jr. H.S.
Orlando, Florida

HOT BUTTERED RUM MIX

1 c. butter, softened
1/2 c. (firmly packed) brown sugar
1 c. confectioners' sugar
2 pt. vanilla ice cream, softened
Rum to taste
Nutmeg (opt.)

Blend butter, sugars and ice cream in bowl. Freeze. Combine 2 tablespoons mixture with 1 cup boiling water and rum. Sprinkle with nutmeg.

Penelope J. Byrd, Elk Grove H.S.
Elk Grove Village, Illinois

FRUITCAKE MUFFINS

1 c. (firmly packed) brown sugar
1/4 c. margarine
1 1/2 c. flour
2 eggs, well beaten
1 1/2 tsp. soda
1 1/2 tbsp. milk
1 tsp. each cinnamon, allspice
1 lb. dates, chopped
1/2 lb. pecans, chopped
1/2 lb. candied cherries, chopped
1/2 lb. candied pineapple, chopped
1 1/2 c. whiskey

Combine first 6 ingredients with spices in large bowl. Add dates, pecans, cherries and pineapple, reserving small amount for garnish. Sprinkle with whiskey; stir well. Line muffin tins with paper baking cups. Fill muffin cups 2/3 full. Arrange reserved fruit and pecans on tops. Bake at 350 degrees for about 20 minutes. Yield: About 30 cupcakes.

Rosie Ynfante, Hargrave H.S.
Huffman, Texas

HIDDEN MARSHMALLOW PUFFS

1/4 c. sugar
1 tsp. cinnamon
2 8-oz. cans refrigerator crescent
*   dinner rolls*
16 lg. marshmallows
1/4 c. margarine, melted
1/2 c. confectioners' sugar
1/2 tsp. vanilla extract
2 to 3 tsp. milk
1/4 c. chopped nuts (opt.)

Combine sugar and cinnamon in small bowl. Separate crescent dough into 16 triangles. Dip marshmallows into margarine. Roll in cinnamon-sugar mixture. Wrap 1 triangle around each dipped marshmallow, completely covering marshmallow; pinch edges. Dip crescent roll in margarine. Place in deep muffin tins. Repeat with remaining marshmallows and triangles. Place muffin pan on cookie sheet. Bake at 375 degrees for 10 to 15 minutes or until golden brown. Remove from pans immediately. Combine remaining ingredients except nuts. Drizzle over warm rolls. Sprinkle with nuts. Yield: 16 servings.

Pam Byce, Greene County H.S.
Greensboro, Georgia

NANCY'S SNOWBALLS

1 c. butter, softened
1/4 c. sugar
1 c. ground nuts
2 c. flour
Confectioners' sugar

Cream butter in mixing bowl. Add sugar, nuts and flour; mix well. Shape into balls using 1 tablespoon dough. Place on ungreased baking sheet. Bake at 300 degrees for 45 minutes or until lightly browned. Roll in confectioners' sugar immediately and again when cooled. Yield: 4 dozen.

Nancy J. Garland, Plymouth Area H.S.
Plymouth, New Hampshire

BANANA-NUT LOAF

1/2 c. shortening
1 1/2 c. sugar
2 eggs
2 c. flour
1 tsp. soda
2 tbsp. buttermilk
4 or 5 med. bananas
1 tsp. vanilla extract

3/4 c. chopped nuts
1 c. confectioners' sugar

Cream shortening and sugar in large bowl. Add eggs; mix well. Sift flour and soda together. Add flour and buttermilk to creamed mixture; beat well. Mash 3 or 4 bananas. Stir into mixture with vanilla and 1/2 cup nuts. Pour into greased loaf pan. Bake at 350 degrees for 45 minutes. Remove from pan. Mash 1 banana in small bowl. Add confectioners' sugar. Blend well. Stir in 1/4 cup nuts. Drizzle over warm loaf.

Elizabeth Neasman, Forest H.S.
Ocala, Florida

CHRISTMAS CARROT LOAF

1 1/4 c. sifted flour
1/2 c. sugar
1/2 tsp. each baking powder, soda
1 tsp. cinnamon
1/2 tsp. each nutmeg, ginger (opt.)
1/4 tsp. salt
2 eggs, beaten
1/4 c. oil
1/4 c. milk
1 c. shredded carrot
3/4 c. coconut
1/4 c. maraschino cherries, chopped,
   drained
1/4 c. raisins
1/4 c. chopped pecans

Sift the flour, sugar, baking powder and soda together with spices in large bowl. Combine eggs, oil and milk in bowl; mix well. Add dry ingredients; beat well. Stir in remaining ingredients. Turn into greased loaf pan. Bake at 350 degrees for 50 to 60 minutes.

Mrs. B. L. Williams, Crescent Heights H.S.
Calgary, Alberta, Canada

NORWEGIAN CARROT BREAD

3 eggs
1/2 c. oil
1/2 c. margarine
3 c. sugar
3 c. flour
1 tsp. each cinnamon, salt and soda
1 tsp. vanilla extract
1 c. crushed pineapple, drained
2 c. grated carrots, firmly packed
1 c. chopped nuts

Combine eggs, oil, margarine and sugar in mixing bowl; mix well. Mix flour and soda with

spices in separate bowl; add to first mixture. Beat well. Stir in vanilla, pineapple, carrots and nuts. Pour into 2 well-greased loaf pans. Bake at 350 degrees for 1 hour. Yield: 2 loaves.

Marian B. Dobbins, Catalina H.S.
Tucson, Arizona

CRANBERRY BREAD

2 1/4 c. sifted flour
1 tbsp. baking powder
1 tsp. salt
1/4 c. butter
3/4 c. (firmly packed) brown sugar
1 egg
7 tbsp. grated orange rind
1/2 c. milk
1/4 c. orange juice
1 c. chopped cranberries

Sift flour, baking powder and salt together. Cream butter and brown sugar in large bowl. Blend in egg and orange rind. Add dry ingredients alternately with milk and orange juice beginning and ending with dry ingredients, blending well after each addition. Fold in cranberries. Pour into greased 9 x 5 x 3-inch baking pan. Bake at 350 degrees for 1 hour. Cool for 10 minutes.

Marilyn Mecham, East H.S.
Lincoln, Nebraska

DILLY BREAD

1 pkg. dry yeast
1 c. cottage cheese
2 tbsp. sugar
1 tbsp. minced onion
1 tbsp. margarine
1 tsp. salt
1/4 tsp. soda
2 tsp. dillseed
1 egg
2 1/2 c. flour

Soften yeast in 1/4 cup warm water. Combine cottage cheese, sugar, onion, margarine, salt, soda, dillseed and egg in large bowl; mix well. Blend in yeast mixture. Add flour gradually, beating well to form stiff dough. Cover. Let rise in warm place until doubled in bulk. Turn onto floured board; knead until smooth and elastic. Place dough into greased loaf pans. Let rise in warm place until doubled in bulk. Bake at 350 degrees for 40 to 50 minutes.

Sandra Whittington, County Line H.S.
Branch, Arkansas

NORWEGIAN CHRISTMAS BREAD

1 c. butter
1 c. sugar
4 1/2 c. milk, scalded
2 pkg. yeast
2 c. raisins
1/4 lb. mixed fruit
1 egg
7 to 8 c. flour

Stir butter and sugar into milk in large bowl. Cool to lukewarm. Add yeast; stir to dissolve. Add remaining ingredients; mix well. Turn onto floured board. Knead until smooth and elastic. Place in greased bowl, turning to grease surface. Cover. Let rise until doubled in bulk. Punch down. Shape into 4 loaves. Place in greased 9 x 5-inch loaf pans. Let rise until doubled in bulk. Bake at 350 degrees for 45 minutes to 1 hour.

Kathy R. Warren, C.M. Goethe Middle School
Sacramento, California

PUMPKIN BREAD

4 c. sugar
4 c. pumpkin
1 c. oil
5 c. flour
4 tsp. soda
1 tsp. cloves
1 tbsp. each cinnamon, salt
1/2 c. chopped nuts
1 c. raisins

Combine first 3 ingredients in large bowl; mix well. Add dry ingredients; blend thoroughly. Stir in nuts and raisins, mixing well. Pour into 3 buttered loaf pans. Bake at 350 degrees for 1 hour. Remove from pans. Cool on rack.

Mabel Valech, Calaroga Jr. H.S.
Hayward, California

FIVE-FLAVOR CAKE

2 sticks butter
1/2 c. shortening
4 c. sugar
5 eggs
3 c. flour
1/2 tsp. baking powder
1 c. milk
2 tsp. each coconut, rum, butter, lemon
and vanilla extracts
1 tsp. almond extract

Cream butter, shortening and 3 cups sugar in large bowl until fluffy. Beat eggs separately until thick and lemon colored, about 5 minutes. Add to creamed mixture, blending well. Combine flour and baking powder. Add to creamed mixture alternately with milk, beating well after each addition. Stir in 1/2 of each of the flavorings except almond extract. Spoon mixture into greased 10-inch tube pan. Bake at 325 degrees for 1 hour and 30 minutes or until cake tests done. Combine remaining sugar and flavorings with 1/2 cup water in heavy saucepan. Bring to a boil, stirring until sugar is dissolved. Spoon slowly over hot cake. Let stand until cool.

Denise Pendergrass, Midlothian H.S.
Midlothian, Virginia
Judy Gebhardt, J.L. Williams Jr. H.S.
Copperas Cove, Texas

CHRISTMAS LANE CAKE

1 3/4 c. butter
3 1/3 c. sugar
1 tsp. vanilla extract
3 1/4 c. flour
1 1/4 tsp. salt
3 1/2 tsp. baking powder
1 c. milk
8 egg whites
12 egg yolks, slightly beaten
1/2 c. Bourbon
1 1/2 c. each chopped pecans, seeded
raisins, fresh grated coconut,
quartered candied red and green
cherries

Cream 1 cup butter and 2 cups sugar in large bowl until fluffy. Add vanilla, mixing well. Sift flour, 3/4 teaspoon salt and baking powder together. Add to creamed mixture alternately with milk, mixing well after each addition. Beat egg whites until soft peaks form. Fold into batter. Pour into 4 prepared layer pans. Bake at 375 degrees until layers test done. Cool. Melt 3/4 cup butter in top of double boiler. Add 1 1/3 cups sugar, 1/2 teaspoon salt and egg yolks; mix well. Cook over simmering water until sugar melts, stirring constantly, and mixture is slightly thick. Do not overcook. Remove from heat. Add Bourbon; beat for 1 minute. Add remaining ingredients; mix well. Cool. Spread between layers and over top of cake. Sprinkle with additional coconut. Decorate with additional green and red cherries.

Patsy C. Gaines, Daleville H.S.
Daleville, Alabama

GRANDMA CARROLL'S FRUITCAKE

2 tsp. soda
1 c. shortening
2 c. sugar
1 16-oz. can applesauce
4 c. flour
1 tsp. salt
2 tsp. cinnamon
1 tsp. nutmeg
1 c. chopped dates
1 c. each candied pineapple, cherries
1 lb. raisins
1 lb. walnuts, chopped

Dissolve soda in 2 teaspoons water. Cream shortening and sugar in large bowl. Add applesauce and soda, mixing well. Combine dry ingredients. Add to creamed mixture, mixing well. Add fruits and walnuts; mix well. Pour into 2 lightly greased 9 x 5-inch loaf pans. Bake at 350 degrees for 1 hour and 30 minutes or until cakes test done.

Susan Owen, Elmhurst H.S.
Fort Wayne, Indiana

HOLIDAY RING CAKE

4 c. sugar
1 c. butter
4 eggs, beaten
4 c. all-purpose flour
1 tsp. soda
1/2 tsp. salt
1 1/2 c. buttermilk
3 tbsp. grated orange rind
8 oz. chopped dates
1 c. pecans
1 c. orange juice

Cream 2 cups sugar and butter together in large bowl. Add eggs; beat well. Sift flour, soda and salt together. Add to creamed mixture alternately with buttermilk, beating well after each addition. Add 1 tablespoon orange rind, dates and pecans; mix well. Pour into greased and floured tube pan. Bake at 325 degrees for 1 hour or until cake tests done. Cool. Do not remove from pan. Punch holes in cake with ice pick. Combine orange juice, 2 tablespoons orange rind and 2 cups sugar in saucepan. Heat until sugar dissolves. Do not boil. Pour over cake, filling holes and dripping down side and center. Let stand in pan for several hours or overnight. Turn onto serving plate. Garnish with additional pecans.

Pearl V. Reed, Justin F. Kimball H.S.
Dallas, Texas

BAVARIAN CHOCOLATE MINTS

3 c. milk chocolate chips
1 sq. unsweetened chocolate
1 tbsp. butter
14 oz. sweetened condensed milk
1 tsp. each peppermint flavoring and
*   vanilla extract*

Melt first 3 ingredients in top of double boiler. Remove from heat. Add next 3 ingredients. Beat on low speed of electric mixer for 1 minute, then on high for 1 minute. Refrigerate for 15 minutes; beat every 5 minutes by hand. Beat on high speed of electric mixer for 2 minutes. Pour into 9 x 13-inch pan. Chill until firm. Cut into squares.

Rita Keller, Gordon H.S.
Gordon, Nebraska

CAROB NUGGET SNACK

1 c. bite-sized cereal
1/2 c. chow mein noodles
2 tsp. butter, melted
1 tsp. Worcestershire sauce
3 drops of Tabasco sauce
1/2 c. dried apricots
1/4 c. carob nuggets
1/2 c. salted peanuts

Combine cereal and noodles in bowl. Blend butter, Worcestershire sauce and Tabasco together. Pour over cereal-noodle mixture; mix well. Add remaining ingredients; toss lightly. Store in airtight container. Yield: 3 cups.

Photograph for this recipe below.

EASY TOFFEE BARS

35 soda crackers, unsalted
1 c. butter
1 c. (firmly packed) brown sugar
1 lg. package semisweet chocolate chips

Line lightly greased 15 1/2 x 10 1/2 x 1-inch jelly roll pan evenly with crackers. Combine butter and brown sugar in heavy 2-quart sauce-pan. Bring to a boil over medium heat, stirring constantly. Boil for 3 minutes, stirring constantly. Pour over crackers. Bake at 375 degrees for 15 minutes or until golden brown. Remove from oven; sprinkle with chocolate chips. Let stand for 5 minutes. Spread melted chocolate over crackers. Cut between crackers. Remove from pan to waxed paper while warm. Yield: 35 pieces.

Nan O. Price, Toombs Central H.S.
Lyons, Georgia

ENGLISH TOFFEE

1/2 c. finely chopped pecans
1 c. butter
1 c. (firmly packed) light brown sugar
1/2 c. semisweet chocolate chips

Sprinkle 1/4 cup pecans over bottom of lightly buttered 9-inch pan. Set aside. Combine butter and brown sugar in heavy saucepan. Cook over medium heat, stirring constantly, to 295 degrees on candy thermometer. Pour over pecans. Sprinkle with chocolate chips. Spread evenly when melted. Sprinkle with remaining pecans; press lightly. Cool completely. Break into pieces. Store in refrigerator in airtight container. Yield: 40 pieces.

Rebecca D. Brown, Troy H.S.
Troy, Texas

MARSHMALLOW CREME FUDGE

3 c. sugar
1 c. evaporated milk
6 tbsp. butter
1 1-pt. jar marshmallow creme
1 c. chopped nuts (opt.)
1 12-oz. package chocolate chips

Place sugar, evaporated milk and butter in saucepan. Bring to a boil. Cook to soft-ball stage or 236 degrees on thermometer, stirring frequently. Remove from heat. Add marsh-mallow creme, nuts and chocolate chips. Stir until ingredients are melted. Pour into 9 x 9-inch buttered pan. Chill until firm. Cut into squares. Yield: 3 pounds.

Lynn Dowdy, Colbert Heights H.S.
Tuscumbia, Alabama

CINNAMON LOGS

1/2 lb. butter
3 tsp. sugar
1 tbsp. cinnamon
1 tsp. almond extract
2 c. flour
Confectioners' sugar

Cream butter, sugar, cinnamon and almond extract in mixing bowl; beat until light and fluffy. Add flour; beat well. Cover. Chill until firm. Shape into 1 1/2-inch logs. Place on greased baking sheet. Bake at 300 degrees for 20 minutes. Cool. Dip logs into confectioners' sugar. Yield: 4 dozen.

Pat Leeser, Montgomery County R-II H.S.
Montgomery City, Missouri

NO-BAKE COCOA-BOURBON BALLS

1 c. finely crushed vanilla wafers
1 c. confectioners' sugar
1 c. chopped pecans
2 tbsp. cocoa
2 tbsp. light corn syrup
1/4 c. Bourbon
Sugar

Combine vanilla wafer crumbs, confectioners' sugar, pecans and cocoa in medium bowl. Add corn syrup and Bourbon; mix well. Shape into 1-inch balls with wet hands. Roll in sugar. Store in airtight container in cool place. Yield: 36 balls.

Linda B. Smith, Avery H.S.
Newland, North Carolina

PASTEL MELT-A-WAYS

Butter, softened
2 c. confectioners' sugar
2 tsp. vanilla extract
2 1/2 c. sifted cake flour
1/4 tsp. salt
Red and green food coloring
Flaked coconut
3 tbsp. cream

Cream 1 cup butter in mixing bowl. Add 1/2 cup confectioners' sugar gradually. Blend in 1 teaspoon vanilla, flour and salt; mix well. Divide dough in half. Tint 1 half pink and 1 half green. Form into finger shapes, using level teaspoons dough. Place on greased cookie sheets. Bake at 350 degrees for 10 to 12 minutes. Cool. Place 1 cup coconut in jar. Add 1 teaspoon food coloring. Cover; shake well. Blend 3 tablespoons butter, 1 1/2 cups confectioners' sugar, cream and 1 teaspoon vanilla in bowl; beat until smooth. Frost cookies. Roll in tinted coconut. Yield: 7 1/2 dozen.

Doris Kruger, Peotone H.S.
Peotone, Illinois

PEPPERMINT STICKS

2 c. all-purpose flour
1 c. sugar
1 c. margarine, softened
1 egg, separated
1 tsp. vanilla extract
1 6-oz. package semisweet chocolate chips
1/2 c. crushed peppermint candy

Combine flour, sugar, margarine, egg yolk and vanilla in large mixing bowl; mix well. Stir in chocolate chips. Press dough into ungreased 15 x 10-inch jelly roll pan. Beat egg white until frothy; brush over dough. Sprinkle with candy. Bake at 350 degrees for 25 to 30 minutes or until golden brown. Cool slightly. Cut into bars. Yield: 40 bars.

Christine L. Ellingson, McClintock H.S.
Tempe, Arizona

CHOCOLATE FUDGE

1 1/4 c. milk
4 oz. unsweetened chocolate
3 c. sugar
2 tbsp. corn syrup
1/4 c. butter
1 tsp. vanilla extract
1 1/2 c. coarsely chopped nuts

Heat milk and chocolate together in heavy saucepan over low heat until chocolate melts, stirring constantly. Add sugar and corn syrup; stir until sugar dissolves. Remove sugar crystals from side of pan with damp cloth wrapped around fork. Cook to soft-ball stage, 234 degrees on candy thermometer, stirring occasionally. Remove from heat; add butter. Cool until lukewarm without stirring. Add vanilla and nuts. Stir until candy holds shape and begins to lose gloss. Pour onto buttered platter.

Cool until set. Cut into squares. Yield: 3 pounds.

Photograph for this recipe on page 142.

CREAMY CARAMELS

2 c. sugar
Pinch of salt
2 c. light corn syrup
1/2 c. butter
2 c. half and half
1 tsp. vanilla extract

Combine sugar, salt and corn syrup in large heavy saucepan. Bring to a boil. Cook to firm-ball stage, 245 degrees on candy thermometer, stirring occasionally. Add butter and cream gradually, so that mixture continues to boil. Cook, stirring constantly, until mixture returns to 245 degrees. Remove from heat. Add vanilla, mixing well. Pour into buttered 9-inch square baking pan. Cool; turn onto waxed paper. Cut into 3/4-inch squares. Wrap individually in waxed paper. Yield: 2 pounds.

Photograph for this recipe on page 142.

ALMOND-FUDGE BARS

2 c. (firmly packed) brown sugar
Butter, softened
2 eggs
4 tsp. vanilla extract
2 1/2 c. baking mix
3 c. quick-cooking oats
1 12-oz. package semisweet chocolate chips
1 c. sweetened condensed milk
1/2 tsp. salt
1 1/2 c. chopped almonds

Combine brown sugar, 3/4 cup butter, eggs and 2 teaspoons vanilla in large bowl; mix well. Add baking mix and oats; stir until of uniform consistency. Heat chocolate chips, condensed milk, 2 tablespoons butter and salt in 2-quart saucepan over low heat, stirring constantly until smooth. Stir in 1/2 cup almonds and 2 teaspoons vanilla. Press 2/3 of the oatmeal mixture with greased hands into greased jelly roll pan. Drizzle chocolate mixture over top. Sprinkle with 1 cup almonds; press lightly into mixture. Bake at 350 degrees for 30 minutes or until lightly browned. Cool completely. Cut into 2 x 1-inch bars. Yield: 70 bars.

Mrs. Helen M. Godwin, Northwest Sr. H.S.
Greensboro, North Carolina

WHITE FUDGE

2 c. sugar
1/2 c. sour cream
1/3 c. light corn syrup
2 tbsp. butter
1/4 tsp. salt
2 tsp. vanilla extract
1/4 c. quartered candied cherries
1 c. chopped pecans (opt.)

Combine first 5 ingredients in saucepan. Bring to a boil over low heat, stirring until sugar dissolves. Boil without stirring over medium heat to 236 degrees on candy thermometer or to soft-ball stage. Remove from heat. Let stand for 15 minutes without stirring. Add vanilla. Beat for about 8 minutes or until mixture starts to lose its gloss. Stir in cherries and pecans; pour quickly into shallow greased pan. Cool. Cut into squares.

Shirley Leslie, J.D. Leftwich H.S.
Magazine, Arkansas

FRUIT-COT CAKES

Light corn syrup
3 c. all-purpose flour
1 1/3 c. sugar
1 tsp. salt
1 tsp. baking powder
2 tsp. ground cinnamon
1 tsp. ground nutmeg
1/2 c. each orange juice, Brandy
1 c. oil
4 eggs
1 c. dark seedless raisins
2 c. diced dried apricots
1 lb. mixed candied fruits
2 c. pecan halves

Combine 1/4 cup corn syrup, dry ingredients, orange juice, Brandy, oil and eggs in large mixer bowl. Blend for 1/2 minute on low speed of electric mixer, scraping bowl constantly. Beat for 3 minutes on high speed, scraping bowl occasionally. Stir in fruits and pecans. Spoon batter into 3 dozen 2 1/2-inch muffin pans, lined with paper baking cups. Bake at 275 degrees for 65 to 70 minutes or until cakes test done. Cool for 5 minutes in pan; place on rack. Cool completely. Heat 1/3 cup corn syrup in small saucepan. Brush over tops of cupcakes. Place cupcakes in container; cover with cheesecloth soaked in Brandy. Store in tightly covered container in cool place, for about 2 weeks. May be frozen for longer storage. Yield: 3 dozen.

Photograph for this recipe on this page.

APRICOT SNOWBALLS

2 c. corn flakes, crushed
1/3 c. diced pitted dates
2/3 c. diced dried apricots
1/2 c. chopped pecans
1/4 c. honey
3 tbsp. butter
1 tsp. vanilla extract
Sugar

Combine corn flakes, dates, apricots and pecans in large bowl; mix well. Melt honey and butter in small saucepan; blend in vanilla. Pour over corn flake mixture; mix thoroughly. Chill for 30 minutes. Shape into balls, using 1 tablespoon mixture for each ball. Roll balls in sugar. Cover; chill until serving time. Yield: 30 balls.

Photograph for this recipe below.

BRANDIED APRICOTS

2 30-oz. cans whole apricots
3/4 c. Brandy
2 cinnamon sticks, broken
6 whole cloves

Drain apricots, reserving 2 cups syrup. Combine syrup with Brandy and spices in medium saucepan. Bring to a boil. Reduce heat; simmer for 15 minutes. Pour hot syrup over apricots in bowl. Cover; chill for 3 to 4 hours or until serving time. Yield: 8 servings.

Photograph for this recipe below.

RUM BALLS

1 box vanilla wafers, crushed
2 c. chopped nuts
4 tbsp. cocoa
Confectioners' sugar
1/2 c. rum
1/4 c. corn syrup
1 stick margarine, melted

Combine first 3 ingredients with 1 box confectioners' sugar in large bowl; mix well. Set aside. Mix rum and corn syrup in small bowl. Add margarine and rum mixture to crumb mixture; blend well. Roll into small balls. Dust with additional confectioners' sugar. Let dry for several hours. Store in tightly covered container. Flavor improves after several days.

Linda W. Skelton, Walterboro Sr. H.S.
Walterboro, South Carolina

BOBBIE'S CHRISTMAS COOKIES

3 egg whites
1/2 c. sugar
1/2 c. flour
1 8-oz. package candied cherries,
*   chopped*
2 c. chopped pecans
3 slices candied pineapple, chopped

Beat egg whites until soft peaks form; add sugar gradually, beating until stiff. Combine flour and remaining ingredients in bowl. Toss well to coat fruit. Fold fruit mixture into egg white mixture. Drop by teaspoonfuls onto greased baking sheet. Bake at 325 degrees for 15 minutes.

Mrs. Bobbie Nix, Kingsville, H.S.
Kingsville, Texas

CANDY CANE COOKIES

1/2 c. margarine, softened
1 1/4 c. sugar
1 egg
2 tsp. vanilla extract
3 1/4 c. flour
4 tsp. baking powder
1 tsp. salt
1/4 c. milk
Red food coloring

Cream margarine and sugar in large bowl. Add egg and vanilla; mix well. Combine dry ingredients. Add to creamed mixture alternately with milk, blending thoroughly. Divide dough in half. Blend small amount of red coloring into 1 half. Pinch off teaspoonful from each half the dough. Roll each 5 inches long. Place red and white ropes side-by-side. Press together lightly; twist. Bend into candy cane shape. Repeat with remaining dough. Place 1 inch apart on ungreased cookie sheet. Bake at 350 degrees for 10 minutes. Remove from cookie sheet immediately. Cool. Store in airtight container. Yield: 5 dozen.

Janice Boeckman, Newcastle Public School
Newcastle, Nebraska

CHRISTMAS HOLLY COOKIES

1/2 c. butter
30 marshmallows
Several drops of green food coloring
4 c. corn flakes
1 sm. package red cinnamon candies

Melt butter and marshmallows in top of double boiler, stirring constantly. Add food coloring until mixture is bright green; stir well. Stir in corn flakes gradually. Drop while hot by spoonfuls onto waxed paper to resemble holly leaves or wreaths. Place 2 or 3 red candies on each cookie. Cool. Yield: 3 dozen.

Marilyn J. Rogers, Roosevelt Jr. H.S.
San Diego, California

FRUITCAKE COOKIES

1/4 c. butter, softened
1/2 c. (firmly packed) brown sugar
1/3 c. jelly
2 eggs
1 tsp. soda
1 1/2 tbsp. buttermilk
1/2 tsp. each allspice, nutmeg, cloves
*   and cinnamon*
1 1/2 c. flour
1/2 lb. each candied cherries, pineapple,
*   chopped*
1 lb. nuts, chopped
1 lb. raisins

Cream butter, brown sugar, jelly and eggs in large mixing bowl. Dissolve soda in buttermilk. Add to creamed mixture, mixing well. Sift spices and 3/4 cup flour together; add to creamed mixture gradually. Dredge fruits and nuts with 3/4 cup flour. Stir in batter; mix well. Drop from teaspoon onto greased and floured cookie sheet. Decorate tops with 1/2 candied cherry. Bake at 300 degrees for 30 to 40 minutes. Bake cookies ahead; allow to ripen like fruitcake.

Johnece Stuard, Mansfield H.S.
Mansfield, Texas

ALMOND CHRISTMAS CUT UPS

1 c. (firmly packed) brown sugar
1/2 c. butter
1 egg
1/2 tsp. vanilla extract
1 3/4 c. flour
1 tsp. baking powder
1/2 c. ground blanched almonds

Cream brown sugar and butter in bowl. Add egg and vanilla, mixing well. Sift flour and baking powder together. Blend into creamed mixture. Stir in almonds. Refrigerate until firm. Roll onto lightly floured surface to 1/8 to 1/4-inch thickness. Cut with floured cookie cutters. Place on greased cookie sheet. Bake at 350 degrees for 8 to 10 minutes.

Ruth S. McMartin, Sprayberry H.S.
Marietta, Georgia

ALMOND STARS

1 lb. butter, softened
Sugar
4 c. flour
1/2 tsp. salt
1/2 lb. almonds, ground
1 tbsp. vanilla extract
Raspberry jelly

Cut butter into 1 cup sugar in large bowl with pastry blender until crumbly. Add remaining ingredients except jelly; mix well. Refrigerate for 1 hour. Roll onto floured pastry cloth. Cut with star cookie cutter. Place on cookie sheet. Bake at 350 degrees for 10 minutes. Spread half the cookies with raspberry jelly while still warm. Top with remaining cookies. Sprinkle with sugar.

Mary Ann Prust, McClintock H.S.
Tempe, Arizona

APRICOT FOLD OVERS

1 1/2 c. butter, softened
4 oz. sharp cheese, grated
1 1/3 c. sifted flour
1 c. dried apricots
1 c. sugar

Cream butter and cheese until light. Blend flour into creamed mixture. Add 2 tablespoons water; mix well. Chill for 4 to 5 hours. Cover apricots with water in saucepan. Cook until tender. Drain. Stir sugar into hot mixture. Cook until mixture boils, stirring vigorously until smooth. Cool. Divide chilled cheese mixture in half. Roll out into 10-inch squares. Cut into 2 1/2-inch squares. Place 1 tablespoon of apricot filling in each 2 1/2-inch square. Bring up corners; seal. Place on ungreased cookie sheet. Bake at 375 degrees for 8 to 10 minutes. Yield: 2 1/2 dozen.

Mrs. Betty M. Deviney, University Jr. H.S.
Waco, Texas

MINT BROWNIE SQUARES

3 1/2 sq. chocolate
3/4 c. margarine
2 eggs
1 c. sugar
1/2 c. nuts
1 tsp. vanilla extract
1/2 c. flour
2 c. confectioners' sugar
2 tbsp. sour cream
1/2 tsp. milk
1/2 tsp. peppermint flavoring
Green food coloring
3/8 c. chocolate bits

Melt 2 squares chocolate and 1/2 cup margarine in small saucepan over low heat. Cool. Combine next 5 ingredients in large mixing bowl; mix well. Add chocolate mixture to egg mixture; blend well. Pour into greased 9 x 9-inch baking pan. Bake at 350 degrees for 25 minutes. Cool. Combine 4 tablespoons margarine and next 4 ingredients in mixer bowl; beat well. Add food coloring; mix well. Spread over brownie layer. Chill for 30 minutes or until firm. Melt 1 1/2 squares chocolate with 1 1/2 heaping tablespoons margarine and chocolate bits in saucepan. Spread over mint topping. Let stand for 1 to 2 hours. Cut into 1 1/2-inch squares. Yield: 36 brownies.

Beate Sacknowitz, R.L. Turner School
Carrollton, Texas

CHRISTMAS SPICE COOKIES

1 c. margarine
1 1/2 c. sugar
1 tbsp. dark syrup
1 egg, beaten
2 tsp. soda
1 tbsp. cinnamon
1 tbsp. cloves
1 tsp. ginger
3 1/4 c. flour

Cream margarine and sugar together in bowl. Add syrup and egg; mix well. Sift together dry ingredients. Add to creamed mixture; mix well. Roll out dough on floured surface until thin. Cut into Christmas shapes. Place on ungreased cookie sheets. Bake at 350 degrees for 10 minutes. Do not overbake. Dough may be refrigerated for several days prior to baking.

Sharon Brozovsky
Scotus Central Catholic School
Columbus, Nebraska

SWEDISH COOKIES

1/2 lb. butter
1 c. sugar
1 egg yolk
1 tsp. dark Karo syrup
1 tsp. cinnamon
1 tsp. soda
2 c. flour

Combine all ingredients in bowl; mix well. Shape into small balls. Place on cookie sheet. Bake at 300 degrees for 22 minutes or until golden brown. Yield: 6 dozen.

Carol Huffstetler, Boca Raton H.S.
Boca Raton, Florida

THREE-GENERATION CHRISTMAS JEWELS

3 1/2 c. flour
1 tsp. soda
1 tsp. salt
1 lb. pitted dates, chopped
2 c. candied red and green cherries,
*   cut into sixths*
2 slices each red and green candied
*   pineapple, chopped*
1 c. white raisins
2 c. coarsely chopped pecans
1 c. butter-flavored oil
1 1-lb. box light brown sugar
2 eggs, well beaten
1/2 c. buttermilk
1/2 tsp. vanilla extract
1/2 tsp. Brandy flavoring

Sift first 3 ingredients together into large bowl. Mix with fruits and pecans, coating completely. Mix oil, brown sugar and eggs in bowl. Stir in buttermilk and flavorings; mix well. Add floured fruits and pecans, blending well. Place in refrigerator container. Refrigerate overnight. Drop dough by rounded teaspoonfuls onto lightly greased cookie sheet about 2 inches apart. Decorate each cookie with pecan half. Bake at 375 degrees for 8 to 10 minutes. Dough may be refrigerated up to 1 week. Flavor improves with age. Yield: 10 dozen.

Ann B. Jones, Mountainburg Public Schools
Mountainburg, Arkansas

SPARKLING CHERRY JELLY

2 c. canned cherry drink
3 1/2 c. sugar
2 tbsp. lemon juice
3 oz. liquid fruit pectin
1/4 tsp. almond extract
4 drops of red food coloring
Paraffin

Combine cherry drink, sugar and lemon juice in large saucepan; mix well. Bring to a hard boil over high heat, stirring constantly. Stir in pectin. Bring to a boil; boil for 1 minute, stirring constantly. Remove from heat. Stir in almond extract and food coloring. Skim. Ladle into hot sterilized jars. Cover immediately with 1/8-inch paraffin. May substitute other fruit drinks for cherry drink with appropriate food coloring. Yield: 5 cups.

Linda Burlingame, Maries County R-II School
Belle, Missouri

CRANBERRY JELLY

1 qt. cranberries
2 c. sugar

Place cranberries in saucepan. Pour 1 cup boiling water over cranberries. Cook for 5 minutes or until cranberries are soft and mushy. Strain into bowl. Add sugar quickly. Stir until sugar dissolves. Pour into sterilized jelly glasses. Store in refrigerator.

Kay Caskey, Manogue H.S.
Reno, Nevada

LINDA'S GREEN PEPPER JELLY

3 lg. bell peppers, seeded
1/4 c. fresh hot peppers
1 1/2 c. white vinegar
6 1/2 c. sugar
1 bottle Certo
3 to 4 drops of green food coloring

Place green peppers and hot peppers in blender container. Add a small amount of vinegar; blend well. Pour into large saucepan. Add sugar and remaining vinegar. Bring to a rolling boil over medium heat; add Certo. Stir for 1 minute. Bring to a boil. Boil for 1 minute. Skim foam from jelly. Add food coloring. Pour into hot sterilized jelly jars. Seal. Serve with crackers and cream cheese. Yield: 4 1/2 pints.

Linda Y. Tuttle, Milwee Middle School
Longwood, Florida

HOMEMADE HONEY

10 c. sugar
1 tsp. alum
66 clover blossoms

Combine sugar and alum with 2 1/2 cups warm water in saucepan; mix thoroughly. Boil gently for 10 minutes over medium heat without stirring. Remove from heat. Drop clover blossoms into hot liquid. Let stand for 10 minutes. Strain. Pour into sterilized jars. Yield: 4 pints.

DeAnn Pence, Chandler H.S.
Chandler, Oklahoma

KRAZY KORN

2 sticks margarine, softened
2 c. (firmly packed) light brown sugar
1/2 c. light corn syrup
1 tsp. salt
2 tsp. soda
1 tsp. vanilla extract
6 to 8 qt. popped popcorn

Mix margarine, brown sugar, corn syrup and salt in saucepan. Stir over low heat until margarine is melted. Bring to a boil, stirring constantly. Boil for 5 minutes. Remove from heat. Add soda and vanilla. Pour mixture over popcorn. Bake at 250 degrees for 1 hour, stirring every 15 minutes. Pour onto waxed paper underlined with newspaper. Cool. Store in tightly covered container.

Lola Enis, Marshall Academy
Holly Springs, Mississippi

HOT BUTTERED NUTS

2 lb. pecans
4 tbsp. butter
2 tbsp. salt

Spread pecans evenly on 2 large shallow baking pans. Dot with butter. Bake at 300 degrees for 10 minutes. Stir pecans, distributing butter evenly. Sprinkle with salt; stir well. Bake for 5 to 10 minutes longer or until pecans are lightly toasted. Cool. Store in airtight jars. Yield: 8 cups.

Marcia Johnson, Prescott H.S.
Prescott, Arkansas

RAINBOW POPCORN BALLS

1 c. light corn syrup
1/2 c. sugar

1 3-oz. package gelatin
1/2 c. popped popcorn

Combine corn syrup and sugar in saucepan; stir over low heat until dissolved. Bring to a full rolling boil. Remove from heat. Add gelatin; stir until dissolved. Pour over popcorn in greased bowl. Form into 16 small balls with greased hands. Wrap well.

Beth A. Archer, Grover Cleveland Jr. H.S.
Zanesville, Ohio

SPICED PECANS

1 c. sugar
1/4 tsp. cream of tartar
1/2 tsp. cinnamon
1/2 tsp. vanilla extract
2 c. pecan halves

Combine sugar, cream of tartar and cinnamon with 1/4 cup water in saucepan. Cook to softball stage or 238 degrees on candy thermometer. Remove from heat; stir in vanilla and pecans. Continue stirring until pecans are coated. Pour onto waxed paper; separate pecans with fork while still warm.

Marilyn Gornto, Perry Jr. H.S.
Perry, Georgia

SUGAR-COATED PEANUTS

4 c. raw peanuts
2 c. sugar

Mix peanuts and sugar with 1 cup water in skillet. Cook, stirring constantly, until mixture crystallizes. Spread onto greased cookie sheet, separating peanuts. Bake at 300 degrees for 20 to 25 minutes. Cool. Store in airtight container.

Grace McDonald, Belton H.S.
Belton, Texas

SWEDISH NUTS

2 egg whites
1 c. sugar
1 to 1 1/2 lb. salted nuts
6 tbsp. butter

Beat egg whites in large bowl until soft peaks form. Add sugar gradually, beating until stiff. Stir in nuts, coating well. Melt butter in jelly roll pan. Spread nut mixture evenly in pan. Bake at 325 degrees for 30 minutes, stirring every 10 minutes. Cool in pan. Store in covered container.

Ruth Larson, Hickman H.S.
Columbia, Missouri

Color Photograph Recipes

DANISH ORANGE DELIGHTS

6 Florida oranges
1/4 tsp. rum extract
1 c. diced pound cake
1/2 c. chopped semisweet chocolate
1/2 c. chopped pecans
1/4 c. whipping cream, whipped

Cut 1-inch slices from tops of four oranges. Cut zigzag edge around tops of oranges with sharp knife. Scoop pulp from reserved shells. Place pulp in blender container. Process on high speed. Strain, reserving juice; discard pulp. Peel remaining 2 oranges; cut into 1/2-inch pieces. Mix orange pieces with 2/3 cup reserved orange juice and rum extract in bowl; cover. Chill for 1 to 2 hours. Add cake, chocolate and pecans; mix well. Spoon into orange shells. Top with whipped cream. Serve immediately. Yield: 4 servings.

Photograph for this recipe on cover.

BAVARIAN COOKIE WREATHS

3 1/2 c. all-purpose flour
1 c. sugar
3 tsp. grated orange rind
1/4 tsp. salt
Butter
1/4 c. Florida orange juice
1/3 c. finely chopped blanched almonds
1 egg white
1 c. confectioners' sugar
1 to 2 tsp. milk
Several drops of green food coloring
Red cinnamon candies

Mix flour, 3/4 cup sugar, 2 teaspoons orange rind and salt in large bowl. Cut in 1 1/3 cups butter and orange juice with pastry blender until mixture holds together. Knead several times. Press into ball. Shape dough into 3/4-inch balls. Roll each lightly into 6-inch strip on floured board. Twist 2 strips together to make rope. Form into circle to make wreath; pinch ends together. Place on lightly greased baking sheet. Mix almonds with remaining 1/4 cup sugar and 1 teaspoon orange rind in dish. Beat egg white with 1 teaspoon water. Brush top of each wreath with egg white mixture. Sprinkle with sugar-almond mixture. Bake at 400 degrees for 8 to 10 minutes or until lightly browned. Cool on wire racks. Mix confectioners' sugar, 2 tablespoons butter, 1 teaspoon milk and food coloring in small bowl. Add additional milk to make frosting of spreading consistency. Spoon into pastry bag fitted with small leaf tip. Decorate each wreath with 3 or 4 leaves and cinnamon candy berries. Yield: 5 dozen cookies.

Photograph for this recipe on cover.

FRESH CAULIFLOWER SOUP

6 tbsp. butter
1/2 c. chopped onion
1 c. chopped celery
1 carrot, thinly sliced
1 head fresh cauliflower, cut into
  flowerets
1 tbsp. chopped parsley
8 c. chicken broth
1 tsp. dried leaf tarragon
1/2 tsp. whole peppercorns
1/2 bay leaf
2/3 c. all-purpose flour
2 c. milk
1 c. light cream
2 tsp. salt
1/2 c. Goldfish Cheddar cheese crackers

Melt 2 tablespoons butter over medium heat in large saucepan. Saute onion until transparent. Add celery and carrot. Cook for 2 minutes. Add cauliflowerets and parsley; cover. Cook slowly for 15 minutes. Add chicken broth. Tie tarragon, peppercorns and bay leaf in cheesecloth. Add to soup. Bring to a boil. Reduce heat; simmer for 5 minutes. Melt remaining 4 tablespoons butter in 2-quart saucepan. Stir in flour. Cook for 1 minute. Stir in milk gradually. Bring to a boil. Cook until mixture thickens, stirring constantly. Stir in cream. Add milk mixture and salt to soup. Simmer for 20 minutes. Remove herbs. Pour into blender container; process to puree soup. Garnish with Goldfish Cheddar cheese crackers. Yield: 8 servings.

Photograph for this recipe on page 1.

CHICKEN WELLINGTON WITH FRESH MUSHROOM DUXELLES

1 1-oz. package chicken marinade mix
1/2 c. dry white wine
2 chicken breasts, skinned, boned, split
1 tbsp. minced onion
2 tbsp. butter
1/2 lb. fresh mushrooms, finely minced
2 tbsp. chopped parsley
2 tbsp. snipped chives
Salt, pepper, ground nutmeg to taste
*4 thin slices boiled ham, 2 x 4-inches
    each*
1/2 c. grated Cheddar cheese
*1 sheet Pepperidge Farm Frozen
    Bake-It-Fresh Puff Pastry*
1 egg

Combine marinade mix with wine and 1/2 cup water in shallow baking dish. Prick chicken breasts deeply all over with fork. Add to marinade; turn to coat. Marinate for 15 minutes, turning twice. Place chicken on ungreased baking sheet. Bake at 425 degrees for 15 minutes. Cool. Saute onion in butter in skillet. Add mushrooms. Cook for 15 to 20 minutes longer, stirring frequently. Add parsley, chives and seasonings. Cut each chicken breast in half horizontally. Spread cut sides of half the chicken with mushroom mixture. Top with ham slice and 2 tablespoons grated cheese. Cover with remaining chicken pieces, cut-side down. Set aside. Thaw pastry for 20 minutes. Unfold. Roll out pastry to measure 12 x 16 inches; trim edges. Cut into 4 rectangles. Place one filled chicken breast in the center of each rectangle. Beat egg with 1 tablespoon water. Moisten edges of pastry with egg mixture. Fold pastry to enclose chicken. Seal edges. Brush with egg mixture. Decorate top with pastry trimmings. Brush with egg mixture. Prick pastry 3 or 4 times for steam vents. Place on ungreased baking sheet. Bake at 425 degrees for 25 to 30 minutes or until golden brown and puffed. Yield: 4 servings.

Photograph for this recipe on page 1.

RED AND GREEN HOLIDAY SALAD

*2 c. torn lettuce leaves, washed, patted
    dry*
2 c. fresh broccoli flowerets
1/2 pt. cherry tomatoes
1/3 c. olive oil
2 tbsp. lemon juice
1/4 tsp. prepared mustard
1/4 tsp. salt
Pinch of pepper
*1/2 c. croutons, seasoned with herbs and
    cheese*

Line salad bowl with lettuce. Arrange broccoli and tomatoes on top. Combine oil, lemon juice, mustard, salt and pepper in small bowl; mix well. Pour over salad. Sprinkle with croutons. Yield: 4 servings.

Photograph for this recipe on page 1.

ORANGE-GLAZED CARROTS AND PARSNIPS

3 med. carrots, sliced 1 in. thick
3 med. parsnips, sliced 1 in. thick
2 tbsp. orange juice
2 tbsp. honey
1 tbsp. butter
1/4 tsp. grated orange rind

Cook carrots and parsnips in 1 inch boiling, salted water in medium saucepan until tender-crisp; drain. Add orange juice, honey, butter and orange rind. Cook over medium heat until vegetables are tender and evenly glazed, tossing occasionally. Yield: 4 servings.

Photograph for this recipe on page 1.

PEARS WITH FRESH CRANBERRY SAUCE

1 3/4 c. orange juice
1 4-in. cinnamon stick
4 firm pears, pared, stems attached
1 c. sugar
1 tsp. freshly grated orange rind
2 c. fresh cranberries

Combine 1 1/4 cups orange juice and cinnamon stick in large saucepan. Add pears. Bring orange juice to a boil. Cover; reduce heat. Simmer for 20 to 25 minutes or until pears are just tender, basting often. Remove pears from saucepan. Chill thoroughly. Discard cinnamon stick. Add sugar and orange rind to orange juice in saucepan. Bring to a boil. Stir in cranberries; reduce heat. Simmer for 10 minutes. Set aside to cool. Pour into blender container; puree until smooth. Force sauce through sieve to remove seeds. Serve sauce over poached pears. Yield: 4 servings.

Photograph for this recipe on page 1.

TWELFTH NIGHT CAKE

2 1/2 c. unsifted all-purpose flour
1 tsp. soda
1 tsp. salt
1/2 tsp. ground cinnamon
3/4 c. butter or margarine
1 3/4 c. sugar
3/4 c. Florida orange juice
1/2 c. milk
2 eggs
1 tbsp. orange rind
1 tsp. vanilla extract
1/2 c. chopped walnuts
1/2 c. golden raisins
1/4 c. currants
1 c. whole blanched almonds

Sift flour, soda, salt and cinnamon together. Cream butter and 1 1/2 cups sugar. Add 1/2 cup orange juice, milk, eggs, orange rind and vanilla. Add flour mixture gradually, beating until well combined. Fold in walnuts, raisins, currants and almonds. Turn into well-greased bundt pan or 10-inch tube pan. Bake at 350 degrees for 55 minutes or until cake tests done. Let cool 15 minutes in pan. Combine remaining 1/4 cup sugar and 1/4 cup orange juice. Bring to a boil. Cool slightly. Prick surface of cake with fork. Slowly pour orange mixture over cake in pan. Cool completely in pan. Remove from pan. Cake is best if allowed to stand overnight. Yield: 12-16 servings.

Photograph for this recipe on page 2.

WASSAIL

1 c. sugar
1/2 c. (firmly packed) brown sugar
4 c. apple cider
1 3-in. stick cinnamon
12 whole cloves
2 c. Florida orange juice
2 c. Florida grapefruit juice
Orange slices
Maraschino cherry halves
Whole cloves

Combine sugar, brown sugar and apple cider in large saucepan. Cook, stirring constantly, until sugars dissolve. Add cinnamon stick and cloves. Bring mixture to a boil over medium heat. Reduce heat. Simmer for 5 minutes. Add juices. Heat; do not boil. Strain. Serve in heatproof mugs with orange slices decorated with cherry halves and whole cloves. Yield: 8 servings.

Photograph for this recipe on page 2.

SPINACH PINWHEELS

2 10-oz. packages frozen chopped
*   spinach, well drained*
2 c. cottage cheese, drained
1/2 c. grated Parmesan cheese
1/2 c. finely cut scallions
2 tbsp. chopped fresh dill
2 tbsp. blue cheese spread
1 tsp. Tabasco sauce
1 tsp. salt
1 pre-rolled sheet frozen puff pastry,
*   thawed*
Packaged dry bread crumbs

Combine first 8 ingredients in bowl; mix well. Cut puff pastry sheet into halves. Roll each half to 8 x 18-inch rectangle. Sprinkle pastry lightly with bread crumbs to within 1 inch of edges. Spread half the spinach mixture lengthwise down center of each rectangle. Fold edges over filling; seal tightly, moistening seams and ends with water. Place on ungreased cookie sheet seam side down. Prick surface with fork. Bake at 400 degrees for 25 minutes or until golden brown. Cut spinach rolls diagonally into 1-inch slices. Serve at once. May be refrigerated or frozen in foil. Bake at 350 degrees until warmed through. Yield: 30 servings.

Photograph for this recipe on page 35.

FIRE ISLAND COCKTAIL SPREAD

1 env. unflavored gelatin
1 10-oz. can condensed tomato soup
1 8-oz. package cream cheese, softened
1 c. mayonnaise
1/2 c. finely chopped celery
1/2 c. finely chopped green pepper
1/2 c. finely chopped cucumber
2 tsp. grated onion
1 1/2 tsp. Worcestershire sauce
1/2 tsp. Tabasco sauce
1/4 tsp. salt
Unpeeled thin cucumber slices

Sprinkle gelatin over 1/2 cup cold water in medium saucepan. Let soften for 1 minute. Warm over medium heat until gelatin is completely dissolved, stirring constantly. Beat together soup and cream cheese in large bowl until smooth. Fold in next 8 ingredients. Stir in gelatin. Spoon into 4-cup mold. Chill until firm. Unmold onto serving plate. Garnish with cucumber slices. Serve with assorted crackers and breads. Yield: 14-16 servings.

Photograph for this recipe on page 35.

SOME-LIKE-IT-HOT SHRIMP

1 egg white, lightly beaten
2 tbsp. dry white wine
1 tsp. cornstarch
1/4 tsp. salt
1 1/2 lb. medium shrimp, peeled,
*   deveined*
Oil for frying
Chopped green onions
1 tbsp. chopped fresh ginger
1/2 c. chicken broth
2 tbsp. catsup
3/4 tsp. Tabasco sauce
1/2 tsp. each salt, sugar
1/2 tsp. sesame oil

Combine egg white, wine, cornstarch and salt in medium bowl; mix well. Add shrimp; stir to coat. Cover. Refrigerate for 1 hour. Drain shrimp, reserving egg white mixture. Pour oil into heavy saucepan to 3-inch depth. Heat to 320 degrees. Fry several shrimp at a time until shrimp turn pink. Drain. Stir-fry 2 tablespoons green onions and ginger in 2 tablespoons pan oil in skillet for 1 minute. Stir in broth, catsup, Tabasco sauce, salt and sugar. Bring to a boil. Add reserved egg white mixture, shrimp and 1/2 cup green onions; mix well. Sprinkle with sesame oil. Spoon into chafing dish. Serve with additional Tabasco sauce. Yield: 16-18 servings.

Photograph for this recipe on page 35.

LAST-OF-THE-RED HOT HAM

3 c. finely chopped ham
1 8-oz. package cream cheese, softened
1/3 c. chopped chutney
1 1/4 tsp. Tabasco sauce
1 c. chopped pecans
Pimento strips
Parsley

Combine ham, cream cheese, chutney and Tabasco sauce in small bowl; mix well. Stir in 2/3 cup pecans. Line 4-cup mold with clear plastic wrap. Pack ham mixture firmly into mold. Refrigerate for 1 to 2 hours. Turn onto serving platter; remove plastic wrap. Press remaining 1/3 cup pecans on sides and top of mold. Decorate with strips of pimento and parsley. Yield: About 4 cups.

Photograph for this recipe on page 35.

CREAMY TUNA-POTATO TOPPER

2 tbsp. butter
3 tbsp. flour
2 1/2 c. milk
1/2 tsp. dry mustard
1/4 tsp. hot pepper sauce
2 7-oz. cans tuna, drained, flaked
1/4 c. chopped pimento
1/4 c. chopped, pitted black olives
4 Idaho potatoes, baked

Melt butter in medium saucepan. Add flour; mix well. Cook over medium heat for 3 minutes, stirring constantly. Remove from heat. Stir in milk gradually. Return to heat. Cook until thickened, stirring constantly. Add mustard and hot pepper sauce; fold in tuna. Stir in pimento and black olives. Cut an X in each potato top with fork. Push some of potato up with slight pressure of fingers on side of potato. Spoon sauce over potatoes. Yield: 4 servings.

Photograph for this recipe on page 36.

RATATOUILLE TOPPING

1 sm. eggplant, cut in 1-inch cubes
1 med. red onion, chopped
3 cloves of garlic, minced
1 lg. green pepper, cut in 1-inch cubes
1 med. red pepper cut in 1-inch cubes
2 lg. tomatoes, cut in 1-inch cubes
1 c. cooked cut green beans
1 zucchini, cut in 1-inch strips
1 c. sliced mushrooms
4 Idaho potatoes, baked

Saute eggplant over medium heat in large skillet. Add onion and garlic. Saute for 1 minute. Add green and red peppers. Cook for 1 minute longer. Add tomatoes and 1/2 cup water. Simmer for 3 minutes. Add green beans, zucchini and mushrooms. Cook until heated through. Cut X in top of each potato with fork. Push some of potato up with slight pressure of fingers on side of potato. Spoon sauce over potatoes. Yield: 4 servings.

Photograph for this recipe on page 36.

SAUSAGE SPECIAL

1 lb. sweet Italian sausages, peeled,
*   sliced*
1 lg. red pepper, sliced
1 lg. green pepper, sliced
1 med. onion, diced
1 to 2 tbsp. curry powder
2 tbsp. Dijon mustard
1 1/2 c. dry white wine
1/2 lb. mushrooms, sliced
1 c. sour cream
4 Idaho potatoes, baked

Saute sausages until lightly browned in medium skillet. Add peppers and onion. Cook for 5 minutes. Stir in curry and mustard. Cook for 5 minutes longer. Add wine. Bring to a boil. Cook until mixture is slightly thickened. Add mushrooms. Stir in sour cream. Cook over low heat until heated through. Cut X in top of each potato with fork. Push some of potato up with slight pressure of fingers on side of potato. Spoon sauce over potatoes. Yield: 4 servings.

Photograph for this recipe on page 36.

SWEET AND SOUR CHICKEN TOPPING

3 tbsp. butter
1 med. onion, thinly sliced
1 lg. green pepper, chopped
2 c. pineapple juice
1/4 c. (firmly packed) dark brown sugar
1/4 c. white vinegar
3 tbsp. soy sauce
Dash of hot pepper sauce
3 tbsp. cornstarch
2 c. cooked, diced chicken
4 Idaho potatoes, baked

Melt butter in large skillet. Add onion and green pepper. Saute over medium heat for 5 minutes. Add 1 3/4 cups pineapple juice. Bring to a boil. Stir in brown sugar, vinegar, soy sauce and hot pepper sauce. Mix cornstarch and remaining 1/4 cup pineapple juice. Stir cornstarch mixture slowly into sauce; mix well. Bring to a boil; reduce heat. Simmer for 3 minutes. Add chicken. Cook until heated through. Cut an X in top of each potato with fork. Push some of potato up with slight pressure of fingers on side of potato. Spoon sauce over potatoes. Yield: 4 servings.

Photograph for this recipe on page 36.

BAKED POTATO WITH DILL-CAPER SAUCE

3 tbsp. butter
1/4 c. finely chopped onion
3 tbsp. flour
2 c. milk
1 tbsp. lemon juice
3 tbsp. snipped fresh dill
1/4 tsp. each salt, pepper
1   7-oz. can salmon, drained, flaked
2 tbsp. drained capers
4 Idaho potatoes, baked
Chopped parsley

Melt butter in medium saucepan. Saute onion until tender. Blend in flour. Stir in milk, lemon juice, dill, salt and pepper. Cook over medium heat until sauce thickens and comes to a boil, stirring constantly. Add salmon and capers. Cook for 1 minute. Remove from heat. Cut X in top of each potato with fork. Push some of potato up with slight pressure of fingers on side of potato. Spoon sauce over potatoes. Sprinkle with chopped parsley. Yield: 4 servings.

Photograph for this recipe on page 36.

TANGERINE STUFFING

2/3 c. sliced scallions
2/3 c. chopped celery
12 slices bread, cubed
1 1/4 tsp. grated Florida tangerine rind
2 c. Florida tangerine sections, pitted,
    cut in thirds
1/4 c. chopped parsley
1/2 c. chicken broth
1/2 tsp. each ground sage, dried crumbled
    leaf thyme and salt
Dash of pepper
4 slices crisp-fried bacon, crumbled

Saute scallions and celery in bacon drippings in skillet until tender. Combine with remaining ingredients in large bowl; mix well. Yield: About 6 cups.

Photograph for this recipe on page 69.

ORANGE-CARROT PUFF

2 lb. carrots, pared
1 c. Florida orange juice
3 eggs, separated
1/4 c. all-purpose flour
1/4 c. butter, melted
2 tbsp. honey
3/4 tsp. grated orange rind
3/4 tsp. each cinnamon, cardamom
1/2 tsp. salt

Cut carrots into 1-inch pieces. Cook for 15 to 20 minutes or until tender in a small amount of boiling, salted water in large covered skillet. Combine 1/3 of the carrots and orange juice in blender container. Process at high speed until carrots are pureed. Repeat process with remaining carrots and juice. Combine pureed carrots with lightly beaten egg yolks, flour, butter, honey, orange rind, cinnamon, cardamom and salt in large bowl; mix well. Beat egg whites until stiff peaks form. Fold into carrot mixture. Pour into buttered 2 1/2-quart casserole. Bake at 350 degrees for 45 minutes. Serve immediately. Yield: 8 servings.

Photograph for this recipe on page 69.

SPICED ORANGES

4 Florida oranges
1 c. sugar
1 c. honey
1/2 c. cider vinegar
6 whole cloves
2 2-in. pieces cinnamon stick

Cut each orange into 8 wedges; remove seeds. Place oranges in large saucepan with water to cover; cover. Simmer for 30 minutes. Drain; rinse well. Return to pan. Add sugar, honey, vinegar, 1/4 cup water, cloves and cinnamon. Simmer for 1 hour, uncovered, until skins are slightly transparent. Cool. Pack slices into hot sterilized jars. Fill with hot syrup. Seal. Yield: 1 quart.

Photograph for this recipe on page 69.

ORANGE HOLIDAY CAKE

8 eggs
Sugar
2 tsp. grated orange rind
Florida orange juice
1/4 tsp. salt
1 c. sifted cake flour
1 orange, sliced
1/4 c. Marsala wine
1/4 c. all-purpose flour
1 c. whipping cream, whipped

Separate 6 eggs. Beat 6 egg yolks in large bowl of electric mixer. Add 3/4 cup sugar, orange rind, 3 tablespoons orange juice and salt. Beat for about 5 minutes. Stir in cake flour gradually. Beat 6 egg whites until stiff peaks form. Fold into egg mixture. Pour into 3 buttered and floured 8-inch round cake pans. Bake at 325 degrees for 30 minutes or until cake tests done. Invert pans onto wire rack. Cool. Remove from pans. Pierce layers with toothpick. Combine 3/4 cup each sugar and water in small saucepan. Bring to a boil, stirring to dissolve sugar. Add orange slices. Simmer for 15 minutes or until liquid measures 2/3 cup. Remove from heat. Remove orange slices. Add wine to liquid. Cool. Pour sauce over layers gradually until absorbed. Combine 2 beaten eggs, 2/3 cup sugar, 1/2 cup orange juice and all-purpose flour in top of double boiler; mix well. Cook over boiling water until thick and smooth, stirring constantly. Refrigerate until chilled. Fold in whipped cream. Spread between layers and over top and side of cake. Garnish with chocolate curls. Yield: 10-12 servings.

Photograph for this recipe on page 69.

CHRISTMAS TREE COFFEE CAKES

4 1/2 to 5 c. all-purpose flour
1/2 c. sugar
1 tsp. salt
2 pkg. dry yeast
1 c. milk
1/2 c. butter
2 eggs
2 tbsp. grated lemon rind
1 tsp. crushed cardamom seed
1/2 c. chopped mixed candied fruits
1/2 c. golden raisins
1 c. sifted confectioners' sugar
2 tbsp. commercial eggnog

Combine 2 cups flour, sugar, salt and yeast in large mixer bowl; mix well. Combine milk and butter in saucepan. Heat to 120 degrees on thermometer. Add to dry ingredients gradually. Beat for 2 minutes at medium speed of electric mixer, scraping side of bowl occasionally. Add eggs, lemon rind, cardamom seed and 1/2 cup flour. Beat for 1 minute at high speed, scraping bowl occasionally. Stir in enough remaining flour to form soft dough. Turn onto lightly floured surface. Knead for about 5 minutes or until smooth and elastic. Place in large buttered bowl, turning to butter surface; cover. Let rise in warm place for 1 hour or until doubled in bulk. Punch down. Turn onto lightly floured surface. Knead in fruits and raisins. Divide in half. Divide each half into fourths. Shape each fourth into 18-inch rope. Arrange 4 ropes on greased cookie sheet in looped figure-8 pattern to form tree. Pinch ends together. Use small ball for tree trunk. Repeat process. Let rise in warm place for 30 minutes or until doubled in bulk. Bake at 350 degrees for 25 to 30 minutes. Combine confectioners' sugar with eggnog in bowl; mix well. Drizzle over cakes. Decorate with additional candied cherries and pineapple. Yield: 2 coffee cakes.

Photograph for this recipe on page 70.

SOUR CREAM YEAST DOUGH

4 1/4 to 4 3/4 c. all-purpose flour
1/3 c. sugar
2 tsp. salt
2 pkg. dry yeast
1/2 c. butter
1 c. sour cream
2 eggs
1 tbsp. grated lemon rind
1 tbsp. granted orange rind

Combine 1 1/2 cups flour, sugar, salt and yeast in large mixing bowl; mix thoroughly. Combine

1/2 cup water, butter and sour cream in saucepan. Heat to 120 degrees on thermometer. Add dry ingredients gradually. Beat for 2 minutes at medium speed of electric mixer, scraping side of bowl occasionally. Add eggs, lemon and orange rinds and 1/2 cup flour. Beat for 2 minutes at high speed, scraping side of bowl occasionally. Stir in enough remaining flour to make soft dough. Turn onto lightly floured surface. Knead for about 5 minutes or until smooth and elastic. Place in buttered bowl; turn to butter surface. Cover. Let rise in warm place for about 1 hour or until doubled in bulk. Punch dough down. Divide in half.

Orange Crown

1/2 c. sugar
2 tbsp. grated orange rind
2 tbsp. orange juice
4 tbsp. butter
1/2 recipe Sour Cream Yeast Dough

Combine 1/4 cup sugar, 1 tablespoon orange rind, orange juice and 2 tablespoons butter in saucepan; mix well. Boil for 2 minutes. Cool. Pour into greased 9-inch fluted tube pan. Shape dough into 1 1/2-inch balls. Melt remaining 2 tablespoons butter. Combine remaining 1/4 cup sugar and 1 tablespoon orange rind. Dip balls into melted butter. Roll in sugar mixture. Place in prepared tube pan in 2 layers. Cover. Let rise for about 30 minutes or until doubled in bulk. Bake at 350 degrees for 35 to 40 minutes. Turn immediately onto large tray. Leave pan over cake for 1 minute. Yield: 1 coffee cake.

Schnecken

Butter
1/2 c. (firmly packed) brown sugar
Pecan halves
Red candied cherries
1/2 recipe Sour Cream Yeast Dough
1/4 c. sugar
2 tsp. cinnamon
1/4 c. raisins

Combine 1/2 cup butter and brown sugar in saucepan. Heat until butter melts, stirring to blend well. Spoon 2 teaspoons into each of 18 greased muffin cups. Place 2 or 3 pecan halves and 1 cherry in each cup. Roll out dough into 13 1/2 x 9-inch rectangle. Spread with 2 tablespoons butter. Combine sugar and cinnamon. Sprinkle over dough. Sprinkle with raisins. Roll as for jelly roll, beginning with long side. Pinch edges to seal. Cut into 18 slices. Place, cut side down, in muffin cups over topping; cover. Let rise for about 30 minutes or until doubled in

bulk. Bake at 375 degrees for 20 to 25 minutes. Turn immediately onto large tray. Leave pan over rolls for 1 minute. Yield: 18 rolls.

Photograph for this recipe on page 70.

BUTTER ROSES

1 stick butter

Cut butter into 6 equal pieces. Let soften for 5 to 10 minutes. Place cut side up on flat surface. Press salad fork against one corner of cube. Press up and toward center while holding opposite corner steady. Repeat for each corner. Repeat process. Dip fork in cold water after each use. Chill. Yield: 6 roses.

Photograph for this recipe on page 70.

POM-POM SALAD

3 c. shredded cabbage
3 c. shredded red cabbage
2 c. shredded carrots
1/2 c. peanuts
1/2 c. raisins
1 c. Wish-Bone Sweet 'n Spicy French or Russian Dressing
1/4 tsp. ground ginger (opt.)

Night Before The Game

Combine vegetables, peanuts and raisins in medium bowl. Toss with sweet, spicy French dressing blended with ginger. Chill. Yield: 8 servings.

Photograph for this recipe on page 103.

SUPER HERO

1 loaf French or Italian bread
Wish-Bone Creamy Bell Pepper Dressing
4 slices cooked turkey
4 slices cooked corned beef
4 slices American cheese, halved
4 tomato slices, halved

Morning of The Game

Make 15 cuts in bread, almost completely through. Spread 1 slice generously with creamy bell pepper dressing; repeat with every other slice. Place 1 slice meat, 1/2 slice cheese and halved tomato slice into each prepared slice. Slice unfilled cuts where necessary to lie flat; wrap in foil. Chill.

At Fourth Quarter

Bake at 350 degrees for 30 minutes or until heated through. Yield: 8 sandwiches.

Photograph for this recipe on page 103.

CHEESE FOOTBALL

1 env. Lipton Onion Soup Mix
2 c. sour cream
1/4 c. port wine
1 8-oz. package cream cheese, softened and cubed
2 c. shredded Cheddar cheese
1/2 c. finely ground soda crackers
1/3 c. chopped cashews or walnuts
Pimento strips

Night Before The Game

Blend soup mix with sour cream. Combine dip with wine in blender or food processor. Add cheeses gradually, stirring and processing until smooth after each addition. Stir in crackers and cashews. Pack into 4-cup bowl; chill.

Before Kickoff

Unmold onto plate. Shape ends to form football. Garnish with pimento to form laces. Yield: 3 1/2 cups spread.

Photograph for this recipe on page 103.

HEARTY ALL-STAR LOAF

2 env. Lipton Beefy Onion Soup Mix
3 1/2 lb. ground beef
1 c. mashed potato flakes
1 1/2 c. beer or water
2 eggs
3/4 tsp. caraway seeds
4 c. hot mashed potatoes

Morning of The Game

Combine all ingredients except hot mashed potatoes in large bowl. Pack into 13 x 9-inch baking dish; chill.

At Third Quarter

Bake at 350 degrees for 1 hour; drain.

After The Game

Frost loaf with hot mashed potatoes. Garnish with cheese "field markings" and carrot "goal posts." Yield: 12 servings.

Photograph for this recipe on page 103.

EGGNOG-RICE PIE

3 c. cooked rice
1 qt. eggnog
1 tbsp. unflavored gelatin
3 tbsp. cream Sherry
1 10-in. chocolate cookie crumb crust
1 2 1/8-oz. package whipped topping mix
1/2 c. milk
1/3 c. crushed peppermint candy

Cook rice in eggnog until creamy but not too thick, about 20 to 25 minutes. Soften gelatin in 2 tablespoons water. Stir into hot rice stirring until gelatin is dissolved. Add Sherry. Cool. Turn into 10-inch crumb crust. Chill. Combine topping mix and milk. Whip until stiff peaks form. Fold in peppermint candy. Swirl on top of pie before serving.

Photograph for this recipe on page 104.

Index

APPETIZERS

bacon
  party
    pizza, 28
    sandwiches, 27
  roll-ups, 27
beef
  hot diggity, 33
  meatballs
    chafing dish, 27
    party, 28
  pizza, 28
cheese
  balls
    and olive, 28
    blue, 28
    four, 29.
    holiday, 29
    hot pepper, 29
    party, 29
    pecan, 29
    pineapple, 30
  chili
    con queso with
      tortillas, 30
    rellenos, 22
  crisps, 30
  herb, 30
  loaf, 28
  molded, liver
    pate, 31
  quiche
    mini, 31
    tarts, 30
  roll, 28
    and olive filling, 31
    chili, 29
    sandwiches, 31
  spread
    carraway-curry, 30
    Cheddar, 31
chicken
  fingers, 32
  party, 32
  snacks, 32
dips
  artichoke, 22
  cheese
    chili, 22
    Christmas, 22
    holiday, 24

  party, 25
    three, dunk, 25
crab, 23
  for vegetables, 23
crispy cashew, 23
curry, 23
dill, 23
dried beef, 23
oyster, 24
shrimp, 24

BEVERAGES

eggnog
  chocolate, 41
  fresh holiday, 41
  too good, 40
  wassail bowl, 45
hot
  cider
    mulled Christmas, 44
    spicy, 44
  pomauder, 44
  spiced tea, 44
    and cider drink, 44
  wassail
    cider, 44
    cranberry, 44
    tea, 45
punch
  banana crush, 41
  Christmas
    Connie's, 41
    Jane's, 41
    sparkling, 43
  Diana's, 41
  holiday
    cheer, 42
    cranberry, 42
    easy, 42
  lime, 42
    evergreen, 42
  nonalcoholic
    mint julep, 42
  pineapple
    Christmas, 43
    golden, 43
    Sue's holiday, 42
  sangria, 43
  strawberry, 43
    sweetheart, 43

BREADS

biscuits
  angel, 96
  dinner cheese, 96
  never fail, 96
coffee cakes
  blueberry holiday, 97
  cherry, 97
  German Christmas, 98
  Kringlers, 98
  Mary's candy cane, 96
  New York Polish
    cheese, 97
  sour cream, 98
coffee can cheese, 96
donuts, easy-do, 130
flatbrod, Norwegian, 100
muffins
  bran, 99
  orange streusel, 99
  refrigerator, 99
  uh-oh, 100
rolls
  Anna's yeast, 100
  butter, 100
  cottage cheese, 100
  Danish puffs, 102
  freezer Kolaches, 102
  pull-apart
    breakfast, 101
sticks, 96
sweet loaves
  anise, 105
  basic, 108
  bishop's, 102
  bran brown, 102
  Christmas towers, 98
  cranberry-orange, 105
    nut, 106
  delicious monkey, 105
  flavorful tomato, 101
  golden
    apple swirl, 108
    jeweled tree, 108
  gumdrop, 106
  holiday
    fruit, 106
    Greek, 106
  nut
    Arniece's, 106

cherry, 105
pumpkin, 107
Jean's, 107
strawberry, 107
zucchini, 107
winter wreath, 108

CAKES

apple
fresh, 121
fruitcake, 120
German, 120
carrot, Chanukah
orange, 121
cranberry, with
butter sauce, 124
gingerbread, Laura's, 124
green velvet, 124
Italian cream, 123
poppy seed, 124
pound
chocolate, 122
Granny's sour
cream, 123
prune, 124
pumpkin, 125
raisin
Amaretta, bundt, 122
German, 123
sour cream coconut, 122
Theola's old-fashioned
fruitcake, 122
Venetian creme torte, 125
yule log, 125

CANDY

caramel
oven corn, 126
yule logs, 126
chocolate
buckeyes, 126
Kay's fudge, 127
millionaires, 126
Christmas wreath, 128
holiday logs, 127
molasses-wheat
germ, 128
orange slices, 129
peanut brittle, 127
pralines, buttermilk, 127
quick and easy, 127
walnuts, panocha, 128

COOKIES

apple-date, 132

apricot brownies, 128
bars
cherry, 128
surprise, 128
lemon, 134
orange
fruitcake, 130
macaroon, 129
pecan pie, 135
quick crescent, 136
brown sugar cut-outs, 132
chocolate
balls
orange, 129
rum, 130
bars
holiday mint, 131
toffee, 132
brownies, 131
cream cheese, 130
unusual, 131
macaroons, 129
no-bake, 130
Christmas, 132
drops, 132
cocoons, 133
cottage cheese, 133
dream, 133
gumdropless, 134
health, 133
holiday wreaths, 134
moon, 134
oatmeal, moist, 134
old-fashioned tea, 136
peanut
butter, rich, 135
sticks, 136
Philly thins, 135
raisin-nut, 131
skillet, 135
snowball, 136
sugar
and spice, 136
stir and drop, 135

cheesecake, 126
Susan's cheese, 126

DESSERTS

ambrosia, Christmas, 112
baked Alaska, special
occasion, 112
blueberry
delight, 113

pizza, 112
cake
Betty cracker, 112
broken glass, 113
rainbow, 119
cherry
in the snow, 114
torte, 113
cheesecake
grasshopper, 114
super, 113
chocolate
fudge meltaways, 114
ice cream
marbled, 115
Oreo, 113
mint, 114
peppermint freezer, 114
cranberry
apple crunch, 115
casserole, 115
fluff, 115
fondue
apple, Cheddary, 26
chocolate, 26
orange custard, 118
fruit
curried, 116
frozen, 116
pizza, 116
gelatin delight, 116
grasshopper, 116
holiday delight, 117
orange-pumpkin
chiffon, 118
pots de creme, 118
peach cream freeze, 118
peppermint, Christmas, 115
pudding
apple
Christmas, 112
steamed, 118
cinnamon-noodle, 117
holiday, 117
pecan, 118
rhubarb, angel, 119
strawberry
angel food, 119
cloud torte, 120
strata surprise, 120
tunnel, cake, 120
torte, jiffy, 117
trifle, easy, 117

EGGS

and sausage, 79

breakfast, 79
Christmas morning, 80
holiday Mornay, 80
omelet, hashed
brown, 80
strata, 80

MAIN DISHES

beef
brisket
barbecued, 64
best-ever, 64
chili, Mexacali, 64
filet, perfect, 64
shish kabobs, 64
steak, holiday Swiss, 64
chicken
and almond, 66
and dressing, 66
apricot, 66
party, 66, 68
rolled breast, 68
sausage, 67
sesame seed, 67
supreme, 65, 67
tetrazzini, 67
thousand dollar, 68
touchdown curry, 65
game birds
duckling, gingered with
orange rice, 78
Sherry and spice, 78
pheasant, braised, 78
ground beef
cannelloni, 68
meatballs
barbecued, 71
casserole, 72
sweet and sour, 71
roll for fifty, 71
stuffed bread, 71
Wyoming straw hats, 72
ham
and cheese, 72
easy souffle, 72
and potato, 73
holiday, 73
pockets, 72
stuffed manicotti, 73
homemade pizza, 79
hot dogs with Coney Island
sauce, 79
pork, stuffed tenderloin, 74
sausage
crepes, 73
zesty squares, 74

seafood
gumbo, 74
shrimp
festive, 75
holiday rice, 74
scampi, 75
turkey
and dressing, 76
enchiladas, 77
festive curried, 76
lasagne, 76
leftover pastry, 76
oriental, 76
pie, 77
roll, 78
stroganoff sandwich, 78

Pancakes, baked, with sausage, 81

PASTRIES

cream puffs, swan, 136
pecan sassies, 141
tarts
cheesecake, 141
sour cream-raisin, 119

PIES

caramel, 137
chocolate
brownie, famous, 138
fudge
peppermint, 138
sundae, 140
mint, 137
cranberry
Bavarian, 137
chiffon, 137
ice cream, 138
French walnut, 138
ice cream, 138
pecan
Mother's, 139
Nancy's, 139
peanut butter, yummy, 140
pineapple
Bavarian, 140
sour cream, 140
pink party, 138
pumpkin
custard, 140
frozen, 140
spicy, 141
white Christmas, 141

QUICHES

Christmas morning pineapple, 80

hamburger, 71
Lorraine, 81
seafood, 75
shrimp, 75
Simple Simon cheese, 81
spinach-mushroom, 81

Relishes
cranberry, 38
conserve, 38
mold, 38
spiced orange, 38

SALADS

fruit
apple, Linda's, 48
applesauce, cinnamon swirl, 51
avocado, 48
guacamole, 48
blueberry, 50
elegant party, 49
red-white-blue, 49
cherry, cheery, 50
Christmas, 56
frozen, 54
garland jelly, 50
lime, 50
Merry, 55
cranberry
apple, 51
checkerboard, 53
Christmas, 51
congealed, 51
gelatin, 51
lemon, 52
mold, 51-52
orange, 52
pecan, 52
pineapple, 52
Waldorf, 52
Diane's, 48
ginger, 48
grapefruit, festive, 54
holiday
cottage cheese, 57
gelatin, 54
pretzel, 54
lime congealed, 54
mandarin orange, 55
medley elegante, 48
noel loaf, 54
old-fashioned, 48
pecan, 55
pear, 55
pink, 49
delight, 55

pistachio
   coconut surprise, 56
   yummy, 56
snow flake, 56
sour cream, 49
strawberry
   cream cheese, 56
   Jell-O, 57
      tri-level, 57
   nut, 57
   yum-yum, 57
meat
   chicken
      fruit, 58
      hot, ring, 58
   crab, elegant olive mousse, 60
   ham, New Year's, 58
   shrimp mold, 59
   taco, 60
   turkey
      macaroni, 59
      super easy, 59
      tiered party mold, 59
pasta, 57
rice, 58
vegetables
   beet, 60
   broccoli, 61
   Cobb, 61
   onion-orange, 60
   spinach, 61
      Katie's, 61
   super bowl, 61

SIDE DISHES

dressing
   Italian, 92
   potato, 93
   sausage-mushroom, 92
   squash, 93
   tropical rice, 77
grits casserole, 93
noodle, sour cream bake, 91
rice
   mushroom, 93
      medley, 93
   wild, 93

SOUPS

bisque, crab, 38
chowder, cheese and vegetable, 38
confetti, 38
French onion, 40
fruit, 39

VEGETABLES

asparagus
   mold, 84
   scalloped, 84
beans
   cheesy Italian, 84
   company, 84
broccoli
   puff, 84
   special, 85
carrots
   cinnamon-glazed, 85
   copper, 85
celery
   en casserole, 86
   far-east, 85
corn, scalloped, 85
holiday, medley, 92
potatoes
   creamy scalloped, 87
   gourmet, 87
   Kugel, 87
   lemon
      onion, 86
      sour cream sauce, 87
   perky mold, 86
sauerkraut, fried
      balls, 88
spinach
   balls, 87
   noodle ring, 88
   torta, 88
squash
   fritters, 89
   glorified, 88
sweet potatoes
   ambrosia, 89
   apple, 91
   balls, 90
   cranberry, 90
   French-fried, 89
   Helen's, 90
   Jo's, 89
   Mary Jo's, 91
   Pam's, 91
   pudding, 90
      old-fashioned, 90
   souffle, 90
   Thanksgiving, with
      topping, 89
spinach
   Diana's, 24
   Milinda's, 24
tomato and green
      onion, 24
vegetable, 25

   holiday, 25
   white spice, 25
eggs
   holiday rolls, 22
   pickled, 37
fondue
   cheese
      creamy Parmesan, 26
      puffs, 26
   Italiano, 27
   sweet-sour, 27
green pepper jelly, 22
ham
   balls
      cocktail, 32
      frosted, 32
   party biscuits, 32
sausage
   pinwheels, 33
   sweet-sour, 33
seafood
   crab
      cheese triangles, 33
      pizza snacks, 33
   Scandinavian
      squares, 34
   St. Jacques, 33
vegetables
   asparagus, hot, 34
   mushrooms
      party-time
         sandwiches, 37
      stuffed, 37
         broiled, 34
         Doris', 37
         microwave, 37
   sauerkraut balls, 34

HOMEMADE GIFTS

beverage mixes
   hot buttered rum, 144
   spiced tea, 144
Brandied apricots, 150
bread
   banana-nut, 144
   carrot
      Christmas, 145
      Norwegian, 145
   cranberry, 145
   dilly, 145
   Norwegian
      Christmas, 146
   pumpkin, 146
cakes
   Christmas lane, 146
   five-flavor, 146

fruitcake, Grandma
        Carroll's, 147
holiday ring, 147
candy
    caramels, creamy, 149
    carob nugget
            snack, 147
    cinnamon logs, 148
    chocolate
        Bavarian mints, 147
        fudge
            almond bars, 149
            marshmallow
                cream, 148
            white, 150
        no-bake Bourbon
                balls, 148
        peppermint
                sticks, 149
        toffee
            easy bars, 148
            English, 148
        pastel melt-a-ways, 148
        rum balls, 151
cookies
    almond
        Christmas
                cut-ups, 152
        stars, 152
    apricot
        fold overs, 152
        fruit, 150
        snowballs, 150
    brownie, mint squares, 152
    candy cane, 151
    Christmas
        Bobbie's, 151

holly, 151
spice, 152
three-generation
        jewels, 153
fruitcake, 151
Nancy's snowballs, 144
Swedish, 153
honey, homemade, 154
jelly
    cherry, sparkling, 153
    cranberry, 153
    green pepper,
            Linda's, 153
muffins, fruitcake, 144
popcorn
    krazy korn, 154
    rainbow balls, 155
nuts
    hot buttered, 154
peanuts, sugar-coated, 154
pecans, spiced, 154
Swedish, 154
puffs, hidden marshmallow, 144

COLOR PHOTOGRAPHS

baked potato with
                dill-caper sauce, 159
Bavarian cookie
                wreaths, 155
butter roses, 161
cheese football, 162
chicken Wellington with
            fresh mushroom
            duxelles, 156
Christmas tree coffee
            cakes, 160

creamy tuna-potato
            topper, 158
Danish orange
            delights, 155
eggnog-rice pie, 162
fire island cocktail
            spread, 157
fresh cauliflower
            soup, 155
hearty all-star loaf, 162
last-of-the-red hot
            ham, 158
orange-carrot puff, 159
orange crown, 161
orange-glazed carrots
            and parsnips, 156
orange holiday cake, 160
pears with fresh cranberry
            sauce, 156
pom-pom salad, 161
ratatouille topping, 158
red and green holiday
            salad, 156
sausage special, 158
Schneken, 161
some-like-it-hot
            shrimp, 158
sour cream yeast
            dough, 160
spiced oranges, 160
spinach pinwheels, 157
super hero, 161
sweet and sour chicken
            topping, 159
tangerine stuffing, 159
twelfth night cake, 157
wassail, 157

PHOTOGRAPHY CREDITS

Cover Design: Tal Howell; Florida Department of Citrus; United Fresh Fruit and Vegetable Assn.; Pepperidge Farm; Idaho Potato Commission; The McIlhenney Company (Tabasco); Rice Council; United Dairy Industry Association; Thomas J. Lipton Company; American Dairy Association; Florida Citrus Commission; Best Foods, A Division of Corn Products Company International, Inc.; Charcoal Briquet Institute; Washington State Apple Commission; The Nestle Company; Campbell Soup Company; Ehlers Spice Company; R. C. Bigelow Teas; National Macaroni Institute; Olive Administrative Commission; The R. T. French Company; California Apricot Advisory Board; Planters Peanut Oil; Pineapple Growers Association; Diamond Walnut Kitchen; American Mushroom Institute; North American Blueberry Council; Peter Pan Peanut Butter Company; California Honey Advisory Board; C & H Sugar Kitchen; California Raisin Advisory Board; National Dairy Council; EL MOLINO — Cara Coa Brand.